MAKING IT!

MAKING IT!

PERSONAL SURVIVAL IN THE CORPORATE WORLD

Steven C. Levi

PRICE STERN SLOAN

Los Angeles

A TERN ENTERPRISE BOOK

© 1990 by Tern Enterprise, Inc.

Published by Price Stern Sloan, Inc.
360 North La Cienega Boulevard, Los Angeles, California 90048

Printed in the United States of America
9 8 7 6 5 4 3 2 1

Library of Congress Cataloging-in-Publication Data

Levi, Steven C.
    Making it! : personal survival in the corporate world / by
Steven Levi.
        p.   cm.
    ISBN 0-89586-770-2. — ISBN 0-89586-807-5 (pbk.)
    1. Success in business. 2. Career development. I. Title.
HF5386.L575 1990
650.14—dc20
                                                                89-70007
                                                                CIP

Making It!
was prepared and produced by
Tern Enterprise, Inc.
15 West 26th Street
New York, New York 10010

Cover design by Paul Matarazzo
Cover Illustration by Donald Richey
Interior Illustrations by Gustav Szabo

TABLE OF CONTENTS

INTRODUCTION

"It's a jungle out there." You've heard it before, but it's true. From business school to the executive suite, the competition is fierce every step of the way. Everybody is looking for that little something to give them an edge over everybody else. More often than not, that little something is a colleague who can give the right advice at the right time, someone to watch over you and show you the ropes.

But what do you do if you don't have a mentor? Usually you do the best you can on your own, succeeding or failing through trial and error. Mostly error. These days you can't afford that. One error too many could mean losing that promotion, making the wrong investment or even watching your business go under.

Think of this book as your mentor. It will be there, in your desk drawer or on your shelf, to turn to when you need a guide to help you cut through the corporate jungle. From office ethics to boardroom politics to investment savvy, it doesn't deal with ideal, perfect-world situations, it deals with reality. Here's the real lowdown from someone who's been there. Here are the answers to questions that might not have even occurred to you. What do you do if someone starts going through your desk or spreading rumors about you? Are you in trouble if your boss says he's hiring a consultant to look over your department? Should you start that small business with your old college pal? Who could you turn to for honest advice in these cases? Your mentor.

But after you've read this book and taken its lessons to heart, you'll still want to keep it within easy reach. With its source-filled sections and the extensive Databank, MAKING IT! is a one-volume, desktop reference library. Government agencies, videotapes, pamphlets, magazines, free material, and book after book are all waiting to help you. You just have to know what's available and where to look. MAKING IT! tells you what the best sources are and exactly where to find them, complete with phone numbers and addresses. In a world where knowledge is power, this kind of knowledge is invaluable.

So, while that other guy in your office is frantically running back and forth to get that important report done, you'll not only know the best way to go about writing it, you'll know where to find the information you need quickly, what to do with the report when it's finished and how to present it. Whom do you think the boss will notice?

Yes, rewarding as it is, the trek through the corporate jungle can be plenty rough. It's easy to get lost, there are different customs and there are even times when the hunter can become the hunted. But you'll have it easier than most. You'll have a guide to lead you through and show you the way.

MAKING IT!

ON THE JOB

1

FINDING THE RIGHT JOB

❖ ❖ ❖

After the tenth or eleventh time one of his salespeople had come in late, the boss cornered the employee and asked if he had a good reason. "Of course I have a good reason," snapped the employee. "It makes the day shorter!"

❖ ❖ ❖

One of the great curses of our time is being nailed into a job that pays you so much money you can't afford to leave it. Mortgage payments, living expenses, health insurance, day-care costs and the expense of keeping up with the Joneses drain us to the point that we are working harder and harder for longer and longer and have fewer and fewer real dollars at our disposal. Gradually, we come to the realization that we are in the same rat race we saw our parents run. The only difference is that now there are more — and stronger — rats in the race.

In the long run, those who say that they "cannot afford to change jobs" are only fooling themselves. These are the very people who cannot afford not to change jobs. Stress, the curse of the corporate worker, will eventually force your hand. It may even kill you.

❖ ❖ ❖

A heart attack is God's way of telling you to slow down.

Psychologists' adage

❖ ❖ ❖

Most people put off changing jobs until the last possible moment. They've put a lot of time into their present job and, as they will be quick to tell you, "a bird in the hand is worth two in the bush." That old saying may be true, but a job you enjoy will lengthen your life by ten years. A job you don't like is just like a bird in the hand; you can't hold onto it too long before you have to either do something with it or let it go.

When you've finally made the decision to change your place of employment, you will be surprised to find that there is a wide array of choices available to you. First, however, you must be aware that there is a great deal of difference between a job and a career. A job is something that earns you money which, in turn, provides you with the time you need to look for something you really want. It's easy to find a job. It's as simple as reading the classified advertisements in your local newspaper and then making a few phone calls. There are always jobs available. You may not like the jobs that are being offered — but they are open.

❖ ❖ ❖

"Nothing is really work unless you would rather be doing something else."

James M. Barrie, creator of Peter Pan

❖ ❖ ❖

When most of us talk of changing jobs, what we actually mean is that we are looking for a different position in the same career path. Lawyers leaving government services usually look at private practice in the same legal area. Pilots usually look for similar work with a different airline. Statistically, the average management person will change employers about five times in his or her career. Thus, change is as much of a maturing process as a fact of corporate life.

LOOKING FOR A CHANGE IN CAREER POSITIONS

Once most people make the decision to change career positions, they usually make at least one of three critical errors. Sometimes they make all three.

The Error of Timing

This error occurs when someone knows he or she wants to change jobs but assumes that this change will be sometime in the "near future," which will eventually become the "future" and thereafter "soon." Keep in mind that the terms "near future," "future" and "soon" have no meaning at all. Exactly when is "soon?" People who refer to their time of departure in these terms either never get around to leaving, or suddenly find themselves out in the cold because of some unexpected corporate gyration. Then it's too late to take the time to properly find a new position.

To avoid falling victim to the error of timing, ask yourself this simple question: "Do I want to be in this position in five years?" If that thought sends shivers up your spine, you had best start looking for a new position immediately. There is no sense in spending another five years where you are. Rather, spend your time building up credibility in a new position.

Jobs for the Future

In order of growth rate, these are going to be the fastest-growing jobs in America during the next decade:

- Paralegal personnel
- Medical assistant
- Physical therapist
- Physical therapist assistant
- Home health aide
- Data processing equipment repairer
- Podiatrist
- Computer systems analyst
- Medical records technician
- Employment interviewer

(Source: U.S. Bureau of Labor Statistics)

The Error of Similarity

When a person decides to change positions, he or she is often just trying to avoid an unpleasant reality of that career field. If you're a soft-hearted soul who happens to be a lawyer and you dislike driving hard bargains in divorce proceedings, you will have problems wherever you go if you stay in legal field. The legal profession is based on confrontation. If you have problems being adversarial, changing to another position in the legal profession will not help you in the long term. Three or four years down the road you will probably have the same problem at your new position that you currently have. If there is some aspect of your profession you cannot handle, either find a new niche in your career field or find a new career altogether. Life is too short to spend it fighting stress instead of a tough opponent on the tennis courts.

The Error of Idiots

It's important to realize that the world is full of people with grotesque personality disorders who, under normal circumstances two hundred years ago, might have been kept in mental institutions. Today they run departments in major corporations. "Only five percent of the population are idiots," as the old saying goes, "but why does one of them always have to be my boss?"

Changing jobs to avoid working with or under one idiot is not a good idea because you're more than likely to end up working with or under another. That's a fact of both life and statistics. If you're reading this chapter because you're trying to escape from an idiot who happens to be your supervisor, you should read chapter 3 first. You're going to have to work with difficult people your whole life, so you had better get used to it. You don't have to like it, you just have to adapt to it and make it work for you.

> ### Information Sources on Occupations
>
> *The Jobs Rated Almanac*, Les Krantz (World Almanac, 1988)
>
> *American Almanac of Jobs and Salaries 1987-1988*, John Wright (Avon, 1987)
>
> *Annual Survey*, U. S. Bureau of Labor Statistics
>
> *Annual Survey*, Administrative Management Society

❖ ❖ ❖

"'Be yourself' is the worse advice you can give to some people."

Tom Masson, American humorist

❖ ❖ ❖

Once you have made the decision to change positions, do what most people do not do. First, take your time and plan your strategy: Where, specifically, do you want to work? Is there a magic moment for you, a date after which you would be willing to leave on a moment's notice? What are you willing to give up when you change positions? What do you want to avoid in your next position? Do you want instead to go back to school? Think all these questions out carefully before you make any moves.

In the long run, you will be better off if you view your occupational change as a two-part decision. The first part is understanding why you want to leave your current position. Make sure it's a good reason. The second part is making certain that where you're going is better than where you are now. Even under the most trying circumstances you should not leave your job unless you've already found a new one. While you may find it intolerable to stay, you at least have the luxuries of time and a paycheck. If it takes three weeks for an option to develop, it's a lot easier on your pocketbook to stay at a job you detest than sit at home gnawing your fingernails to the bone. Furthermore, as many a sadder-but-wiser veteran of the street can tell you, it is a lot harder to find a job when you are unemployed then when you are employed. Remember, just as banks tend to give loans to people who don't need the money, employers tend to hire people who don't need a job.

LOOKING FOR A CHANGE OF CAREER

Many Americans need more than just a change of jobs. They need a change of career. Perhaps they went to college expecting to be in business and took nothing but business classes. Now, successful as stockbrokers, insurance agents, lawyers, property managers, or investment counselors, they want something more than an ongoing grind. It's not that they want to go back to school and start from scratch. They just need something else in life, but really don't know where to turn.

Average Starting Salaries for College Grads by Profession

Accounting	$22,838
Marketing/Sales	$21,472
Financial Administration	$20,778
General Business Admin.	$20,335
Personnel Administration	$19,319
Advertising	$18,983
Hotel/Restaurant Mgmt.	$18,693
Retailing	$17,035

(Source: Society for the Advancement of Education)

If you happen to be in this group, take heart. Right now there are thousands just like you sitting at their desks making sixty or seventy thousand dollars a year, but wishing they were someplace else.

If you know that you want to leave your current job and aren't particularly thrilled with your occupation, you might want to take a few personality tests to see how well you really know yourself. These tests are important because what you are really lacking is an occupational sense of direction. You know that you want to be working in another field, but you're just not sure what that field is. Understanding yourself better is the first step toward making that decision.

These personality tests don't measure acceptability or talent. Rather, they give you an indication of your personal strengths and weaknesses, likes and dislikes. These tests are relatively inexpensive, about $50 each, are available through most counseling services — including university or community college career placement centers — and can be scored at home.

Some of the most popular indicators are:

Myers-Briggs Type Indicator — Provides a measure of your personal dispositions and preferences. The indicator will place you in one of sixteen personality types and give you a brief glimpse at how you view problems and how you go about developing solutions. (Consulting Press, 577 College Avenue, Palo Alto, California 94306-1490; tel. 415-857-1444)

Strong Interest Inventory — Assesses your interests and compares them with those of people happily employed in a wide variety of occupations. (tel. 1-800-624-1765)

Guilford-Zimmerman Interest Inventory — Measures your interests in ten fields: mechanical, natural, aesthetic, service, clerical, mercantile, leadership, literary, scientific and creative. (tel. 415-857-1444; FAX orders, 415-493-2130)

FIRO B Awareness Scale — Evaluates interpersonal relationships and your needs for inclusion, control and affection. (Consulting Psychologists Press Inc., 577 College Avenue, Palo Alto, California 94306-1490; tel. 415-857-1444)

Taylor-Johnson Temperament Analysis — Assesses general levels of adjustment and adequacy of personal, interpersonal, social, academic and vocational functioning. (Consulting Psychologists Press Inc., 577 College Avenue, Palo Alto, California 94306-1490; tel. 415-857-1444)

Career Development Inventory — Gauges knowledge and attitudes regarding career choices. (tel. 1-800-624-1765; California residents, 415-857-1444)

California Psychological Inventory — A multipurpose questionnaire assessing normal personality characteristics important to everyday survival. (Consulting Psychologists Press Inc., 577 College Avenue, Palo Alto, California 94306-1490; tel. 415-857-1444)

Some of these tests can be taken and scored in the privacy of your home; others require a short class. Some will provide an analysis sheet; with others you may need assistance. Each test is different. Before you order a test, be sure to ask if it comes with a self-analysis section. If it doesn't, contact a local counselor. You can find one in the Yellow Pages or at any college or university.

If you have a hard time finding any of these tests at a counseling center or college placement center, there are firms which specialize in vocational testing by mail. Most of these firms not only sell the test but provide an analysis of the results and recommendations.

Palmer Testing Service, 93 Main Street, Andover, Massachusetts 01810 (tel. 1-800-225-5800) offers both an Executive Personality and a Personal Resources test for under $50.

Chronicle Guidance Publications, P.O. Box 1190, Moravia, New York 13118 (tel. 315-497-0330) offers Career Interest and Ability Inventory tests for under $35.

You can order the Strong Campbell Interest Inventory and the California Psychological Inventory from **Behaviordyne**, 994 San Antonio Road, Palo Alto, California 94303 (tel. 415-857-0111) for under $35.

"Self-Directed Search" by John Holland is a vocational test which allows for do-it-yourself scoring and analysis for under $10 from **Psychological Assessment Resources**, P.O. Box 998, Odessa, Florida 33556 (tel. 813-968-3003).

While taking an IQ test is probably not necessary, you might consider it simply to reinforce the fact that you have every mental ability needed to succeed in today's corporate world. If you're interested in finding out just how smart you are (and want something you can put on your résumé), you may want to take the MENSA test. MENSA is a national organization of individuals who have an IQ that is at least 145. These people are, quite literally, card-carrying geniuses. The MENSA test is offered in most communities on a regular basis and costs about $25. For more information on MENSA, contact the organization at 2626 East 14th Street, Brooklyn, New York 11285-3992.

If you really want to feel humbled, consider taking "The Mega Test" which divides the smart from the ultra-smart. Available from Ronald K. Hoeflin, 439 West 50th Street, New York, New York 10019. The test is free but there is a $25 scoring fee.

Perhaps the most important benefit of testing is that the results will help you choose an occupational direction. Corporate America is full of competent, dedicated and aggressive people who are lost in the maze.

They want to advance but don't even know their options. Psychological testing will not hand you an answer, but it will show you your strengths. Using these as an guide, you can change positions without jumping from the frying pan into the fire.

KEY DATES WHEN JOB HUNTING

When you are looking for a job, set deadlines for yourself, then think in reverse. Suppose, for instance, that you want to start working at a new job by November 1. Follow this schedule.

August 1 — Begin researching companies in your chosen field. Read the professional journals. Go to the library.

September 1 — Send out twenty personal letters with résumés to those companies that you would most like to work for. Depending on your level of confidence and the type of job you want, you might consider hiring an employment agency at this point. (See elsewhere in this chapter for advice on employment agencies.) Start reading and responding to want ads in the newspapers and professional journals.

September 7 — Call the twenty companies to whom you have sent letters to make certain they have arrived. Continue to read want ads.

September 14 — Send out letters stating your continued interest in those companies that have not responded to your initial letters. Also, send out letters and résumés to your twenty second-favorite companies. If you have not registered with an employment agency as of yet, do so now. Continue to read want ads.

September 21 — Call the second twenty companies to be sure your letters have arrived. Call those of the original twenty that still have not responded. Continue to read want ads.

October 1 — By now, you will most likely have received requests for interviews. Send out letters of continued interest to all firms that have not yet responded. If you have not recieved any positive response from any of the forty companies, either you are seeking an inappropriate job, or the economy is in very poor condition. Either way, be warned that it will take you longer than usual to find the position you are looking for.

It is a good idea, now, to broaden your range of acceptable positions. Inform your employment agent that you have adjusted your strategy. If you can remain at your old job, you should consider postponing your date of departure. Continue to read want ads.

October 14 — By this point, you have probably received a number of interviews and/or offers. If no offers have yet come in, something is definitely wrong. Send a last round of letters of continuing interest to companies that have not responded. Tell your employment agent that you will now consider ANY job.

CHANGING FRONTIERS OF EMPLOYMENT IN AMERICA

If you haven't gone job hunting in a while, you're going to find that there's been a profound change in the American job market over the past decade. It's a new world out there. Ten years ago, corporate responsibility meant paying a lot of money to new employees and never having manufactured Agent Orange. It has a great deal more meaning today.

One of the changes you will notice immediately is that competent women and minorities have a larger say in the corporate world than ever before.

You will also find that computers have invaded the workplace in staggering numbers. FAX is no longer a four-letter word and corporate gobbledygook has been replaced by computer double-talk. Access lines stretch from public libraries to offices and then around the world to other corporate offices. The pace of communications has increased dramatically. Reading, long considered an art form that faded with the advent of television, has now become vitally important. Professional publications — previously thought to be dull and dry — are now becoming as important to their industries as the Wall Street Journal is to stock-brokers.

Perhaps more important still is the the changing focus of world trade. At the beginning of this century, President Theodore Roosevelt noted that the Mediterranean was the ocean of the past and the Atlantic the ocean of the present. But the ocean of the future, he observed, was the Pacific. America's political and economic future lies within what is known as the Pacific

Average Salaries by Degree	
Accounting	$22,838
Doctorate (Ph.D.)	$31,479
Master of Business Administration (MBA)	$31,265
Master of Arts or Sciences (MA or MS)	$27,712
Bachelor of Arts or Sciences (BA or BS)	$22,609
(Source: Society for the Advancement of Education)	

Rim, the collection of nations that share the Pacific Ocean.

Japan is now America's second largest trading partner and the focus of world power is shifting accordingly. In the long term, there will be a shifting of America's international emphasis as well. More and more corporations will see that the future lies with the nations of the Pacific Rim rather than Europe. Japanese, Chinese and Korean will be the languages to learn. Business trips will be to Tokyo, Seoul and Beijing rather than Paris, London and Zurich.

If you are in your mid-forties or younger, within your working lifetime the focus of American business will complete the shift from the Atlantic to the Pacific. This will mean a vast new market for American corporations. Business opportunities abound. Horace Greeley was right when he said, "Go west, young man. Go west."

As you look toward the long term for your own career, keep in mind that America is changing dramatically. Whether you like it or not, you are part of that change. You can ride the crest of innovation, adapt to the computer and the FAX machine, adjust your thinking to incorporate the Pacific Rim — or you can ignore the signs of change and continue on with business as usual. The choice is yours.

RESUMES

Once you've decided what job you want, the next thing to do is write three résumés. Why three? Because most people expect a single résumé to be all things to all people. That is a mistake. That's like using a shotgun to shoot anything that moves, from grouse to grizzly. Hunters who hunt like that only come home with wildlife citations and claw marks on their back.

Unless you live in a small community where you're very well known and are applying for a job that you already have "in the bag," you are going to need a résumé. Statistically, ninety-five percent of all employment interviews are given only AFTER a résumé has been read.

But why three résumés? Because the best résumés are those tailored to specific openings. Let a prospective employer know the job he's offering is exactly the one you want. Don't forget, when your résumé hits someone's desk, he or she most likely doesn't know you. His or her first impression of you will be based entirely on that résumé. If your résumé looks generic — as most résumés do — you've reduced your chances of getting an interview significantly.

Take the time to develop your résumés. First, focus on your experience. Let whoever reads your résumé know that you're the best candidate. Most Americans over the age of thirty have had a wide range of experience, even if they've been in a fairly specific field. You've got experience. Show it!

Second, keep your résumé as short as possible. This does not mean trimming three pages of specific experience down to one page of general rambling. Be precise. Be brief. You probably don't like reading office memos that are three pages long, so why would a personnel director like to go through two hundred résumés, each that long. Chances are, if your résumé looks too long, the personnel director will simply skip it and go on to the next.

When it comes to details, be selective. Do not put in items such as age, Social Security number, salary history, salary expectations, names of previous supervisors, references, marital status or shoe size. Nor should you include anything that indicates your religious beliefs, political affiliation or any reference to ethnic background. If you want to make these known later, fine, but the résumé is not the place for it. Learn the meaning of the word "succinct." Stick to the point.

Career Information for Special Groups

The organizations below provide information on career planning and job hunting techniques for special groups:

U.S. Department of Labor, Women's Bureau, 200 Constitution Avenue NW, Washington, D.C. 20210 (tel. 202-523-6652).

Wider Opportunities for Women, 1325 G Street NW, Lower Level, Washington, D.C. 20005 (tel. 202-638-3143).

Department of Veteran's Benefits, Veteran's Administration Central Office, 810 Vermont Avenue NW, Washington, D.C. 20420 (tel. 202-872-1151).

League of United Latin American Citizens, National Educational Service Centers Inc., 400 First Street NW, Suite 716, Washington, D.C. 20001 (tel. 202-347-1652).

National Association for the Advancement of Colored People, 4805 Mount Hope Drive, Baltimore, MD 21215-3297 (tel. 301-358-8900).

National Association of Older Workers Employment, c/o National Council on Aging, 600 Maryland Avenue SW, Washington, D.C. 20024 (tel. 202-479-1200).

President's Committee on Employment of the Handicapped, 1111 20th Street NW, Room 636, Washington, D.C. 20036 (tel. 202-653-5044).

Third, be different. Most of the serious candidates' résumés will look similar. They will be laser printed on eggshell-white paper and specifically tailored for the position being advertised. How do you make your résumé different? What you do not do is send it by FAX, put it on colored paper or submit it on an odd-sized sheet. What you can do is add a "Miscellaneous" section at the bottom of your résumé and include those things that make you different from everyone else in that pile of résumés. Are you MENSA? Were you an All-American swimmer in 1969? Do you speak French? Are you the author of six adventure novels? Anything that you put in the "Miscellaneous" section will draw attention to you as a person. You never know what will strike a responsive chord in someone. No matter how good your résumé is, you won't get the job if no one remembers reading it.

For more detailed information on writing résumés, read:

The Perfect Résumé, Tom Jackson (Doubleday, 1981)

The Résumé Kit, Richard H. Beatty (John Wiley & Sons, 1984)

The Résumé Catalog, Yana Parker (Ten Speed Press, 1988)

The Complete Résumé Guide, Marian Faux (Prentice-Hall, 1988)

Résumés for Computer Professionals, William F. Shanahan (Arco, 1983)

The Best Résumés for Scientists and Engineers, Adele Lewis (John Wiley & Sons, 1987)

The Executive Résumé Handbook, Harold Dickhut (Prentice-Hall, 1987)

What Color is Your Parachute?, Richard Nelson Bolles (Ten Speed Press, 1971)

(These and all other books recommended in this book are available either in bookstores or major libraries.)

Developing Hidden Personal Talents

Overall, when people say they have "no talent," what they really mean is that nothing has stimulated the talent that they do have — yet. To discover the hidden talents inside you, look for new experiences that will develop your awareness of those hidden talents.

Develop a hobby. Sometimes people discover that they can get more satisfaction from a hobby than from a job.

Don't limit yourself. For instance, suppose you're an accountant. A friend of yours is putting together a magazine venture and they need someone to help with the accounting end of a business plan. Don't say "No, I don't do magazines." Say, "Sure, I'll give it a shot." You may find that you have a hidden talent for magazines.

Volunteer to help with Junior Achievement, the local chamber of commerce, or your local chapter of the Economic Development Council. Each of these groups will offer you the chance to work with businesses other than those connected to your line of work.

Do not cut yourself off from unexpected opportunity. To discover your hidden talents you have to put yourself in different settings. Vary your schedule. Take lunch in a different part of town. Get involved with the community. Go places you would not usually go. Read magazines you would not normally read.

USING A HEADHUNTER OR EMPLOYMENT AGENCY

When it comes to finding a new job — not a career, but a job — the first call most corporate people make is to a placement agency, colloquially known as a "headhunter." These are agencies which specialize in placing highly qualified people in high-paying jobs. An agency that places people in more common jobs is called simply an employment agency. Since this is basically a question of degree, I will use the terms interchangeably. The advice given here pertains equally to both.

There is nothing wrong with using a headhunter — as long as you keep three things in mind:

First, never use a headhunter if you are unhappy with your occupation in general. If you don't like the insurance business, changing to another insurance position is not going to make you happy. It is going to make you miserable because now you'll have paid $2500 to get another job that's causing you just as much gastric distress as your previous one. The headhunter can only find you a job; he can't choose your career for you.

Second, shop around before you sign up with any headhunters. Some firms will require money up front as a "registration fee" or other such expense. Be careful. The world is full of people who swear they can get you a high-paying job but "it's going to cost you."

Just as in buying a car or a home, purchasing the services of a headhunter requires caution. "Buyer beware" is an important concept to keep in mind. In most states, anyone with twenty-five dollars and the ability to sign his or her name can form an executive recruitment company. Certainly there are many legitimate businesses that provide quality executive recruiting services, but there are many fly-by-night companies as well.

If you don't know of the headhunting firm personally through someone who has used it, check whether the firm is a member of the Professional Association of Executive Recruiters. Check with your library. They will have a number of excellent directories listing executive recruiters, some even specifically designed for women.

Third, even though you may not actively be looking for a new job, you may get a call from a headhunting agency. Headhunters are often looking for clients to fill positions at companies they represent. But if you get a call out of the blue, be very careful. While all calls are supposed to be confidential, that's not always true. There are no secrets in this world and if you don't know to whom you are talking, you could be placing yourself in a great deal of jeopardy. As you know, word does "get out."

If you get a call from a headhunter, listen to what he or she has to say and then set up an appointment at his or her agency. Once again, if you have never heard of the firm, check them out at the library. Get a reference if you can and call the person before your meeting with the headhunter.

If word does leak, don't deny it. Honesty is always the best policy. Besides, no one is going to believe that you did not get a call if they have information to the contrary. In fact, Jim Kennedy, publisher of *Executive Recruiter News*, even suggests that you tell your boss that recruiters frequently call you but you have no plans to change positions. You will then be viewed as a more valuable asset.

On the other hand, if you are not getting calls from headhunters when you aren't looking, you had better get on someone's list. "If you don't get four calls a year," a former General Electric executive noted, "you're in trouble." Keep your name active with a headhunting firm even if you are not planning on leaving — just yet. No one knows what the future will bring and, like a good scout, you should be prepared.

Also, if you do get an interview through a search firm, don't try to go around them. These men and women are professionals. They are often paid by a firm on an ongoing basis to provide competent executives. The client trusts the headhunters and undoubtedly has a long-term arrangement with them. He has faith in them. If you try to go around the headhunter, you'll probably find yourself out in the cold. The company won't deal with you, and the headhunter will cut you from his or her call list.

Keep in mind that each headhunter has his or her own clients. If you want to work for a particular corporation, find out from your contacts which headhunter placed the executives in the department where you want to work. You can also raise your profile by participating in high-visibility roles, such as volunteering for nonprofit organizations or participating in worthy community causes. Headhunters are looking for people who stand out; it's easier to "sell" a person who has high visibility and a dedication to identifiable goals.

GENERAL TIPS ON DEALING WITH HEADHUNTERS AND AGENCIES

1. Remember that all headhunters were not created equal. Before you sign with any agency, check around. Call a few of them. What do they specialize in? How much is the placement fee? Who pays the placement fee? If you pay the fee, how must it be paid: in a lump sum or can you stretch the payments over six months?

2. Read everything before you sign any document. Make sure you understand what you are paying for. Make certain that if you find a job under your own steam, even in the company you already work for, you won't have to pay an agency fee.

3. Don't apply to every employment agency in the book, under the mistaken impression that the more agencies that are looking, the more likely you are to find a job. What may happen is that you will find a job with one agency and discover that another agency claims you owe them a finder's fee because you "really" got the job through their lead.

4. Contact the agency as soon as possible. Even if you don't expect to start looking for six months, let them know. The longer the agency has to present your résumé, the better your chances of finding that "perfect" job.

5. Work with your agent by giving tips. If you know, for instance, that you would fit in perfectly at a certain company, tell your agent. It's his/her job to track down new leads. Make your agent's job easier.

6. Don't neglect the possibility of temporary work. Should the right job not be available right now, a temporary position will keep your bills paid until the perfect job comes along.

7. Keep all appointments that your agent sets up for you. Be prompt, professional and courteous. Being rude, late or unprepared may very well keep you from getting another interview. After all, from the agent's point of view, he or she only makes money if you get the job.

NETWORKING FOR A NEW JOB

While it's all fine and dandy to talk about headhunting, agencies and dressing for success, the actual fact of the matter is that about ninety percent of the jobs in America are found through networking. Say you are looking for a job and your friend Charlene knows of one at Consolidated Electric Enterprises. Charlene tells you, and you make a call. You get an interview. That's networking. Often it's just that simple. Here are some networking tips from the experts:

1. The moment you know you are going to be looking for a job, call everyone you know at other companies. Casually tell them you're looking for a job and see what happens.

2. Choose the companies where you would like to work and then create an excuse to go there. Check out the bulletin boards. Is there a social function coming up? Is there a softball game or a volunteer activity? Don't look like a gate-crasher, but join in the fun and meet the people — then subtly drop the hint that you're looking for a new job.

3. Go to social functions such as concerts, operas, art shows and other such meetings that sophisticated business people would attend. Mingle with the crowd and make friends.

4. Many cities have networking groups. Ask around. Join the Chamber of Commerce and get involved with its committees. Join Rotary.

5. If you're looking for specific professional groups locally, but can't make contact, go to the library and look them up in the *Encyclopedia of Associations* (Gale Research).

6. Don't overlook the possibility of volunteer work. An influential headhunter reports: "One of my best sources of leads over the years has come from networking. I network with health organizations by doing volunteer work. I choose three health organizations and spend my time getting to know the staff and the board. Do you know who is on those boards? Those people aren't the tire-kickers, they're the ones who sign the checks: my kind of people."

Remember, personal contacts come before business contacts. Don't expect to network in another company unless you can get to know someone there.

INTERNSHIPS

An internship is generally a short-term position that pays little or nothing, but which provides a great deal of experience. It also provides a foot in the door to many otherwise inaccessible companies. If you are seriously interested in finding an internship, contact your reference librarian for annual guides to internship programs.

If you're thinking of the possibility of an internship, do not wait for a "convenient" time to go to the library. Most of the internship programs have deadlines, and putting together your application may require more than just your name, address and a copy of your résumé. Competition for these intern slots is fierce, so you should expect to spend quite a bit of time on your application.

If you are interested in contacting an active program to find out more about it, below are some programs which were highlighted in the February, 1989 issue of *Black Enterprise*.

Linda Alexander
National Urban/Rural Fellowships
570 Seventh Avenue
Suite 905
New York, New York 10018
tel. 212-221-7090

James W. Barge
Accounting Fellow Program
Office of the Chief Accountant
Securities and Exchange Commission
450 Fifth Street NW
Washington, D.C. 20549
tel. 202-272-2158

Ann W. Lavin
President's Commission on White House Fellowships
712 Jackson Place NW
Washington, D. C. 20503
tel. 202-395-4522

Maureen S. Myers
The Kellogg National Fellowship Program
W. K. Kellogg Foundation
400 North Avenue
Battle Creek, MI 49017-3398
tel. 616-968-1611

Stephen D. Nelson
Congressional Science and Engineering Fellows Program
American Advancement of Science
1333 H Street NW
Washington, D. C. 20005
tel. 202-326-6600

Jenifer Renzel, Director
Stanford Sloan Program
Graduate School of Business
Stanford University
Stanford, California 94305-2144
tel. 415-723-2144

Alan F. White
Alfred P. Sloan School of Management
Massachusetts Institute of Technology
50 Memorial Drive
Cambridge, Massachusetts 02139
tel. 617-253-7166

Rotary Foundation of Rotary International
Group Study Exchange Program
l Rotary Center
1560 Sherman Avenue
Evanston, Illinois 60201
tel. 312-866-3000

HOW TO READ WANT ADS

When looking for a job, do not neglect the most important tool at your
disposal — the newspaper.

   After reading the business section to see which businesses are
expanding, go immediately to the want ads. These are jobs that really do
exist and will most probably be filled.

1.   Be skeptical of any jobs that promise too much. No one is
     offering a job for $1500 a week in the Want Ads. If the ad says
     "no experience necessary," wonder about it.

2.   Be wary of jobs being advertised through employment
     agencies. Think. Why would an employment agency be
     advertising a job? It could be so bad that they could not place
     any of the people they handle. Before you send any
     paperwork in, call the agency and ask how long the job has
     been vacant. If it's been a while, think twice.

3.   Government jobs, by regulations, have to be advertised. Don't
     get your hopes up. File your résumé and wait.

4.   There is nothing wrong with applying to a post-office box or
     blank address. It does make preparing for an interview more
     difficult, however.

5.   Look for hotline numbers. Many large companies have so
     many jobs open so often that they have a recording to list their
     vacancies. These numbers are often listed in the paper. Write
     the phone numbers down and make it a ritual to call the
     hotline on the FIRST day it changes. Don't find out on
     Thursday that the job you wanted opened the previous

Monday. When looking for a job you need all the advantages you can get.

6. Keep in mind that you don't have to respond to questions concerning your age, marital status or a number of other personal questions. Also, be wary of giving your Social Security number to anyone over the phone. If they want it, let them ask for it on the employment application.

7. Don't give names of references unless you are specifically asked. If someone is serious, fine. If not, you don't want to annoy your references by having four or five prospective employers calling them for no reason.

8. Experts disagree as to whether or not you should ask about salary before you fill out an application. Some feel you shouldn't waste your time on a job that doesn't pay enough. Others recommend not discussing salary until the job has actually been offered to you. You will have to eventually decide for yourself. You might want to determine the general range beforehand and leave the specific numbers until the end.

9. What does the want ad NOT say? Is there something suspicious about it? Has this job been advertised before? If so, why is it open again?

10. Keep track of the ads to which you have sent inquiries, particularly if there is a company name in the ad. Don't end up with an interview for a job that you can't remember applying for.

11. Finally, there is no shame in sending a résumé out to every possible job lead. All you're wasting is a stamp, an envelope and a résumé. Remember, about 70 percent of your inquiries will go unanswered, and roughly 85 percent of those that do answer will be negative. Sad but true.

USING A COLLEGE PLACEMENT OFFICE

One of the best ways to get a new career is at the placement office of your local college or university.

Traditionally, a college placement office is where students are put in contact with people who have part-time work. But this has been changing over the years. With so many students going to night school, full-time or almost-full-time jobs are often listed on the employment board alongside temporary jobs.

Even better, at the end of each academic session, recruiters from all over the country converge on colleges to find the best and the brightest for their companies. You can take advantage of this opportunity by signing up for an interview. In most cases you do not have to be a student at the college, though it certainly helps. Get your appointment with the college placement officer and then do your research at the college library.

By the way, if you're looking for a new job, you might also look at the employment office of the college itself. Colleges hire a wide variety of professionals. Even though your experience may be in the business world, there are plenty of opportunities for business professionals in colleges.

THE INTERVIEW

If all goes well, be it through networking, agencies or whatever, you will be offered an interview. After looking over your résumé and\or talking with a headhunter, a corporation may want to call you in. But do not be fooled. This does not necessarily mean that there is a job for you or, for that matter, that there is even a job available. But it *does* mean that you're being seriously considered for a position of some kind.

There is a television commercial aired for a shampoo that's message is "You never get a second chance to make a first impression." When it comes to an interview, that is definitely the truth. That interview is your moment to shine, personally and occupationally. If you're hired because "you were the best that we could find on short notice," you will always be viewed as someone who got the job only because you happened to be in the right place at the right time. Once you are viewed as a lightweight, that's exactly how you will be treated.

On the other hand, if you go into an interview and really make an impression, your superiors will have no choice but to feel fortunate that they were in the right place at the right time to pick you up. You rose above their level of expectation. They will treat you like a heavyweight because they view you as one.

As far as you are concerned, the mechanics of the interview should start long before you ever walk into the room. First, immediately after you make your appointment for the interview, research the company. You may want to contact a newspaper clipping service in your city for

Are You Prepared for a Tough Interview?

While you're doing your research for your next interview, be sure you can answer the following ten questions:

- What is your weakest point?
- Why should you be hired to work here?
- Why are you leaving your present job?
- Do you have a personality conflict with anyone at your current job and, if so, why?
- What are you worth?
- What can you bring to this company?
- How much volunteer work do you do in your spare time?
- Have you had any personal problems that have caused you to miss work over the last three years?
- Why do you change jobs so frequently?
- How do you operate under stress?

every news article that has been written about your prospective new employer in the past year. You can find clipping services listed in the Yellow Pages of your city's phone book. Additionally, if you have the money for it, there are companies that specialize in monitoring television news broadcasts on both national and local stations. You can find these through the clipping services or by looking up "broadcast monitoring" in the Yellow Pages.

The more you know about the company that interviews you, the more it looks like you really care about working for them, and the better your image will be. Take the time to do your research. A one-hundred-dollar-investment for a clipping service is a small price to pay for making a good impression on a company that may be paying you $60,000 or more plus benefits for the next twelve months.

Second, choose your interview clothes at least a week before the meeting. Stick to conservative colors like blue and gray. Follow the guidelines of John T. Molloy's classic work, *Dress for Success* (Warner, 1978). Even if you are applying for a job where clothing has nothing to do with work — such as in an art department — dress conservatively. There is more riding on your appearance than you think. Superficial as it seems, people will often form first impressions based on your appearance. If you're a sloppy dresser, you will look like a sloppy worker.

These days, there's another reason to dress well. The interviewer will be considering how you will act in public. More and more companies expect their employees to become part of the community — to serve on nonprofit boards or with charitable associations. High profile employees mean a high profile for the company. In the corporate world, this is called free advertising. But no company wants its reputation tarnished because some employee makes the company look like a collection of cowboys. Every company feels that its image is at stake every time it hires a new executive. You're not just applying for a job, you're asking to be part of a corporate image. Sad though you may find it, if you don't fit the image you may not get the job, even if you're more than qualified to do the work.

So be very careful about your interview clothes. Are they clean? Are they still in style? When was the last time you wore them? Don't leave anything to chance. If the shirt is faded or stained, even slightly, get a new one. The same goes for the tie. Don't risk a $60,000 job on a ten dollar tie. Shine your shoes.

If you wear glasses, think about the frames. Heavy, black, plastic frames may make you look out of place. Green or red framed glasses may make you look ridiculous. Round lenses may make your face look owlish. Look in fashion magazines to see what kinds of frames are available. While this may not seem like much to you, it's important to a corporation interested in image. If you do get new glasses, make sure that they're non-glare. The extra forty dollars will be well worth your effort down the road. When someone's eyes cannot be seen, there is a tendency to believe that they're lying. A forty-dollar expense now could be worth your job later.

Get your hair done no later than three days before the interview. You want your hair to look good, but not to have that "just cut" look. Avoid tints and shades. Stick to your natural color and a conventional hairstyle. If that's not your usual style, suffer. Spiked hair, no matter how carefully done, is not going to leave a positive impression in the corporate world.

On the day of the interview, leave plenty of time to make it to the appointment and find parking, even if you have to walk around downstairs in the lobby for ten minutes. Arrive about five minutes early so you can use the restroom and check your hair and clothing. After you have told the receptionist who you are, sit down and pick up a magazine. You don't want to walk into the room gasping for breath as if you've just dashed up ten flights of stairs.

When you walk into the interview, try to relax. There is nothing else you can do but be yourself. Be comfortable. If you're offered coffee, accept it if you wish. That's fine. But don't smoke — unless you're being interviewed by R. J. Reynolds. Even if one of the interviewers is smoking, it's still not a good idea.

While there are scores of books on how to do well in an interview, the truth is quite simple: Be yourself. Companies hire more than just a warm body to sit at a desk from nine to five. They hire human beings with personalities. Let your personality shine through. That's your salesperson. Let that salesperson do his or her job.

Answer the questions fully. Don't lie. If something is proprietary, say so. Don't talk about personalities even if everyone in the room knows the same people. Don't assume you have the job and that this interview is just *pro forma*. On the other hand, don't walk into an interview assuming you were damn lucky to have gotten this far. What you feel will be expressed in your body language. Make sure you are sending strong, positive messages. If you are unsure what that means, read *Body Language* by Julius Fast (Pocket, 1979).

Once the interview is finished, leave the office immediately. Do not stop off and see a friend before you go, or visit the bookstore on the tenth floor. Treat the interview as what it was, a very important business meeting. If the interviewers know you're stopping off to see a friend that works for the company, it may appear as a tidbit of pressure. If they know you are going to a bookstore upstairs, it may appear that you don't view this interview as a serious matter, just something on your laundry lists of "things to do today." If the interview is important to you, treat it that way.

If You're Having Trouble Finding a Job...

- Redo your résumé.
- Extend your networking efforts. Go to meetings and lunches you would not usually attend. Go to cultural events and volunteer meetings.
- Keep a positive attitude. Many people get fired and many people are unemployed. It's going to take time to find another job. If you think negatively, it will show in your attitude.
- Dress professionally.
- Avoid the generic. Don't send in photocopied cover letters or make phone calls that have no purpose other than to "keep your name and face fresh."
- Work a full day, every day, looking for a job.

- Prepare for your interviews. Read up on your prospective employer. Follow the corporation's stock for the last six months.
- Be honest in an interview. Lying will not necessarily get you a job but it will probably get you fired should the lie ever be discovered.
- Examine every job carefully. Even though you're eager for a job, do not accept something just because it's offered. You may find yourself with a job you hate but cannot leave.
- Expand your job search far and wide. Reading the want ads and the industry publications will only inform you of a fraction of the jobs available. Almost all of the private sector jobs are never advertised. You'll find those jobs by meeting the people who know there are positions open. The greater the number of people who know you're looking, the greater your chance of being employed.

2

CORPORATE SURVIVAL

❖ ❖ ❖

"Now this is my kind of job," a disgruntled employee snarled as he read the want ads. "This corporation says they're looking for someone who's responsible. Hell, every time anything goes wrong around here, I'm responsible!"

❖ ❖ ❖

One of the facts of life is that when you work, you must work with people. And as we all know, people are, well, people. There are moments when they are vain, moody, greedy, excitable and unpredictable. In short, "they" are just like us. While most of us have no difficulty loving humanity, we have a great deal of trouble always getting along with people.

Knowing how people really are, it's hard to work with them and still keep your sanity and your job. But whether these people are your co-workers, assistants, competitors or clients, dealing with them can be the most important job you have. There are thousands of people who cannot cope with the pressure. Stress, mental fatigue and career burnout are the result. If you don't have the time or money for a mental breakdown, then you had better learn to get along with people as soon as possible.

❖ ❖ ❖

"Man — a creature made at the end of the week's work when God was tired."

Mark Twain

❖ ❖ ❖

29

To successfully deal with people, though many of us refuse to recognize it, we must first learn to deal with ourselves. The better each of us knows who we are, the better equipped we are to deal with the corporate world. While this may sound like a passage from a "feel-good-about-the-world" paperback, look at it another way: Every day at the office you are going to have to interact professionally and effectively with a wide variety of personalties in a bizarre spectrum of moods. On any particular day you may have to contend with an edgy client, a moody public relations director who has never liked you but just asked you to "do lunch" and "talk over some concepts" and a chain-smoking marketing representative who is always in a crisis mode. And that's just before lunch. Who knows what the afternoon holds in store for you.

Regardless of your mood, personality or job description, you are going to have to deal with each of these people on a personal, professional and protracted basis before the sun goes down. That's life in the corporate world. You have two choices: 1) You can do it and like it, or 2) you can do it and not like it. The choice is entirely up to you.

To keep your sanity and job, you should know the basics of self-preservation. While no one can tell you all the rules, here are some basic ones.

THE FIRST RULE OF CORPORATE SELF-PRESERVATION

Be yourself. To understand this rule, think of the best salesperson you ever met. Most likely it was someone who got along with everyone, regardless of their personality. He or she could make a sale even with the hardest nut in the buyer's seat. That salesperson wasn't just good; he or she was great. Being a good salesperson means being able to read people like a book. Since everyone is different, each person must be treated differently.

For example, there are some clients who appreciate a dirty joke. There are others who will be upset if the word "damn" is said in their presence. There are some people who would rather talk about fishing than advertising. Others just want to talk business.

Knowing that is what makes this person a good salesperson. What makes this salesperson a survivor is this: Even though he or she is dealing with a wide variety of individuals every hour of every working day, the salesperson's personality is not changed. When the day is through, the salesperson is still a unique individual. During the day, the salesperson must be flexible to deal with the spectrum of people with whom he or she must communicate. But the basic personality of the salesperson, his or her individuality, is not affected.

It is important to note that "being flexible" does not mean the salesperson is all things to all people. What it does mean is that the successful businessperson realizes that different people respond differently. People are individuals and have to be treated as such. To get ahead in business, you have to deal effectively with the individual signing the checks. To be a survivor, you have to deal effectively with the individual inside of you.

❖ ❖ ❖

"This above all, to thine own self be true."

Polonius, Hamlet, *Act I, Sc. 3*

❖ ❖ ❖

When it comes to source material on dealing with people, most libraries in America have a wide spectrum of books. Some of the better ones include:

I'm OK; You're OK, Thomas Anthony Harris (Harper & Row, 1969)

Huddling, The Informal Way to Management Success, V. Dallas Merrell (Books on Demand, 1979)

The First Book of Common Sense Management, Diane Tracy (William Morrow, 1989)

Why Work? Leading the New Generation, Michael Maccoby (Simon & Schuster, 1988)

The Gamesman, Michael Maccoby (Simon & Schuster, 1976)

The Naked Manager, Games Executives Play, Robert Heller (E.P. Dutton, 1985)

Three other books that are worthy of note that fit peripherally in this subject are:

The Peter Pyramid, L. J. Peter (William Morrow, 1986)

Thriving on Chaos, Thomas Peters (Alfred A. Knopf, 1988)

Games Mother Never Taught You, Betty L. Harragan (Warner, 1987)

THE SECOND RULE OF
CORPORATE SELF-PRESERVATION

Know what is expected of you. One of the biggest causes of competent people getting fired is that they have confused their job description with their actual duties.

❖ ❖ ❖

"Expecting the job description to match the job being done is like signing an elephant to play shortstop for the Chicago Bears."

Warren Sitka, humorist

❖ ❖ ❖

For your own sanity and survival, be like most parents on Christmas Eve: Throw away all the directions and figure it out for yourself. Don't believe what people tell you; find out what's really true. Only as a last resort should you try to go by the instructions.

A job description is simply an outline used to hire someone. You just happened to be that someone. Individuals may be hired on the basis of how their credentials and experience match the job description — sometimes — but once they're hired their duties are, as the fine print says, "as required."

To survive in the corporate world, your first task is to understand exactly what is expected of you. Look around. Open your eyes. Think. What do you see? Who are the power brokers in your department? Who really does the work? Who's close to retirement and how much work are they doing? Are there pending legal problems? Are your co-workers finishing projects or have the projects died of neglect? If you are in a sales position, are your co-workers closing? Have sales been slipping? Has there been a change in the market that will affect performance in the months ahead? (If you followed the advice in the previous chapter and bought a year's worth of newspaper clippings, you would know.)

Don't be afraid to look even deeper. If you've been hired to be in charge of half a department, who runs the other half? Is there a functional reason for the department to be divided as it is? If not, you have another job unmentioned in the interview. How old is your co-supervisor? Is he competent? Who handles money? When was the last audit? Who does the auditing? Which lower-level managers seem to have greater responsibilities than you would have expected? Why? Are you a minority? If so, are there any other minorities in your department? Are you in a "window" position for the public?

If you start your first day on the job with a turf war, that's a pretty good indication that you have not been hired just to do your job. You have also been hired to keep someone on their toes or, sad to say, force someone out. Is there an "experience" flaw in your co-supervisor? Is your co-supervisor on the way up or out?

Your first obligation in any new position is to discover for yourself exactly what your real job is. Not what you were told it was, but what it really is.

THE THIRD RULE OF CORPORATE SELF-PRESERVATION

Always C Y A: cover your ass. The cliche is true: Corporate America can be a jungle. There are very few rules in the corporate world and most of them are broken frequently. Your goal is to survive with your sanity intact.

Be careful. When you're slogging it out in the trenches, it's very easy to believe that the higher up you are in the corporation, the more rules you can break. That is a myth. No one is immune from the repercussions of bad decisions. Corporations fold from bad management decisions. People are fired because of bad decisions. There is only one group of people who profit from those who break the rules: federal investigators.

Don't be a fool. Follow the rules. It may seem boring, but to be on the safe side, CYA. And make absolutely sure that while you are following the rules, you are not being set up for someone else's mistakes.

While CYA tips could take an entire book, below are a handful that will help get you through your first year:

Memos — Whenever you participate in a meeting in which you're given an assignment, even a nebulous assignment, write a memo indicating how you understand the project and when you expect the project to be completed. When it is completed, write another memo. *Keep a copy!*

Calls — Make every call you have to make as soon as possible after you have been assigned to make the call. The less important the call *appears* to be, the more important it is. If you think the call is a waste of time, be careful, someone could be using you as the fall guy. Then, if there is any trouble, you could be blamed for not having made call. *Log your calls!*

Secrets — If you believe there is a such a thing as a secret, you should also believe in the Easter Bunny and Santa Claus.

Meetings — About ninety percent of all meetings are not worth attending. The problem is that no one knows which ten percent will be the important ones. So don't miss any of them.

The tell 'em rule — Even if you have never been in the Army, follow the military procedure when giving instruction. Tell someone what you're going to tell them. Tell them. Then tell them what you've told them.

cc — If you write a letter at the request of someone and sign your name, send a copy of the correspondence to everyone involved in the process as well as their brothers, uncles and anyone else remotely concerned. Once your name is on a piece of paper, YOU will be held responsible for any repercussions from it.

Copies — Keep a copy of every CYA memo and letter you write. It might even be a good idea to keep the copies at home. Never underestimate what someone will do to cover themselves when their job is at stake.

The phone rule — If you wouldn't say it in the office, don't say it on the phone. People overhear things. There are extensions, and even bugs.

Keys — The fewer you have, the better off you are. The more keys you have, the greater the chance of having to explain what you were doing when something disappeared from a room to which you have one of the keys.

Cash — Don't touch it. Even if it comes with a receipt, don't touch it.

Checks — Make sure there's a paper trail for every check you handle. This means a receipt, copies of the letter with which it came, and copies of your letter with which you sent it along. If there is no paper trail, don't touch the check.

Read — Read what you sign. Think about what you're reading. Sign it only if you have read and understood it. Keep a copy.

Lying — Don't. Remember that every one of your co-workers that is intelligent has a personal copy of their critical memos and letters.

Unfairness — Life is unfair. Learn to live with it.

Guess — Don't.

Assume — Don't.

Pawn — Don't be one. When something doesn't seem right, it probably isn't.

I don't know — The three most important words you can say when you really don't know.

Ways to Commit Corporate Suicide

- Start rumors.
- Lie.
- Go for the "Quick Fix."
- Blame others for your mistakes.
- Violate a confidence.
- Drink to excess, or use drugs for any non-medicinal purpose.
- Miss meetings.
- Firmly believe that your private life, even on your own time, is of no concern to the corporation.
- Don't bother to read memos.

While numbers one to nine are part of a generic list that most of us have seen for years, number ten is new. It does not fit in conveniently with the rest, but it may be the easiest way of all to commit corporate suicide.

- Believe there is objective reality.

Remember, what you view as reality, others view as your opinion. Perception is reality. What people see, or think they see, they believe to be true. When you work for a corporation, follow the Roman adage: "Avoid the appearance of evil."

DEALING WITH MEMBERS OF THE OPPOSITE SEX

Around the office, it's always best to be purely professional in your dealings with the opposite sex. Use common sense and remember that even if you act with only the best intentions, people can still misinterpret what you do. This is equally true whether you are a man or a woman. In a worst case scenario, you can be liable to charges of sexual harassment. But even in lesser instances, your reputation and esteem will suffer if people think of you as sexist.

Keep in mind that perfectly innocent requests can be interpreted as harassment. If you are a man, asking a woman to make coffee is generally insulting. If you are a woman, asking a man to perform janitorial or maintenance duties is just as bad. Make certain that any instructions you give do not have the slightest hint of sexism.

Socializing with an employee of the opposite sex is risky. It inevitably opens the door to suggestions of impropriety. Many companies will take official steps to prevent intra-office relationships from forming or continuing.

In general, we are in a transitional era where the rules of what is and is not sexual harassment have yet to be set. An action that you may consider harmless may just hit the wrong button in someone else. For the moment, at least, the best advice is simply think about your actions. Be considerate of the other person's feelings. And make certain that you don't inadvertently offend anyone.

Sexual Harassment

Charges of sexual harassment are becoming a fact of life in American corporations. What was accepted as standard practice is now considered grounds for lawsuits. Play it safe.

- Don't call women in your department "honey," "sweetheart," "darling," "bitch" or make any sexual innuendos. Even if you're a woman.
- Don't make sexually suggestive remarks, even in jest. The person you are speaking to may understand that you are being funny, but others may not. Your behavior could end up as an example of sexism in the workplace.
- Don't touch other people.
- Don't make any evaluations of personnel that carry, or seem to carry, sexist overtones.
- Do read *Corporate Romance* by Leslie Aldridge Westoff (Times, 1985) if you are getting serious with, or married to, someone with whom you work.
- Do read *Games Mother Never Taught You* by Betty Harragan (Warner, 1987).
- Do understand that the world is changing. There is an ever-expanding list of individuals who fall under the category of "minorities." Guidelines for dealing with people will be getting far more complicated before they get easier.

The rector of the church frequented by Jay Gould, financier and railroad magnate, wanted to invest his $30,000 life savings. The rector asked for a stock market tip and Gould suggested Missouri Pacific but told the rector not to mention it to anyone else.

True to Gould's word, the price of Missouri Pacific stock rose rapidly but several months later, fell dramatically. The rector lost his entire life savings.

Much to the rector's surprise, soon after the stock crashed Gould gave him $40,000. The rector thanked the magnate profusely and then stated, guiltily, that he had also told some other members of the congregation about Gould's tip on Missouri Pacific.

"Oh, I know that!" Gould replied. "They were the ones I was after!"

❖ ❖ ❖

CORPORATE POLITICS

❖ ❖ ❖

Corporation: an ingenious device for obtaining individual profit
without individual responsibility.

The Devil's Dictionary, *Ambrose Bierce*

❖ ❖ ❖

Keeping your sanity and job requires more than just CYA. It requires an understanding of the nuts-and-bolts of corporate politics. Difficult? Not really. You just have to understand that there are basically three games being played at the same time. The first is the primary function of the corporation: make money. It's crude but it's true. Period. The bottom line is top end and black ink is gold.

The second game is just as crude. It's to keep other corporations from increasing their slice of the market pie.

The third battle is yours. It's the day-to-day battle to keep the corporation operational and operating. You are expected to keep your expenses down, the competition in the dark, and, at the same time, "maintain the integrity of the corporate system." That means that you are supposed to be a team player, keep the lights on, provide the brain boys upstairs with all the research they want, avoid embarrassing the corporation in public and keep your department under budget every reporting period and on time every day.

Your job is made even more difficult by sometimes having to work with people who are idiots, have no desire to advance in the corporation, cannot advance in the corporation, refuse to work overtime, display symptoms of budding psychological disorders or who spend so much time crawling up your back that you feel you should have a plastic surgeon implant a ladder.

What does this have to do with corporate politics? Regardless of what anyone tells you, advancement in corporate America, academic America and small-business America has little to do with talent and ability. It has more to do with networking, Machiavellian subversion and end-around-runs.

Just as assuredly, your advancement will also be based on your understanding of the three games being played. If you don't understand the "big picture" and can't get along with your co-workers, you will not advance. It's easy to say that someone got a promotion because they "had a friend upstairs." But that might not be true. What is true is that if you continue to believe that just knowing someone will get you up the corporate ladder, you are in for a rude awakening.

Required reading for understanding the corporate game is extensive.

For the best books, read *The Prince*, Niccolo Machiavelli (New American Library, 1952); *Power: How to Get it; How to Keep it*, Michael Korda (Ballantine, 1976); *Up the Organization*, Robert Townsend (Alfred A. Knopf, 1970); and *The Peter Principle*, Laurence J. Peter and Raymond Hull (Bantam, 1984).

Office Politics

Office politics is a deadly serious business. Playing it poorly will not only ruin your chances of advancement within the corporation, it may even put you out of the corporation altogether. Here are some basic rules for down and dirty survival in the trenches:

Maintain ongoing, semi-personal relationships with the other people at the office. Meet at least three times a week to "shoot the breeze" with your colleagues. This networking will keep you informed as to what is happening, and, more importantly, give you a chance to stop any rumors about you that are starting.

Beware of empty praise. If you're suddenly being praised, be careful. Somebody may be setting you up.

Watch for changes in personality. If your supervisor starts taking long lunches or sitting in his or her office with the door closed, it could be a sign that he or she is on the way out. Be very careful.

Mentors are good to have when you need them, but when they go down, so do you. It's your choice; but don't make that choice lightly.

In and Out groups change. He who is in today may be out tomorrow. Choose your friends wisely.

Profit when you must make an enemy. If you have no choice but to deal with someone harshly, don't do it on the spur of the moment. Make sure you get something out of it. That enemy is going to be waiting in the bushes to do you dirt for years to come. If you have to watch your step, you might as well profit from the confrontation.

Beware of committees. Committees are appointed because someone doesn't want to make a decision. Usually a committee will develop a solution that's worse than the original problem.

Consultants are not hired to solve a problem. Their job is to do the bidding of the person who hired them. Do not argue with consultants. But don't believe them either.

"Marching Orders" are what you are supposed to be doing. Listen carefully and you will be told.

Affairs of the heart at the office are never a good idea. Try to avoid them yourself, but if you see someone else's affair causing problems, keep your mouth shut.

Joke telling is fine if it isn't in a sterile business setting. Be sensitive to the feelings of others. Racial jokes are never proper, no matter how funny you think they are. Sarcasm, too, should be avoided; it's too easy to be misconstrued.

Loyalty is highly valued in a corporation, regardless of what you may think of it. Do not be disloyal. If your boss is in trouble and you appear to be pulling the rug out from beneath her feet, no one is ever going to trust you again.

Beware of any social changes in your office. If suddenly people aren't talking to you, find out why.

Give credit where credit is due. Don't end up with someone on your staff disliking you because you used one of his ideas and never bothered to thank him for it.

Getting rid of a hazard is a very dangerous game, and should only be done as a last resort. If you do not know how to play the corporate game, live with the hazard. Getting someone moved off the playing field is a game for the experts. Read the section on Damage Control if you are in *deep* trouble.

DEALING WITH BUREAUCRACY

An unavoidable aspect of corporate politics is having to deal with bureaucracy. Remember your worst experience with government bureaucrats? Corporate bureaucracy is worse because you have to deal with these people and this system everyday.

First of all, it is important to remember that a bureaucrat is basically someone with turf to protect. These people are given responsibility for a tiny piece of corporate ground, and they intend to make good use of it. Try not to get annoyed if they tend to lord it over every one else, or if they don't use their corporate turf wisely.

The best way to deal with frustrating bureaucracy is to find someone in that department who is competent and deal with them, even if that's not the person you're *supposed* to deal with. Keep in mind that bureaucracy was not developed to drive you crazy. It's just some of the people in it that get to you. So deal with other people.

Second, understand that discretion is much more effective than a memo or complaint. Always try to work through people not over them. Going over somebody's head may help in one case, but it will make it much harder when you run into that bureaucrat the next time.

Be extremely careful when you run into a bureaucratic roadblock. There might be a very good reason why you're not getting the information you're looking for. Check out the situation. You may be stepping on delicate toes.

Finally, cultivate connections with capable people. In the long run, they will rise in the corporate structure. Never lose contact with those who have helped you, even if it's only once.

What to Expect from a Good Assistant

Everybody who's anybody has an assistant. They can run the office, or they can ruin your career. What should you expect from a good assistant? It goes without saying that your assistant should be able to communicate effectively, take notes, check for typos and see a project through to completion. But what are the more important, subtler things to look for?

- Loyalty. Loyalty does not mean putting his or her job on the line for you. It means living with the decisions you make and not "bad-mouthing" you at the office, at home or on the street.
- Honesty. Face it, not every idea you've ever dreamed up is a good one. The higher up you are in a corporation, the fewer people there are that will tell you when your idea is junk. Finding people to tell you your ideas are stunning is easy. Finding someone who will honestly tell you when you are

being stupid is very difficult. If your assistant isn't being honest with you, find another one — QUICKLY.

- Good Phone Manners. Your assistant is your representative to the rest of the world. When your assistant is rude on the phone YOU pay for that.
- Resourcefulness. How long does it take your assistant to find something out of the ordinary? When you need something quickly, how long is "quickly?" Can your assistant use the library competently? Does your assistant know how to use the FAX machine? Does your assistant have to ask other people for help with his or her work? Remember, there are very few secrets in an office. The more people that have access to your paperwork, the fewer secrets you'll be able to keep.
- Amiability. Does your assistant get along with the rest of the people in the office? If not, you are being cut out of a lot of useful networking information.

FINAL PLACEMENT

❖ ❖ ❖

"In a hierarchy every employee tends to rise to his level of incompetence [and the] work is achieved by those employees who have not yet reached their level of incompetence."

L. J. Peter, author of The Peter Principle

❖ ❖ ❖

Final placement, as L. J. Peters notes, is when form becomes more important than function. People who have achieved final placement have reached the top rung of their ladder at that corporation. They probably won't be fired, but they will never rise any higher. Around the office, these people are probably known as twits, losers, backsliders or a variety of other terms many of which could not be printed in this book. They may have the personality of a log and the work ethic of a three-toed sloth or they could be very personable and seem to do a lot of work around the office. They could be part of a federal matchgrant or even the son or daughter of a close friend of the CEO. Whatever they are, they are in your department, and often they are your supervisors.

It's very easy to spot someone who has reached their highest possible position in the corporation. The easiest way is to compare how they act to what they do. Where are they when work has to be done? Where are they on payday? What time do they come into the office? What time do they leave?

On a positive note, these people are great for moving desks around the office and finding waste baskets. They are even better at delegating responsibility and blame. They are best at leaving early on Fridays. They are the kind of people who would never be missed. Essentially they are nothing more than conduits, like assistant commissioners. They are highly-paid employees who simply pass instructions down from the corporate officers and channel the results up from mid-management. ... as they ... have to initial memos, make sure ... rooms are clean, ... weather reports and harass secretaries ... later than 10 A.M. ...

"The head of the department ... old guy who had been with ... teen or nineteen years. Nobody upstairs wanted to fire him but nobody trusted him to do any work. So he would show up and walk into his perfect office and clean desk, close ... during ... all day. We just worked around him. But what upset me was that he was pulling down $50,000 a year and I was ... to have friends upstairs."

typical lament

Final-placement employees are very bad for morale. They make quite a bit of money and do less work than the secretaries — who often do almost all of the work. Worse, most of them spend the day wandering around or poking their noses into other people's projects, which only reinforces the distaste the rest of the staff has for them.

Be particularly careful of people in final placement. If they are still working, someone higher up is protecting them. The more incompetent they are, the higher up their protection. If you are unused to the corporate game, stay away from these people. While Hollywood has done an admirable job in showing how these people can be used — see if you can find the old but still applicable musical *How to Succeed in Business Without Really Trying* — the fact of that matter is that people in final placement are time bombs.

Regardless of what L. J. Peter may say in *The Peter Principle* and *The Peter Prescription,* individuals in final placement are not passive parts of the corporate network. If you tickle them out of their comatose state, they could come out and actually do some work. This invariably results in at least one of three disastrous consequences:

1. The person will step out of his or her office and do the job they were hired to do — generally messing the system up very badly. They have neither kept up with the professional advancements over the years nor the changing texture of their office. But they have the corporate muscle to force their point of view. The project they choose to supervise will immediately disintegrate, the staff will hold you personally responsible for the disaster and it will take six months to pull the project back to its original state and three more months to get the person back into his or her office.

2. The project will be so far along that it will succeed in spite of the person's questionable supervision. This will immediately inspire him or her to take charge of the next project which will immediately disintegrate. The staff will hold you personally responsible for the disaster and it will take six months to straighten the project out and three more months to get the person back into his or her office.

3. The person will be asked to use his or her influence to suggest a project for the department. He or she will make the suggestion to his friend in corporate management along with some additions that he or she thought were good ideas. The idea will be accepted with the suggested additions. The project immediately disintegrates because the suggested additions are not workable. The staff will hold you personally responsible for the disaster and it will take six months to redirect the project and three more months to get the person back into his or her office.

Unless you are a very shrewd corporate manipulator, stay away from people in final placement.

❖ ❖ ❖

"So much of what we call management consists in making it difficult for people to work."

Peter Drucker, author of Frontiers in Management

❖ ❖ ❖

Consultants

Far too often a consultant is hired to implement a political point of view rather than clean up a mess. How can you tell the difference between a hack and a qualified harbinger of change? You can't. But you can survive a consultant if you:

- Listen carefully to what the consultant is telling you. Just because you suspect him or her does not mean that the person is wrong.
- Remember that most corporations will resist change. But don't develop the attitude that any change is bad.
- Consider that while things may be going well in your department, they could be falling apart in another. Just because a consultant shows up in your department doesn't mean that your department is in trouble.
- Look around your own department. Are you as efficient as you could be? If not, then maybe there's a very good reason for the consultant to be there — regardless of whether he or she is a hack.
- Count the number of people in final placement in your department. If you have a lot, you're in trouble. These people are deadwood. They are a drain on the budget and an embarrassment to the corporation. If you are in charge and a consultant shows up, you'd better be thinking of giving these people a lateral transfer — or you might get a terminal transfer yourself.
- Provide all the information a consultant requires, even if you think the consultant is doing a hatchet job on you and the department. Remember, the consultant has been hired to do a job. He is also making more than you are, and that is a direct expense to the corporation. Don't make it difficult for the consultant, or the consultant could make it very difficult for you.
- Hands-on is the way most consultants like to handle problems. Don't expect a team of consultants to sit in a back room and go through old office memos. Expect them to be out and around the department.

- Remember the "Punk Rule of Consulting." Many consultants will tell you (off the record, of course) that someone in the company usually knows what has to be done. No one is listening to that person because they consider him or her to be a punk, a lightweight or a royal pain. A smart consultant always looks for that "punk."

By the same token, if you have a problem, solve it the same way the consultants do. Find that person who can solve the problem. You might find that most informed source is the office worker you dislike the most.

ETHICS

❖ ❖ ❖

"An ethical man is a Christian holding four aces."

Mark Twain

❖ ❖ ❖

Yes, there is such a thing as business ethics. While most business books skim over the subject as if it were a swamp, ethics is just as much a part of business as an accounting department or public relations program. It's a large part of staying sane and employed in the corporate world.

Damage Control And Security

There are some real slimeballs out there. You may work with one of them. It's a big corporation and there are a lot of people gunning for your job. Strange things are happening at the office. Major changes are coming. Some of your paperwork is being waylaid and changed. You think your office is being snooped. Your phone makes funny clicks. Obviously this is not simply office politics. This is a very serious and extreme situation. You're sure you're not being paranoid; someone actually is out to get you. What do you do?

- Take your sensitive work home with you.
- Vary your schedule so that no one can predict when you will be in the office.
- Take items of great personal value home. Also take home any personalized stamp pads, checks even if they're canceled, any extra clothing and items that are traceable to you.
- Clean your computer's hard disk onto diskettes and take the diskettes home each night.
- If things *really* get bad: Report any illegal activity, no matter how minor, to the police. Do not lie to the police, and do not exaggerate what happened. But if anything does happen, you want to make absolutely, positively sure that there is a paper trail that shows you reported illegal activities very early.

Do not do anything illegal yourself. You have no idea how much worse things can be if you break the law.

❖ ❖ ❖

"If you want to know what God thinks of money, look at the people he gave it to."

popular saying

❖ ❖ ❖

Staying ethical in an unethical world is not easy. If it were profitable, everyone would be ethical. But it isn't. On the contrary, having ethics is very expensive. It can slow down your advancement in the corporation, and force you to forgive people who make mistakes. But it can keep you out of jail. "Greed is good," Ivan Boesky, convicted Wall Street swindler, is reputed to have said, and look what a lack of ethics did for him.

Some people depend on the teachings of the Bible to guide them through a corrupt world; others depend on their experience. Whatever their model, those who try to maintain ethical standards have a number of beliefs in common.

What Goes Around, Comes Around

Just as you treat people, so shall you be treated. It may take some time for your reputation to circulate, but it will.

If you expect to make your way up the corporate ladder by

destroying people on your way up, you can expect to be destroyed in the same fashion. The longer it takes, the more disastrous will be the consequences.

Beware of the Quick Fix

When you are working on a project, do it right the first time no matter how long it takes.

Doing it right the first time means more than doing a quality job. It means making sure that the project is done with the long term in mind. If you do something that is "good enough for government work" and will last six or seven weeks, don't forget that six weeks later you are going to have to do it again.

❖ ❖ ❖

"When we first started putting our marketing files in order, we didn't bother to make a master file," a rueful employee laments. "Each person had their own clients and the dockets were filed by salesperson's name and then by client. None of the paperwork in the files was alphabetical or chronological. Each salesperson filed the paperwork the way they wanted. Why didn't we make the files uniform? We didn't think there was enough activity to make it worthwhile. Then, as salespeople came and went, the system became unworkable. Finally we had to stop sales for a month just to straighten out the filing system. That was our lowest sales month in years and did we catch hell from upstairs. It would have been a lot easier to start putting the files in order right from the start."

❖ ❖ ❖

If you are interested in more information on the disastrous consequences of the quick fix, you might want to get a copy of *American Business and the Quick Fix*, by Michael McGill (Henry Holt, 1988). McGill looks at management practice fads of the last forty years and how they were packaged and sold to America's business community. This book is must-reading for anyone in a supervisory capacity. It's particularly critical reading for managers because, as McGill observes, when employees lose faith in management, "no fad or fix, regardless of how popular, can remedy the situation."

Believe in the Law of Inevitabilities

With every decision that is made, there is an inevitable consequence. If you want to play fast and loose with the facts to make a sale, you are most certainly going to have to live up to the promises you made.

If an alcoholic refuses to reform, he will die. If drunk-driving arrests, canceled auto insurance, jail time, rehabilitation sessions and the loss of his wife and family don't cure him, death will.

What does this have to do with ethics? Along the corporate trail, you may be tempted to violate ethical standards. You may be able to get away with the violations a few times, but sooner or later you are going to be caught. That's known as the "Law of Big Numbers." If your chances of being caught are one in ten, and you cheat ten times, you are going to be caught.

The people who have severe ethics problems are those who continue to cheat after they have been caught the first time. If caught again, the punishment will be more severe. If they continue to cheat, they could very well be out of the company.

The problem with a section on ethics is that no matter how it's written, someone will always say, "Hey. That's a bunch of hogwash. I believe in the old-fashioned way. Do unto others before they do unto you." Reasoning like this has made the corporate world a jungle. It will allow you to survive in the short term. But it will not help you in the long run. Set your goals high, and work to achieve those goals. Spending your time doing unto others before they do unto you is *wasting* your time. Spend your time doing a good job and moving up in the corporation.

Handling a Snoop

All the world may love a lover, but all the world hates a snoop. The scary thing is that snooping is far more widespread than you may think. Hopefully, you'll never have to deal with one of these corporate creeps, but you just might. Here's what to do if you think there's a snoop in YOUR office:

- Private correspondence and papers should be kept under lock and key.
- Wastebaskets are a terrible place to dump important papers. If you don't have a shredder, tear your important papers in two. You might even deposit one half in your wastebasket, and the other half somewhere else.
- Locks on your desk are made to be used. If someone asks why you lock your desk, ask them how they know your drawer is locked.
- Vary your break and lunch schedules. This will make it

harder for someone to predict when you'll be away from your desk.

- Shrewd corporate players occasionally come back to their offices unexpectedly. Perhaps they announce loudly that they're going out for a long lunch, and then five minutes later come rushing back for an umbrella.
- Catching someone in the act of snooping requires you to keep your sense of humor. Ask if they are looking for anything in particular. If a person is snooping they will probably mumble something stupid. Let it pass. But keep an eye on them.
- Reporting snoops is never a good idea. Don't assume that the snooping is being done for the personal gratification for the snoop alone.

CREATIVE ESCAPES

There comes a time, we all know, when we are forced into that uncomfortable position of having to answer a question for which the most appropriate answer is a lie. Don't do it. No matter how much easier it seems, you will be found out eventually. So what do you do? First, read the alternatives in the rest of this chapter. Then follow the advice in a very timely fashion — immediately.

Statistics

One of the easiest ways to present a cohesive argument is to gather statistics that accurately prove your point.

Where do you find the statistics? Go immediately to the reference desk of your local library. Even if your library is the size of a walnut, most of the basic business statistic books are available.

But when you go to the library, go the reference section first, NOT the card catalog. Why? Because people have been known to become lost and never return from book stacks. Further, if you do what everyone else would normally do, your results will look just like theirs. Follow the old adage: Be bold, be different, but be first!

Once you're in the reference section, go to the business books. (Go to the 330s. If that doesn't make any sense, your library is not using the Dewey Decimal System.) Look over those first. Next, before you go to the card catalog, go the *Reader's Guide to Periodical Literature*. For those not familiar with the library, this is an annual catalog of all articles printed in major newspapers and magazines on all subjects. Follow the *Reader's*

Guide to the actual articles in the magazines — often on microfiche. With any luck at all, you can put together a comprehensive report using just the reference material and the *Reader's Guide* within two hours.

Case Studies

Along with statistics, case studies are the best weapons in your arsenal. A case study can illustrate that someone somewhere else did the same thing your company is trying to do and made a WHALE of a mess.

Where do you find case studies? The best place to start is once again the *Reader's Guide to Periodical Literature.* If you check over the past three years you'll probably find a number of articles which specifically relate to the decision your corporation has made.

"Fine," you say, "now that I've got all of the statistics and case study material together, what do I do with it?" Good question.

Orphaning an Idea

If you have an idea that, for some reason, you do not want associated with your name, you can "orphan" it, or allow your idea to become someone else's without them ever knowing that it was yours. Say, for example, your idea is in conflict with one your boss had a month ago, or that it's a risk for which you don't want to be held responsible. Then you orphan it.

The process of orphaning is simple. You can take your entire package, drop it on your supervisor's desk or put it in his mailbox. For better results, put a memo on it that says "Read" and scribble some illegible initials on it.

If you work in an office where anonymity isn't possible, put your work together and go to see your supervisor. Say something clever like, "I just heard about the new policy. I did all this research that probably won't work now." Drop the envelope with the research on your supervisor's desk and change the subject. Then leave without the envelope.

If your supervisor gives you the envelope back unread, send it upstairs anonymously.

You can also send the envelope to your supervisor's home with no return address — Federal Express makes it seem even more important.

When I used to work as a legislative aide, I would often take my ideas — carefully packaged — and present them as something I had "found" in the hallway. Then I would give my boss a don't-ask-me-about-it look and drop it on his desk. If that didn't work, I would pass it around among the other aides for comments, knowing full well that eventually one of them would pass it along as their idea.

For those who say, "Well, that means that someone else is getting credit for my idea," the response is "So what?" If you are clever enough to come up with one good presentation, you will have no trouble doing it again. Whoever steals the credit for that report will only be able to do it once. They will have to come back to you for the next one.

Then it's time to talk turkey.

Horizon Thinking

If you have trouble with the office sleight-of-hand that's

Effective Memo Writing

- Be short.
- Be succinct.
- Be factual.
- Be finished.

If the memos you write are not being read, it could be because they were poorly written. Find a copy of Cheryl Reimold's *How to Write a Million Dollar Memo* (Dell, 1984) for some tips.

---

necessary to orphan an idea, or you feel that you always want to be identified with the solutions you propose, then you fight bad ideas with *horizon thinking.*

Remembering that most ideas are for the solution of short term problems, look for ammunition in the long term. Ask yourself, how is this going to affect the company in the long term? Find the weaknesses. Once you have found the weaknesses, put stress on them.

Take, for instance, a situation where company profits are going up but stocks are going down. To stop the downward sweep of stock prices, management decides to launch a public relations campaign. You don't think this is a good idea because you work for an oil company and there has just been a major spill in Alaska.

Being a horizon thinker, you suspect that stock prices are going down because of the reaction to the oil spill. A public relations campaign is only going to be an expensive way of reminding potential stock buyers just how much they hate the oil industry.

What you do is look to the long term. You know that those people selling their stock are short-term investors. You really don't need them for the long term. What the corporation needs are stockholders who have faith in the long term economic viability of the company.

Develop your own idea of an effective campaign and present it. Don't just whisper it, present the complete package. If you're going to take heat anyway, it might as well be for a whole proposal as for a single idea.

Maintaining your sanity and keeping your job day by day is not an easy task. Even with the advice in this chapter it can still be difficult. However, all of the tools you need are at your fingertips, or readily available. All you have to do is reach out.

Meeting Etiquette

- Meetings are a bore. Even important meetings are a bore. Live with that fact. Be on time and stay awake.
- At each meeting, expect the "heavyweights" to spend the first couple of minutes talking amongst themselves. This is normal even if they have just been talking a few minutes before the meeting. It's part of showing their corporate muscle. Don't interrupt them.
- Go to the bathroom before a meeting, even if you don't "feel the urge." You don't want to have to leave halfway through an important discussion.
- Stay away from coffee and cigarettes if they make you hyperactive. Liquor of any kind before a meeting is a very bad idea. Remember, every meeting is potentially a battleground; don't go into that battle without that competitive edge.
- Always have a pad and pencil, even if you won't need them. It makes you look efficient.
- Depending on your personal habits, be wary of pens. Pencil marks can be erased; ink cannot. On the other hand, inked notes make a better impression on someone casually looking at your notepad. But when you try to cover something up with a pen, it is very visible.
- If you doodle, keep the doodles clean. Don't write obscene words on the pad, and don't include any insignias or logos that you don't want everyone in the room to see. Keep in mind that doodles tell quite a bit about the person. If you are in a violent turf war with someone else in the office, you could be releasing valuable personal information.
- Never talk about your dreams to anyone. They also release quite a bit of valuable, personal, psychological information about yourself.

- Choose your seat carefully. In the days of old, the deadliest enemy of the king sat on the king's left. The king's closest ally (his "right hand man") sat on the king's right. Why? Because that way the king had control of his enemy's right hand, the sword hand, and the king's sword hand was protected by his closest ally. Today, the best seat is still to the right of the power broker.
- Think before you open your mouth. Have marching orders been given? What were they? Where do you fit in the big picture?
- Arrive early and leave late. Socialize with your co-workers. It's a way of networking and stopping rumors. No one has nice things to say about someone who arrives fashionably late and leaves early as if they had to go to another appointment.
- Be suspicious of the unexpected. Meetings are the fertile ground where the seeds of disaster are sown.
- Ducks should always be in a row. If they are not, don't bring your idea up. Period.

CAREER BURNOUT

Regardless of how well you've mastered the art of corporate survival, there may come a time when you feel trapped, bored or just downright miserable. It could be burnout. You've seen it happen. An ambitious, intelligent, competent individual is working hard, when suddenly, for no apparent reason, his or her output begins to lose its spin. The work just isn't as good, but no one seems to know why. It's frustrating for him or her to see the drop in quality. In particularly bad cases, it may even lead to problems at home, drinking or drugs.

Many times, the person who exhibits these symp-toms is suffering from career burnout. What is even sadder is that sometimes the victim may recognize the problem as burnout, but not know what to do about it.

The initial step to combatting burnout is to recognize the disease. Frequently it's caused by spending too much time performing the same function. If you have been doing the same job in the same company for a long time, ask yourself the following questions.

Do I want to come to work as badly now as I did a few years ago?

Do I look forward to the challenge of more work?

Has the quality of my work improved as much in the last two years as it did the two years before that? Or has it gotten worse?

Am I spending more time working than fooling around at the office?

Have I taken a real two-week vacation that has nothing to do with work in the last few years?

If you answered "no" to two or more of these questions, you are a prime candidate for career burnout. What can you do about it? Take action immediately. If you decide you don't like your company or career, the answer is easier; start looking for a new one. If you like the company or the career you are in, talk to your boss about restructuring your job to include more challenging tasks. If that doesn't work, start looking for another job where you are or in the same field. You've gotten bored and tired of doing the same thing over and over again.

Second, take a real vacation. If you think, "I wish I could," or "I can't afford to take the time now," then that's all the more reason to take that vacation *now*. All work and no play will not only make you a dull boy or girl, it will burn you right out of your career.

Third, start looking for mental stimulation in your life. Visit museums during your lunch hour. Get involved with a local community group. Take up a sport. Sign up for a class. Keep in mind that you are trying to stimulate your mind, to recharge those mental batteries. You might not realize it right away, but this will gradually give you a new perspective. You have to do something to liven up your life, and snap you out of those doldrums before it's too late. Then you can get back to enjoying your work.

Briefcases, Business Cards and Stationery

Before you spend hundreds of dollars on briefcases, business cards and stationery, look at what other people have. Use your head. Yes, individuality will get you noticed, but that's not always a good idea. Remember, you want to be seen as a team player.

Business cards are a must. In most corporations you will be given a card. If not, see if there are standards.

Then, depending on your position and personality, decide how you want your card to look. You'll have to walk a thin line here. Inside the corporation you will be expected to conform. But the fact of the matter is that the only way most people outside the corporation will remember you is by your card. If your card is generic, you're forgotten a week after you've passed it along. So stay within the bounds of decorum, but do something different. Run the script up and down instead of side-to-side. Put a drawing on it. Be clever. If you don't know how to be clever, open the Yellow Pages to "graphic artists." These people are paid to be clever. It may seem a trivial point, but your business card will say a lot about you. Make it say good things.

Don't let titles fool you. Outside of one's own corporation, titles mean very little. "Vice president," for instance, is a title that is given out quite freely in some corporations. With so many corporations giving advancement in titles rather than in cash, "vice president" is a fairly generic term.

On the other hand, be very careful of someone who gives you a business card which has no title. You never know who you are really talking to. People with no titles are either very influential or not influential at all. Also beware of people whose cards say "special projects" or "operations." Once again, these titles can mean a great deal or nothing at all, but rarely something in between.

Whenever you think of personalized stationery, don't. Unless you can keep track of every single sheet of paper, you're putting yourself at undue risk. It may have that nice personal touch, but any letter written on that stationery will be assumed to be from you, even if you didn't write it. Personalized memo pads are also a bad idea. Anyone can forge your initials. Live with the indignity of having to sign off on corporation stationery.

A briefcase looks good even if it's never used. If you decide to carry a briefcase, make sure you open it frequently enough that people assume that you're actually using it. Make sure there is company material in the briefcase. And locking the briefcase is a good idea, just in case there is a snoop.

LONG-TERM PERSONAL PLANNING

Career burnout is often the result of poor long term personal planning. Perhaps you've stayed too long in one job simply because you don't know where to go next. It's always a good idea to keep the long term, the next five to ten years, in mind. You don't have to be incredibly specific, but you should have a general concept of your goals. Then, plan your life in reverse. First picture where you want to be, then figure out how to get there.

Suppose, for instance, your goal is to be a department head in five years. Chart your course. How many jobs are between you and your goal? How did the people who hold these jobs get there? Do they have graduate degrees? What kind of experience?

Now, to be fair, look at the downside. What hours do they work? Are there responsibilities you wouldn't want? Is there more pressure than you can deal with? Don't work hard to get somewhere only to find out you hate the job.

Bare vs. Cluttered Desk

If you have a sick mind, are looking for a new job or are the CEO, you're free to have a cluttered desk. If you're trying to make a good impression, make sure your desk is tastefully bare. A cluttered desk doesn't make you seem hard-working, it makes you seem sloppy and unorganized.

Then ask yourself how much you are willing to put up with to move into each slot. You're going to have to pay your dues each step of the way. What makes paying those dues bearable is knowing that you are on the way up. If it were easy, everyone would do it.

Once you've determined what your goals are and what you have to do to achieve them, always keep them in mind. Be on the lookout for any oppor-tunity that will help you on your way. Don't slow yourself down by staying too long in a job that was just a step on the ladder. Don't get sidetracked, or you could watch as your goals get less and less likely.

CORPORATE TRAVEL AND ENTERTAINING

CREDIT AND CREDIT CARDS

Credit cards are a fact of business life. They are essential to even the most basic transactions such as writing a check at the grocery store. They're a blessing insofar as they provide us with a means of buying goods and services without using cash. They save us when our car breaks down or when we accidentally end up with the dinner check.

But credit cards can also be a curse. Since spending is so much easier than saving, the cards have a tendency to, well, fill up. Worse, many of us don't pay off the total amount. This leaves us with a debt at an interest rate of fifteen to twenty percent a year.

Like money, credit cards can be a slave or a master. Which of these they become depends on the person in whose hands the cards fall. Here are some simple rules for keeping your credit under control:

1. Credit cards provide the best receipts for your business expenses. But you can have problems with the IRS if you mix your personal expenses with business expenses. Do not use the

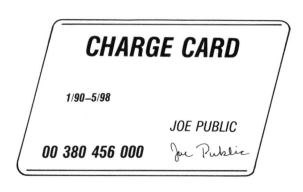

same card for both. The IRS will want all of your receipts to have an indication of the reason for the expense. That's why the receipts have room on the back for you to make notes.

If you have never written on the back of a receipt, try it before going out of town. Many credit card receipts have a wax on the back on which it is difficult to write. Make certain you have a pen that will leave a mark on the receipt *before* you go out of town on a business trip.

2. As long as you pay off your credit cards before the end of the billing period, usually a month, there is no interest charge. If you can pay off your bills by that time, the credit card, therefore, offers you a "float." You are, in essence, using someone else's money for a period of time. This is to your advantage. The downside, of course, is that most people don't pay in full by the end of the month, and end up paying interest. That's why banks like credit cards.

3. Keep all of your receipts, at least until the end of the billing period. When you get your bill, *check* your charges. This does not mean giving the bill a cursory look. It means looking at each of the signatures to make sure they are yours and that the amounts are correct. Don't be trusting. There are disreputable merchants who will add on charges.

4. *Check* for "post charges." These are charges that are added onto your bill *after* you have left the establishment. These are often legal, but you can complain. Check your receipts.

5. If there is a question on any bill, do not pay the amount of the receipt in dispute. Inform the credit card company why you are short in your payment. Make it clear that there is a problem you are trying to work out. Contact the establishment which has made the charges. If you're not satisfied that all is correct, inform the credit card company that you will not pay.

6. Be very careful about releasing your credit card number over the phone. If you don't know to whom you are giving your number, you may be in for a rude surprise.

7. Most credit companies have an insurance policy against stolen cards. Before you buy it, check your state laws. You may be paying for something that, legally, the credit companies are forced to provide any way. In some states, you are already liable for only up to fifty dollars of unlawful charges. Don't pay if you're covered free of charge.

8. When traveling, don't keep all your credit cards in the same billfold or purse. If you have more than one, leave at least one in your hotel room. What are you going to do

if you get robbed? American Express may be able to get you one in twenty-four hours, but there are three meals in every twenty-four hours and if you're on a business trip there could be other expenses as well.

TEN TRAVEL TIPS

1. For short trips, use carry-on luggage only.

2. For long trips, check your luggage at the airline gate, and let them see to it that it gets transferred if you have to change planes. Some car rental agencies will even handle your luggage right from their counter. Check with your travel agent.

3. Get your airline boarding pass and seat assignment from your travel agent. This will save time at the airport — particularly if you often arrive late.

4. Keep the confirmation numbers for all of your hotel and car reservations handy. You may need them to resolve any last-minute mix-ups.

5. Unless you enjoy talking on your flight, bring along something to read. Bring a novel or a magazine for when you are sitting in the airport waiting for your flight and more intensive work to do on the flight itself.

6. Choose your travel dates carefully. Traveling over the holidays or traditional vacation times may mean flight delays, crowded restaurants and overbooked hotels. It will also mean that the art museums or public galleries you were intending to visit will be closed.

7. Get a travel book on the city you are going to visit. Don't depend on the handout material that may or may not be in your room.

8. Bring your own alarm clock. You can't always trust the hotel's wake-up service.

9. With the exception of your business suits, which should be carried in a suit bag, bring and wear clothing that is wrinkle resistant. Sweaters and knits are good choices. If you have to carry ties in a bag, roll them up with your socks.

10. If you wear glasses, take along an extra pair as well as some sunglasses.

SURVIVING JET LAG

1. Adjust your thinking to the time zone where you will leave the plane. Lock your mind on that time. If you jog for an hour at noon, when it is noon at your destination, if possible, go jogging. Try to have breakfast even though you would be eating dinner on your old time clock. This will get you psychologically "in tune" with your destination.

2. Follow the anti-jet lag diet outlined in *Overcoming Jet Lag,* by Dr. Charles F. Ehret and Lynne W. Scanlon (Berkley, 1986). Experiments show that your body reacts in certain ways to the physical act of long-term flying. This diet prepares you physically for the ordeal ahead of you. Three days before leaving, "feast" on a high-protein breakfast and lunch — eggs, meat, fish, fowl — and follow with a high-carbohydrate dinner — pasta, fruit, salad.

    Two days before you go, "fast" with light meals but still keeping breakfast and lunch high in proteins and dinner high in carbohydrates.

    The day before you go, repeat the "feast," and on the day you leave, "fast." Then, "feast" at the time that is appropriate in your city of destination.

3. Avoid coffee and alcohol.

4. Get out in the daylight as soon as you arrive at your destination — assuming there is daylight to be had. Daylight will help you adjust — except in places like Alaska and Scandinavia, where the sun can shine through most of the night.

5. If you have problems with stress and stiffness, try "Fitness in Flight," a cassette of exercises you can do in an airplane seat, from Washington Healthcare Corporation, Room 8102, East Building, l00 Irving Street NW Washington, D. C. 200l0 (Under ten dollars).

A QUICK GUIDE TO WINES

Choosing the proper wine for your meal is not easy. It takes years of rather enjoyable practice. For the person who is going out to dinner in an hour and doesn't know anything at all about wines, here are some tips:

1. When you first get your wine list, look at it intelligently. Are most of the wines from California? If so, stick to California wines. You will have a wider variety from which to choose. The few French or Italian wines might be special vintages for the connoisseur. (That also means these wines are more expensive.)

2. Keep in mind that the wine you drink must add to the meal. Stick with white wines for fish, poultry and shellfish. Red wines go well with game, beef, lamb and heavy pasta dishes with tomato-based sauces.

   Beyond the color of the wine, ask the wine steward for a recommendation. If you are going to have a spicy dish, you want to make sure that the taste of the wine is not obscured. On the other hand, if you are going to have shellfish, you might want your wine to have a bit of a tart taste.

   If you have more than an hour, go to your local library and find a copy of the article "What's My Wine" by Steven Raichlen. It appeared in *Boston Magazine,* February 1986. Not only does Raichlen have specific recommendations for the proper wine, he also provides a list of "Good Vintages" (page 209).

   Another excellent source to help you with wine is the *Esquire* video, "The Wine Advisor." It costs about thirty dollars and can be ordered from Esquire Video, P.O. Box 648, Holmes, Pennsylvania 19043 or, if you're in a rush, call 1-800-345-8112.

3. When it comes to vintage, a good rule of thumb is to drink white wine within two years of its bottling, but the older the red wine, the better. If you are ordering more than one wine, follow the traditional drinking sequence of white wines before red and dry wines before sweet.

4. Before the wine steward opens the bottle, check the label. Did you get what you ordered? Mistakes can happen. If you wanted a twenty-five-dollar bottle of wine, make sure

you didn't end up with a one-hundred-dollar bottle instead.

5. When the wine steward opens the bottle, sniff the cork. Does it smell like vinegar? If it has a strong vinegar smell, ask for another bottle. Is the cork moist or dry? If it is dry, air could have seeped into the wine. Squeeze the cork. If it is dry and pieces of cork fall off, consider another bottle.

   Examine the wine against the white tablecloth. Is it clear? Cloudy wine indicates problems. A white or red wine that bubbles could also be bad.

   If it appears suitable, swirl the wine in your glass and smell its bouquet. Then take a sip. Swallow.

   Don't make too big a production out of this. Remember, you're not tasting for the quality of the wine — just to be sure it hasn't spoiled, that it's being served at the right temperature, and that it's the wine you ordered. Statistically, the chance of getting a spoiled wine is about one-tenth of one percent.

6. If you're buying a very expensive wine, you may want it decanted. Decanting performs two functions. First, any residue can be strained off before the wine is set at your table. Second, it allows the wine to breathe.

   The older the wine, the more time you must give it to breathe. With very old wine, that time could be two or three days. If you are going to have a special meal with a very expensive wine, talk to the restaurant's wine steward well in advance so that your wine can breathe properly.

7. If the wine is acceptable, just nod your head. Then enjoy the vintage.

8. If you are looking for a before-dinner drink, consider sherry. Cognac or brandy is best for after dinner.

9. Also keep in mind that if you are planning on drinking before, during and after your meal, you should be taking a cab home. Don't risk driving drunk.

10. Don't forget to tip your wine steward fifteen percent of the cost of the wine.

TEN ANNOYING HABITS TO AVOID AT A TABLE

Business lunches and dinners can be quite productive because you and your client are in a neutral location — not at your office nor at his or hers. It's a casual setting, rather than the stiff confines of a boardroom, and you're more inclined to be relaxed.

However, you can quickly turn a lunch or dinner meeting unproductive if you happen to have a personality quirk that grates. People are very particular about their food. Watching you pour a mountain of pepper on your steak could turn a client's stomach, and seriously affect his or her opinion of you. Everyone has quirks, but here are a few you should avoid:

1. Don't comb your hair or apply makeup at the table. If there is food on the table you could find yourself in the embarrassing position of trying to explain why some of your hair got into your client's minestrone. If you need to freshen your lipstick, excuse yourself, and go to the restroom.

2. Be sparing with the salt, pepper, butter, steak sauce or any other dressing on the table. Watch what your client does, and follow his or her lead. It's always a good idea to taste your food before you reach for the salt or pepper.

3. Let your client choose the table. This will give you a clue as to whether he or she smokes. Don't smoke unless your client smokes — even if your client says that smoke doesn't bother him. Smoke always bothers non-smokers.

4. Be very careful about drinking alcohol. When in doubt, don't. Alcohol will dull your sensibilities, exactly what you do not need in a business discussion. And you

still have to get home. Driving drunk is not smart, safe or legal.

5. Unless you know wines very well, let your client choose. If he or she doesn't know wines any better than you, let the wine steward make the decision for you. Don't try to bluff your way out of it. It will look very bad if your client does know wines.

6. Brush your teeth and use mouthwash before going to dinner. Eating will not hide bad breath. Be careful of your perfume, aftershave and deodorant as well. Remember, you're going to be in close contact with someone for at least an hour. Don't allow your fragrance to overpower the food you are eating.

7. Stay away from chicken with bones and soup. Chicken is hard to eat and you end up picking your way around bones. No matter how you eat soup, you have a tendency to slurp. Avoid fish with small bones, too.

8. Don't kick your shoes off under the table.

9. If you have a choice, sit facing a wall. While Wild Bill Hickock may have preferred to sit with his back to a wall so he could survey the faces in the bar, don't let your client think he's not important because you look up at each person that comes in.

10. If you're going to pay the bill, do it subtly. Don't put up a fight over the bill. Don't be stingy with the tip. How would you feel if you went out to a business dinner and saw your host cheat the waiter out of his fifteen percent?

HANDLING EMBARRASSING MOMENTS

No matter how closely you plan, embarrassing moments will arrive. Drunks stumble into your party, wine spills on your tuxedo, your client's husband cracks a dirty joke, you spill your buffet on the floor.
    Are you prepared? If not, here are some suggestions:

1. Have a repertoire of good, clean jokes or anecdotes that you can use when the situation gets tense. Save your old copies of *Reader's Digest* and buy all the funny books you can find. Read them. Buy books of anecdotes such as

The Little, Brown Book of Anecdotes, edited by Clifton Fadiman (Little, Brown, 1985) and commit to memory some of the better tidbits.

2. When something embarrassing happens, don't get flustered. Try to laugh it off, making a joke if possible. Let people laugh WITH you, not at you. Turn the situation to your advantage.

3. Do what good airplane pilots do: Play the "what if" game. While flying along they suddenly say to themselves, "What would I do if the right engine went out?" or "What would I do if a cargo door suddenly blew off?" They are constantly playing this game with themselves. But what they are really doing is preparing for an emergency.

4. Keep up with the news. If you can't remember jokes, at least you will have something current and nonbusiness-like to use as a distraction.

5. Keep a supply of emergency paraphernalia in your purse, briefcase or glove compartment. Be sure to include safety pins, styptic pencils, aspirin, dimes and nickels, facial tissue, tweezers, small scissors, clippers, deodorant, breath mints and whatever else you feel should be included.

   You should also keep a working flashlight in your glove compartment. To make sure the batteries stay fresh, put the batteries in backwards. When you need the flashlight, reverse the batteries.

ENTERTAINING AT HOME

Here are some common sense tips for a successful evening:

1. Subtly check with your guests if there are any foods that they do not eat such as pork, fish or meat. There are people who cannot drink milk, others who cannot handle seeds. Plan your meal carefully.

   Stay away from high-cholesterol hors d'oeuvres. If the party is going to be semi-formal or formal, stay away from foods that leave fingers sticky.

   If you are not a gourmet cook but would like to be, consider getting a copy of the *Esquire* video, "The Short

Order Gourmet." It costs under thirty dollars and can be ordered from Esquire Video, P.O. Box 648, Holmes, Pennsylvania 19043. You can also order it by phone (1-800-345-8112).

2. Make sure you have enough furniture for everyone to sit. Put coasters on all the tables. That's a strong hint that you do not want drinks placed directly on the surface.

3. Plan to have smokers, but be sure they have someplace they can smoke away from the crowd. Also be sure to supply enough ashtrays for everyone.

4. Count on someone using your phone. Be sure to clean any room with a phone in it, just in case.

5. Clear your living room of items that are of particular importance to you. Not because someone might steal them, but because they may end up broken or with wine on them.

6. Draw a map for your guests. No matter how simple it is for you to find your home, some guests will have problems. On that map, be sure to list the time you expect them, your phone number in case they get lost, and an indication of where parking is available.

7. If you want your guests to remove their shoes to protect your rug or floor, have slippers available. Few people feel comfortable standing in stocking feet in someone else's living room.

8. If you don't have a hall closet, expect to place coats on a bed. Keep in mind that if it rains or snows on the day of the party, your guests will have wet overcoats when they arrive. Plan for that. They may also have wet galoshes; plan for that as well.

9. Have a good supply of nonalcoholic beverages, both hot and cold, on hand. Don't pressure any guest to drink alcohol.

DINING OUT OF TOWN

Dining out of town is always an adventure, even for someone who does it frequently. To make the most of your adventure:

1. If your heart is set on a specific restaurant, call ahead for

reservations. Ask if anything special is happening that evening. If you are expecting a quiet, romantic evening and a victorious soccer club has reserved half the restaurant, you might want to go elsewhere.

If you're a wine connoisseur, make sure you call the steward in advance. Don't assume the wine you want is going to be available. Make arrangements for your wine to breathe if necessary.

2. Plan to arrive fifteen or twenty minutes early. This will allow for any freeway slowdown or subway delays.

3. Make certain that everyone knows where you're going. This includes the name of the restaurant, the address, the phone number, the time of the reservation and the name under which the reservation is made.

The restaurant's phone number is important because you'll have to phone the restaurant if you're delayed. Don't let the restaurant assume that you're a no-show, and give away your table.

4. Develop a Plan B. If you are going in more than one car, choose a place to meet if something goes wrong. Suppose the restaurant had a fire and is closed for repairs. Where are you going to meet the rest of your party?

5. If you plan on drinking, take a cab. If you want to arrive in style, take a limousine. But whatever you do, don't end up taking a DWI test.

6. If you have a tendency to have gastric difficulties, take along some medicine to help you.

7. Don't play explorer. If you haven't been there before, get a map.

If you're driving, make sure you have a flashlight that works and your spare tire is not flat. You might also buy a few of the slow-leak repair aerosol cans that sell for under five dollars. Flares are not a bad idea either. Toss an extra jacket and a blanket in the trunk.

8. Make sure everybody has the same time.

TIPS ON BUYING LUGGAGE

If you want to know true misery, take the wrong luggage with you on a trip. When you travel, luggage is your most important concern. It can make the difference between arriving at your meeting fresh, and running in, gasping for breath.

1. Choose your luggage on the basis of how you travel most often. Look for a lightweight, durable material if you do most of your traveling by plane. Airports have a tendency to damage or lose luggage, so don't spend money on expensive fabric. Also keep in mind that expensive suitcases attract thieves.

2. Stay away from white. No matter how well you clean it, it always looks dirty. Black is another color to avoid. Keep in mind the old adage that there are only two kinds of dirt: white dirt that clings to black objects and black dirt that clings to white objects. Neutral colors like grey or tan are always a safe bet.

3. If you can buy luggage with pockets inside, all the better. The pockets keep small items from running all over the inside. If you travel with ties, some suitcases have small compartments to keep your ties flat. These work reasonably well, and keep your ties a lot fresher than rolling them inside your socks.

4. Use matching luggage. This makes it easy to spot coming down the luggage ramp.

5. When you buy your luggage, make certain that at least one piece can slide under an airplane seat. If you can carry all of your luggage on board, you won't waste time waiting at the baggage claim area.

6. This may come as a shock to many travelers but there are garment bags that actually keep suits and shirts hanging upright! Spend some time looking at garment bags. Many travelers find that the best buys in garment bags are in the advertising section of the inflight magazines. When buying a bag, make certain that your clothes will hang, and not fall into the bottom of the bag. Also make certain that it's light so you won't be red-faced and sweaty as you lumber through the airport.

    If you travel frequently, spend the money for a good garment bag — getting a shirt pressed by room service is quick and inexpensive. Getting a suit repaired is another matter altogether.

7. If you can't fit everything you need — not want but NEED — into your suitcase and garment bag, you had better be on a long trip. If you think you're saving money by buying a larger suitcase that will hold more but has to be checked through, you'll find out how expensive it is to buy a suit in a strange town when you make it to Denver two days ahead of your luggage.

HOTEL ROOM SERVICE

One of the most overlooked services in a hotel is room service. Room service is more than just an expensive way to get breakfast in bed. It can shine your shoes, press your clothes, replace buttons, provide medical services and run errands.

While you may not THINK you need room service that much, consider how many times you have needed a ruler, pen, dictionary, map or pad of paper in your hotel. Most people just put on their jacket and head out the door. But that takes time. Room service is just a phone call away.

True, room service is expensive, but what is your time worth? Do you want to spend your time looking for a ruler or in your room working?

Room service may not respond quickly or get you what you want if they don't know you. If you spend more time getting to know them, they will respond faster to you and your needs. Hint: A good way for them to remember you is by your tips. However, examine your meal checks. Often, a fifteen-percent gratuity is already added.

Remember, too, that if room service does not have what you need, there may be a giftshop in the hotel that can accommodate you.

DEALING WITH YOUR BOSS

❖ ❖ ❖

It was the staff assistant's first day on the job. Handing the staffer an industrial stapler, the supervisor said, "I'll get the pages of the pamphlet together. When I nod my head, you staple it."

The apprentice did exactly as he was told and it took the supervisor half an hour to get his toupee off.

❖ ❖ ❖

The world is full of idiots. There is no escape from them. They sell shoes, real estate, stocks and bonds, advertising and office furniture. They write books. They work in offices. They act on stage. Some are rich, some are poor, some are male, some are female, but all are a royal pain.

While there are many breeds and brands of idiots, the worst idiot is the one that is your boss. He is a total and complete idiot. But he's also in charge of an entire department. He believes that everyone is entitled to an opinion and he states that opinion frequently. Worse, rather than just slink back into his office and close the door, he takes an active part in all projects. You can't work with him and he won't let you work without him. Staff turnover is high, and morale is low. What can you do if you find yourself in a situation like this?

"Smile, your mother said. Things could be worse. So I smiled. And you know what? Things got worse."

old saying from an old man, my father

Things could be worse, of course. Your boss could be a snoop, having a not-so-private affair with one of the research staff, or under the gun to implement an idea the CEO developed while she was up all night with a migraine.

Playing office politics is tough enough without having to deal with a difficult person. It can be virtually impossible when that difficult person is your supervisor. But that does not mean you have to live with stress, abandon your career or make a voodoo doll to keep in your drawer.

Remember, you're not alone. There comes a time in virtually everyone's corporate life when they have to deal with a difficult boss. If you are faced with this situation, remember that having an overpowering boss does not mean that you have to twist your personality into something it's not just to please him or her. What it does mean is that you must recognize that there are moments when you can be yourself, and others when you must take a back seat and keep your mouth shut.

Immediately, some people will claim this is duplicity. Not so. A wise individual knows that there are times to be vocal and times to be silent, times to talk and times to listen. Timing is the key. While you may feel that your boss is overpowering, he or she may see it another way. If the boss wants a moment to seem overpowering, fine. Just remember that you can have your moment, too.

STANDING TALL FOR YOUR IDEAS

At some point, no matter how delicately you treat your boss, you will inveitably have to make a clear-cut choice. You can continue to go along with your boss's ideas, which you know to be wrong, or you can stand up for your own ideas. How you handle this challenge may mean the difference between moving up or out.

For most people, standing tall for an idea that is not the boss's is a very dangerous position. After all he or she *is* the boss, and you *are* the employee. The boss has the experience, and you're the new kid on the block. And, of course, you could get fired if the boss doesn't like your idea. That is a risk you will have to face based on your personality, that of your boss and the subject in dispute.

If you are willing to take that risk, first be very sure that the idea you are presenting has been carefully considered. Have someone play devil's advocate to make absolutely certain you have covered all the angels. Don't bring up any idea you haven't thought about long and hard.

Second, tactfully bring up the fatal flaw in your boss's idea. If his or her idea is flawed, you have an obligation to at least point out the short comings. Diplomatically. Don't stand up in a meeting and announce, "That's a dumb idea beacuse..." Rather, say something non-threatening like, "Gee, that's a great idea, but what about..."

Third, remember to show that not only is the boss's idea flawed, but that yours is better. There has to be a burning reason for the boss to vote in favor of your idea, not just change his or her own. If you can't adequately illustrate both points of view, don't bring the subject up. Just sit there and be quiet. But if you handle this situation well, with diplomacy, tact and intelligence, not only will you find that your boss isn't nearly as impossible as you thought, but you'll pick up some credit as well.

❖ ❖ ❖

"The incompetent with nothing to do can still make a mess of it."

L. J. Peter

❖ ❖ ❖

But say you can't get your boss to think about your ideas, or even consider the possibility that he or she is wrong. Now what do you do? Before you make any kind of a career move, either out of the department or to another job, make certain of two things. First, that this person *really* is as bad as you think he or she is. Be honest. Is this person doing the job they are *supposed* to be doing? How do you know? Who does the job performance reviews? When was the last one done? When is the next one expected? Has there been a change in this person's behavior in the meantime? Is this person under the gun?

If the difficult person in question appears to be in a precarious situation, don't change jobs or positions. Just wait it out. There may be a reason that he or she is under the gun. The person you find difficult might be the pawn of a shrewd corporate manipulator. This unknown manipulator may be placing a hindrance to his or her own career in an uncomfortable position. Then, as these pawns fail to perform, they can be fired — usually by someone other than the corporate manipulator.

How can you tell if the difficult person is being programmed for failure? Open your eyes and pretend that you have nothing at risk. As we all know, it's easy to solve someone else's problems. That's because we're divorced from their realities. Do the same when you examine your own problems. Be open minded. What is really happening?

Has your supervisor been given a job that is impossible to do? Has someone said it is possible? Who said it? Is there a deadline to finish the project? Is there enough equipment and staff to do the project? If not, who controls the hiring of more staff or the buying of new equipment? Is anyone taking some unexpected time off at this moment or has someone announced plans on being gone in the next few weeks? If so, that could be when the boom is lowered.

If the person you hate most is also hated by almost everyone else in the department, step lightly. If she is being protected by a higher-up, how you treat her will determine your future. If she is being set up to be fired, how you treat her will determine your future as well. Be loyal, be honest, but be distant.

If your supervisor doesn't appear in any danger of being fired, there is the possibility that *you* are in danger of being fired. Your supervisor might be acting this way not out of stupidity, but malice. Are you being given an impossible task? Are you meeting all of your time and task benchmarks? If not, why not? Is someone acting as a bottleneck? Is this unusual for that person? Has that person had a behavior change lately? What does that person have to gain by having you leave? Don't ever assume that innocence or ignorance is coincidental.

❖ ❖ ❖

"Once you have eliminated all that is impossible, that which remains, however improbable, is the truth."

Sherlock Holmes

❖ ❖ ❖

Once you have eliminated the possibility that your supervisor is not going to be fired and that you are not in danger of losing your job either, you are stuck with the truth. He is incompetent and you are not. Incompetent, please note, in this case doesn't just mean he can't do HIS job; it might mean that no one else can do theirs efficiently while he's around. In the corporate world, this is incompetence, too, because you lose that "team spirit." As *esprit de corps* goes, so goes the department. As the department goes, then surely so goes the corporation.

Now what? Your first option is to work around your supervisor. This usually works because there is often an "escape valve" in every department. That is, there is always someone who has a friend higher up in the corporation. What usually happens in a case of incompetence is that the word "gets upstairs" that there is a problem with the chain of command. Then one of two things happens:

1. The incompetent is left in charge in name only. His supervisory functions are moved laterally and a *de facto* boss is put in charge. This person will be calling the shots in the department even though he or she may not have the title. The supervisor is in final placement, but at least his function has been shifted.

By the way, if you're hired into an office where it's quite apparent that the supervisor is already in final placement, stay awake. Even if you have nothing to do with him, when he gets fired or retired, the whole department might get cleaned out. It also means that someone you don't know is actually in charge. Find out who that is before you start trying to use any muscle. If you play it shrewdly, you could be promoted into your boss's position after he's fired.

2. The department is split in two. The old supervisor is given a meaningless task while the real work of the department is being done by the hard-core old timers. When you see this happen, work like hell to get on the side of the hard-core old timers. If you don't, when the corporation cleans house, you'll be the baby tossed out with the bathwater.

OFFICE TERRORISM

But suppose neither of these things happen. The incompetent supervisor puts up a struggle and won't give up his position or authority. He demands to be left in charge of his department and won't take a raise in pay, advancement or a lateral shift. He wants to stay in charge. You still can't work with him, and now you can't move around him.

This can be an intolerable situation. You can live with it or you can change it. Try to live with it. If you absolutely can't, there is one final alternative. You don't have to quit; you just have to get creative. But you also must want to continue in the corporation for the long term. Remember, this is an absolutely last-ditch move. What you are going to do is, for want of a better term, office terrorism. You are going to cause serious damage to the office structure and a lot of good people are going to quit. There will be real damage here, particularly if corporate heads refuse to step in. But then again, if the heavyweights don't step in, the corporation gets what it deserves.

Be very careful. Do not start the following activities unless you're absolutely committed to staying in the corporation for the duration *and* you can count on your co-workers to join in unasked. This will be a gut feeling. *Don't ask for help. Let it come naturally.* Further, understand that once these activities begin, everyone will be under scrutiny. If your boss discovers you are the ringleader, you WILL be fired. (Making sure that your Plan B is operational, check with your headhunter to see what's happening "on the street.")

First, realize that you don't have to take the stress. Since your supervisor is so sure that he is in charge, let him be in charge. Pull back on things you used to do out of the goodness of your heart. Let things fall through the cracks. Then make sure that someone higher up *sees* that all is not well in Lilliput.

Second, start transferring the stress back from where it came. That's only fair. This is known as sharing. You have been taking stress from

How to Avoid Getting Fired

- Understand where you fit in the big picture. You're more than just a little cog in a big wheel; you're a valuable person in the corporate structure. In most cases, so long as you perform as expected, you won't be at risk.
- Understand that people are different. Don't try to treat all people the same. Learn to deal with each of your co-workers on their terms, not necessarily yours.
- Review your work critically. Are you working up to your ability? What will make you a better worker? Are you spending the time you should to improve yourself?
- Listen carefully.
- Find a mentor, a more established person in the corporate ladder who can assist your career.
- Be yourself. No one likes a phony. No one trusts a phony.

your boss's actions — or inaction — now force it back to him. Finish your section of a project early and let it be known that you've done your part. Now it's his turn. If you're lucky, the rest of the department will get the message. Without being told, everyone will begin finishing early. Now the work is piling up on his desk. He'll soon be buried.

Third, follow the book. If there is a question, ask it. Don't ask stupid questions. Make them important, complicated and time-consuming. Let him take care of those items you used to handle. Stress that the decision is too important for you to make. Let him make it. Let him sign off on it. Let him take the heat you were willing to take a few weeks earlier. Sooner or later everyone will be asking questions.

Fourth, force your supervisor to arrive on time and keep him late. If he wants to run the department, fine. Make sure he's there to do it. Develop schemes for holding meetings early. Create complex problems that have to be resolved immediately, and don't present them until 3:30 in the afternoon.

Fifth, keep up the pressure. If the entire department maintains a rigorous onslaught, your supervisor is going to wonder just what was so great about this job anyway.

If you need more ideas, read Michael Korda's *Power: How to Get It, How to Keep It* (Ballantine, 1976).

As a side note, don't assume that you would be a great boss just because your current boss is incompetent. Dell Books puts out a series called Clear & Simple series which features books for specific business problems. *Being a Boss* by Cheryl Reimold (Dell, 1984) is an excellent book, as is *Think Like an MBA* by Marian Colwell (Dell, 1984). Being a boss is not easy; don't assume that it is.

THE OLD GUARD

❖ ❖ ❖

"The older I grow, the more I distrust the familiar doctrine that age brings wisdom."

H. L. Mencken

❖ ❖ ❖

When it comes to power in the corporation, the *real* power, not the man with the title or the woman with a large office, those that have it are called the Old Guard. Regardless of what you may think, these people are very competent. They got to where they are by being the most competent people in the company. You may not at first regard them as particularly bright, creative or dynamic, but, after all, they're still in the corporation and still drawing a paycheck.

The first mistake in corporate politics is to believe that the Old Guard are all part and parcel of the same mind set. That is a strategic error. Corporations are made up of people. That's all. Just people. Corporate leaders are just as concerned about their careers as you. They have financial problems, cheating spouses, drug-addicted children, carnivorous compeers and aspirations for advancement that may never be fulfilled.

Whether you like your corporate heads or not, there will be no advancing if you cannot get along with at least one or two members of the Old Guard. This does not mean that you find a mentor, toady up to anyone or change the way you think. What it does mean is that you have to find a member of the Old Guard who "thinks" like you. You will only advance on the merits of your ideas if your they're allowed the room to be presented and tested.

If you think office politics is rugged at the department level, wait until you get upstairs. Department politics will seem nothing more than a tempest in a teapot by comparison. The Old Guard plays very rough. They are not dumb. They've been around the block many times and they're shrewd. If they weren't, they would not have survived to become the Old Guard.

The best way to deal with the Old Guard is to be competent and innovative. Be political. These people are the real power brokers. They can't necessarily advance your career but they can kill it.

Dealing with the Old Guard is easy. Be competent, be accessible and don't be a "yes-person."

ROADBLOCKS

The Old Guard has to produce and, in their position, they have learned to take advantage of those around them. This last statement can be viewed as both a negative and a positive. The Old Guard is interested in staying employed. So are you. Don't stand in their way.

If you hit a roadblock in the Old Guard, you will find it a difficult obstacle indeed. At the departmental level you can, for example, effectively orphan an idea. With the Old Guard, orphaning an idea is much more difficult. Why?

First, remember these are the professionals of the corporation. No one in the Old Guard is going to put his or her credibility on the line for an idea that he or she has not thought through. There is too much personal danger.

If you have presented an idea to the Old Guard — and it had better be a good idea with plenty of competent research — wait. Watch carefully. Any power broker worth his salt will eyeball an idea and mull it over in his mind. Good ideas get better with rumination; bad ideas stink after two days. Be careful, too, that your boss doesn't know you are dealing directly with the Old Guard. He or she may not like you going over his or her head.

Second, when dealing with the Old Guard, keep in mind the "WIIFM" principle ("What's In It For Me?"). While doing good for the company is a noble sentiment, it doesn't play well with the Old Guard. That's talk for the mailroom. These men and women are looking for advancement and keeping their backs covered.

If you want to propose an idea to the Old Guard, there has to be something in it for the person who's going to push your idea. After all, why should someone push your idea? What does he get out of it? If it succeeds, you get the glory. If it fails, he get the blame. If there isn't a burning reason for someone to carry your idea forward, he won't. To be successful, you are going to have to add a sweetener.

If you present your idea and it gets rejected, don't give up. But wait a while. Make sure it wasn't your personality or approach that was in error. Was there "something in the air" that made your idea unworkable at this moment? Who would benefit from this idea? Who wouldn't? More important, who ends up with the responsibility to follow this idea through if implemented? Out of whose budget will the money come?

Re-examine your great idea from a different angle. What's the matter with it? The faster you got it back, the more glaring the miscalculation. Until you figure out what went wrong with the presentation, don't present it again.

Finally, what *wasn't* in that proposal? Think about that before you submit it again.

LEAVING WHILE THE NEST IS STILL WARM

You've fought very hard to succeed in your job. You've mastered the art of corporate survival. You've dealt with impossible co-workers and overbearing bosses. But it may still be time to quit. Anyone can get fired. Anyone can get career burnout. But not everyone is smart enough to leave the nest while it is still warm.

Leaving a job at the right time is an art form. Since it is quite likely that when you leave you will remain in the same field you are in now, it's important to leave on friendly terms. After all, you never know when the contacts you developed at your old job will be needed.

Here are some factors to consider, even if you like your job:

1. How old is your boss? If you work for a fairly young company, you might find that your climb up the corporate ladder is right behind your boss. As he or she is promoted, so are you. But if the boss is only a few years older than you, and the next person up the line is only a few years older than that, you may have to wait quite a long time for any openings or promotions to come along. Are you willing to wait?

2. How well do you get along with the people at the office? If you are having personality conflicts, particularly with superiors, you might consider leaving. Keep in mind that your advancement depends on other people letting you move up.

3. How old is your mentor? Is he or she about to retire? Is he or she strong enough to survive a power struggle? If your mentor is old or in a poor political postion, you should think about leaving now.

4. How is the company doing in general? If the company is doing well, and promotions aren't coming along as fast as you would expect, be careful. There's something you aren't being told. On the other hand, if the company isn't doing well, start looking around.

How Do You Know When Your Job Is at Risk?

- Are your raises or bonuses below average?
- Is your corporation acquiring debt?
- Are your corporation's earnings dropping?
- Is your corporation losing market share?
- Is management playing the "executive shuffle," with people changing responsibilities as fast as the business cards can be printed?
- Are top-notch people leaving, often with no apparent reason?
- Are people from outside the company being hired over you, and are they bringing in their own people?
- Are restrictions being placed on items that were previously allowed, such as travel, petty cash, time off or phone calls?
- Is your mentor in disfavor?
- Does the management of your corporation know what it's doing?
- Is your company selling some of its assets or making other major cutbacks?

If you answered yes to three or more of these questions, you might want to read the chapter on finding a new job.

4

DEALING WITH THE PUBLIC

No matter how lucky you are, sooner or later you are probably going to have some sort of dealings with the public. It may not be to dedicate a bridge or cut the ribbon at the opening of a children's hospital, but it will be important — because any public appearance you make is important. If you are not used to it you can make a fool of yourself.

This, however, does not mean that you should not be seen in public. You *should* be out in public and you should be there frequently. The more you're out and about, the higher a profile you cut. That's good for your image, your salary and your chances of promotion. Further, it's good for the organizations you represent. The American Diabetes Association, March of Dimes, Special Olympics, Chamber of Commerce, and the Civic Opera all need support from the business community that doesn't necessarily come in dollars.

When appearing in public, remember to disbelieve the old Hollywood adage that "there is no such thing as bad publicity." That is a lie. There *is* such a thing as bad publicity and it can kill your career.

Fortunately, bad publicity is easy to avoid. The first rule is to avoid people who are working at receiving bad publicity. Don't associate with groups run by people with questionable reputations.

The only other rule of public appearances is to be a professional. When you sit on a board of directors, do what is professional, not what is political. Political decisions have a tendency to come back to haunt you. Professional decisions do not.

If you keep these two rules in mind, you'll be surprised by the benefits you will reap from public appearances. They enhance your visibility, open new avenues for networking, allow you to meet new clients and, at the same time, affiliate you with a worthy cause.

If there is a downside it is that occasionally you're asked to make a speech. That's right, a *speech*!

HOW TO WRITE A GREAT SPEECH

Inevitably, being a public person means giving a speech. Usually you don't *ask* to give a speech, you suddenly find that you've been volunteered. Giving a great speech starts with writing a great speech. The rest is just performance.

Ten Ways to Succeed When Giving a Speech

- Prepare your speech well in advance, and double-check your figures.
- Develop hand-out material even if it doesn't seem absolutely necessary. Include a bibliography.
- Before your speech, visit the room where you'll be speaking to make certain that you know how to use the microphone and that there's room for your paper on the podium and a place for a glass of water.
- Underline the im-portant points in your speech with red ink.
- Relax your aud-ience with some personal comments or questions before you begin.
- Speak clearly and slowly, using words that a high school graduate can un-derstand.
- Refer to the hand-out material, and wait for people to find their place before you continue.
- Keep it simple. Make your points clearly. Be sure to sum up at the end of the speech.

- Use visual aids.
- Leave time for questions.

If you have time, you should consider getting a copy of the *Esquire* video "Persuasive Speaking." It costs under thirty dollars and can be ordered from Esquire Video, P.O. Box 648, Holmes, PA 19043 (tel. 1-800-345-8112).

"My father gave me these hints on speechmaking: 'Be sincere, be brief, be seated.'"

James Roosevelt, son of Theodore Roosevelt

"The best audience is one that is intelligent, well educated — and a little drunk."

Alban W. Barkley, Vice President under Harry Truman

In preparing a speech, follow the "KISS" principle: "Keep It Simple, Stupid." Write your speech so that even a Chairman of the Board can understand it. Keep it focused and to the point. And keep it short.

1. When preparing a speech, ignore the time you have been asked to fill. Don't write a fifteen-minute speech to express a thirty-second idea. When you step up to the podium, you're in charge. Do it your way.

2. Write your speech backwards. Write the conclusion first. Once you have done that you will have a clear target for your ideas.

3. Make certain that you have a single point to make.

4. Make certain that your anecdotes and jokes fit your speech.

    They must be guideposts on the route to your conclusion. Don't include a joke just because it's funny.

5. Keep your speech focused. Having minor points is fine, just make sure every sentence in the speech points toward your inevitable conclusion.

6. Don't confuse the issue with irrelevant or redundant facts. Be clear and concise.

7. When organizing your speech, break in into four parts. Follow the "HAPL" rule:

H is for Hook. Begin your speech with something catchy. In modern parlance, that means a "sound bite," something that is worth reporting the paper. Say you happen to be raising money for a wildlife museum. You might start your speech by saying something like "I'm here on behalf of a lot of dead animals."

A is for Angle. The angle of your speech is the direction you take to reach your conclusion. If you are speaking on behalf of Junior Achievement, for instance, you might want to talk generally — and briefly — about the overall necessity of educating and training the youth of today for the world of tomorrow. Feel free to speak philosophically, but not for long.

P is for peg. A peg is a fact. Your speech will be a real bore if you don't have some juicy facts to report. If you're speaking for Crime Stoppers, give a few concrete examples of the program's success. However, don't give more than three examples. Highlight each of the incidents, making certain that each of the actions has a relevant point that will tie into your concluding statement.

L is for lift. Don't finish a speech by saying, in essence, "that's all I've got to say." Finish with a light note. If you have trouble coming up with a light note, check out a book of anecdotes or quotes from your library and find one that is appropriate. If you're stuck for a finish, refer back to your opening anecdote — you had one, didn't you? — and tie your speech together that way.

Sources of Quips Jokes and Anecdotes

Reader's Digest and *Reader's Digest* collections
The Little, Brown Book of Anecdotes, edited by Clifton Fadiman, (Little, Brown, 1985)
The Devil's Dictionary, Ambrose Bierce (Dover, 1911)
Peter's Quotations, Laurence J. Peter (Bantam, 1979)
Any book by Robert Orben
Bartlett's Familiar Quotations, John Bartlett (Little, Brown & Co., 1980)

Tips to Feel Comfortable When Giving a Speech

The biggest problem most speechmakers have is feeling uncomfortable in front of a group of people. Writing the speech is not a problem, but giving the speech to a room of people just makes them freeze. Here are some quick tips for getting used to speaking to large groups of people:

- Have a few friends listen to your speech informally. Have them move about the room, talk and laugh. Play the stereo while you give your speech. This will let you rehearse, get used to people, and learn to ignore the noise in the lecture hall, all at the same time.
- Internalize the technique of addressing only select places in the room. Choose just six places to look while giving your speech. In this way you can convince yourself psychologically that there are only six people in the room.
- Develop a great three-minute introduction with jokes and anecdotes about the subject of your speech. Nothing warms an audience up and calms you down like laughter.
- On the day of the speech, see if you can give an announcement. This will help you break the ice.
- Ask the audience questions. This gives you and the audience a chance to become acquainted.

❖ ❖ ❖

"A speech is a solemn responsibility. The man who makes a bad thirty minute speech to two hundred people wastes only a half hour of his own time. But he wastes one hundred hours of his audience's time — more than four days — which should be hanging offense."

Reverend Jenkin Lloyd Jones, head of Henry Ford's Peace Party

❖ ❖ ❖

Dealing with the Press

- Do not call the press unless you have a story.
- Do not call the press unless your story is completely researched.
- Try to find black-and-white photographs to support the story.
- When you call the switchboard at the newspaper or magazine, ask for the business reporter. Then write the name down.
- When you talk to the business reporter, be prepared to say *why* your story is important. Don't assume that the reporter can figure it out.
- If the business reporter decides to handle the story over the phone, let him or her. But send your material down to the newsroom anyway. Be sure to include a note and your business card.
- After the story comes out, call and thank the reporter.
- If the story comes out wrong, *do not* call the reporter to yell and scream. *Do* call the reporter and set the record straight. Ask the newspaper to print a retraction. Then forget it.

WHAT TO WEAR FOR TV

Depending on your position, you may even have the chance to appear on television. Going public on television is a bit different than giving a speech. First of all, how you look is just as important as what you say. When you stand up in front of the Chamber of Commerce, no one has a close-up view of you. As long as you're wearing a suit and tie, you are appropriately dressed. On television, there is a little more required.

When appearing on television, think "Civil War" and stick to light blues and light grays; they show up best on camera. Stay away from starched whites and flashy colors. These have a tendency to reflect light. Stay away from black as well; it will make you look heavy. Television has a tendency to make you look ten pounds heavier anyway. If you wear black, you'll look fatter still.

Even if you're a man, you should also wear make-up. You don't have to go overboard, but you should use a bit of powder. This will cut down on the light reflected on your face. If you are bald or have thinning hair, you should also put some powder on your pate.

Whether you are male or female, an eyebrow pencil is a good idea if your eyebrows are light. Eye shadow works well, but only for women. Don't wear a hat.

❖ ❖ ❖

"TV — chewing gum for the eyes."

Frank Lloyd Wright

❖ ❖ ❖

Once you're on television, decide whether you are going to address the audience or the person asking the question. If you want to speak to the audience, look for the television camera with the red light. That's the camera that's operating. Either way, make absolutely *sure* you know what you're going to say before the words slip out of your mouth. A loose statement will do more damage in three seconds than you can repair in a year.

HANDLING THE PRESS IN PERSON

Another medium that you'll probably be in contact with as a public person is the newspaper. In most cases, your contact will be in the form of a press release. You will send it in and the newspaper won't print it. That's called "Freedom of the Press."

To get a press release printed, follow the same "HAPL" rule outlined earlier. But in the case of the press release, be short. Very short.

A good press release is short and to the point, sometimes as brief as four or five lines. It also has a very good reason for being presented. One of the reasons *good* press releases get printed is that there are so many self-serving ones being sent in. A president of a company suddenly wants some press coverage and orders some low level staffer to make up a press release. Since there is no good reason for the press release to be written, the newspapers will probably not take it. These are the types of press releases you are competing with. It's also a good idea to go with a bit of the human touch; enclose a photograph with the release.

Occasionally you may get a call from the press — and it may not be pleasant. Newspaper reporters look for stories and if your name pops up in connection to a story, you will be called. You may not know anything about the subject of their investigations but, second only to police, newspaper reporters are the most suspicious of professionals. Dealing with the press under adverse conditions is dangerous. You could find yourself implicated in something you had nothing to do with. If you are not careful, you could find your name in a very negative article.

If you are faced with a hostile reporter, here are some tips for getting your side of the story out:

1. Do not lie. Tell the truth as you know it. If you do tell a lie, the reporter is quite likely to discover it. Reporters hate loose ends. They will follow each clue to its natural conclusion. If the reporter discovers you've lied, you're in REAL trouble.

2. Do not volunteer any information. Answer the questions you are asked, period. Don't put yourself at a legal risk.

3. If you're caught unprepared, say that you're busy and will call back. This is perfectly acceptable — as long as you call back. *Be sure you call back.* This will give you time to pull your thoughts together.

4. You may not want your name to appear in the press. If you're being called by an investigative reporter, tell the reporter you will only speak "off the record." Nothing you say will be directly attributed to you.

If the reporter wants an "on the record" comment on a hot story, tell the reporter you will call back. Write down exactly what you intend to say. Then *read* your comment to the reporter.

HOW TO ANSWER TOUGH QUESTIONS IN PUBLIC

Handling tough questions in public is just as tough as talking to a reporter who's convinced you're lying. Worse yet, you're caught out of your office and don't have the luxury of taking a few moments to pull your thoughts together.

Most frequently, the toughest question will come at the worst possible moment. That's because people who ask embarrassing questions wait until exactly the right moment to ask the question in front of the greatest number of people.

❖ ❖ ❖

"Why shouldn't truth be stranger than fiction. Fiction, after all, has to make sense."

Mark Twain

❖ ❖ ❖

"I never give them hell. I just tell the truth and they think it's hell."

Harry S Truman

❖ ❖ ❖

When you get hit with a tough question at an unexpected moment, you can be sure of one thing: Whoever is asking the question either already has the answer or has a very good idea what the answer is. What do you do?

First of all, don't guess. If you don't know, say that you don't know and that you'll find out. This has a tendency to defuse hostility. That's your first priority. Once you've shown a willingness to handle this person's problem, your audience will be sympathetic.

Get the person's name and number and say you'll get back to them. Get an answer and then keep your promise. The next time they ask, you'll be able to say, "I answered that for you last week and the answer is still the same."

If it's a legal question, refer them to the corporation's legal counsel. If it's a public-affairs question, direct them to the public-affairs office. If it is a question of corporate policy, direct them to the responsible department.

❖ ❖ ❖

"The credibility gap is so wide that our suspicions are confirmed by any official denial."

L. J. Peter

❖ ❖ ❖

ON YOUR OWN

5

STARTING YOUR OWN BUSINESS

❖ ❖ ❖

"There are three ways to do everything," many a boss has said to a new employee, "the right way, the wrong way and *my* way. Always do it my way!"

❖ ❖ ❖

Everybody wants it their way. There will come a point in your career when you may seriously want to do it *your* way. You might find that you have been laterally and politically promoted to a position that didn't exist two weeks ago. On the other hand, perhaps you're so good that you have been promoted to a position where there is no reasonable slot above you into which you can advance. Or like more and more Americans, you're tired of having a boss and now you want to *be* a boss.

If you're reading this chapter, chances are you're thinking about going into business for yourself. You've probably thought long and hard about the reasons you *should* start your own business, but how seriously have you thought about why you *shouldn't*? Sitting at your desk looking out the window, you may think that starting your own business is a romantic idea. It is just that, a romantic idea. But the accent is on the idea part of the phrase. Being your own boss can be absolutely wonderful, but a good dose of reality might change your mind. Starting a business is very risky. The fatality rate for businesses is about fifty percent the first year and ninety percent within five years. Quite a few good people have lost a lot of money trying to start their own businesses.

Before you think about starting off on your own, go back and re-read the chapter on finding a new job in this book. Starting a new business is, in essence, exactly the same as looking for a new job. Make certain that you're not violating any of the laws that were mentioned there. You're going to be spending a lot of time and money trying to stay alive as a business owner. Think before you make that decision.

HIRING AND FIRING

Sooner or later you're going to be need to hire or fire someone. Neither is easy, particularly the first time. If you're queasy about hiring or firing, just look at the task as one of the growing pains of private enterprise.

Firing

Once you decide to fire someone, do it immediately. The longer you wait, the harder it is going to be for everyone concerned.

Expect office morale to take a plunge when someone is fired, regardless of the reason. After you have fired someone, call a meeting, reassure everyone that there are not more firings in the wind, and get on with business as usual.

Do not threaten someone with firing unless you're willing to do it.

If you have told someone that they are going to be replaced, give them a definite time to be gone. Be reasonable. Be professional. Assume that it's going to take them about one week for each $10,000 of their salary. Then add two weeks just to be fair. Remember, what goes around, comes around.

When firing someone, be bold, be honest and be quick.

Consider repainting or redecorating the office of the fired person. At least move the furniture around. As long as that office remains the way it did when the person was fired, it will remind the rest of the office of what happened.

Hiring

Hiring someone means checking their credentials. Go back at least five years. The more important the job, the further back you should check.

Be suspicious of someone who walks on water. If you get a sterling recommendation, ask yourself: Why is this person's current employer letting him or her leave? Don't be a sucker; This person could be so bad that only a good recommendation will get rid of him or her.

Vacuum thinking will work best when looking at a resume. What is *not* there? Before you look over any resume, go down to personnel and look at the resumes of some highly-qualified people. How does your candidate compare? If the comparison is poor, someone is pushing this prospective employee too hard. In that case, be careful.

Don't ask questions that have obvious answers, because that's the kind of answers you're going to get.

Ask questions that require brains to answer. Remember, anyone can do what the job description says. What you need is a competent individual who is not going to get you in trouble for what they do or don't do. If you have the power to sign off on the person, you will take the blame if something goes wrong.

For instance, if you're interviewing prospective secretaries, ask them to respond to the following three situations. Inform the candidates that they have to react immediately and cannot think about the situation for a few minutes.

"Pretend you have one of our largest clients on hold. He wants to talk to me, he's impatient and you've already told him I'm in the office. I tell you that I don't want to speak to him yet because I'm still waiting for the report I was waiting for the last time I talked to him, and I really don't know when it's going to get here." What would you do if you found yourself in this situation?

or

"Tell the marketing rep on the phone that I think he is a clown and I don't want to buy his product or consider his service. I'm tired of talking to him and dodging his calls and I would be very happy if the earth opened up and swallowed him alive and immediately." Again, what would you do?

or

"I'm at a long lunch with a person you don't know and you suspect that I'm going to have a drink with my salad. The president calls, wants to see me immediately, can't believe I'd have taken a long lunch on this particular day, can't believe you don't know where I am, and is madder than hell." How would you react?

CYA is the rule when hiring. Whomever you hire must be willing, able, and intelligent enough to cover you as well as themselves. Look for this in their responses. You can always find a secretary to type a letter. You can never recover from a secretary that makes you look bad every time he or she picks up the phone — particularly if you did the hiring.

Hiring or Subcontracting

At some time in your career you will have to hire temporary help. Temporary help can be a blessing in disguise or it can be the worst decision of your professional career.

- Dont just accept the luck of the draw when hiring temporary workers. Before you put anyone in your office, look over their resume. Interview at least two or three people before selecting one.
- Look for people who are "just passing through." Temporary services often have people who are just biding their time. Perhaps they have a job that starts in two months. Or maybe they are just "testing the waters" to see if they want to return to work after having raised two children. These people are an incredible bargain. Try to find them.
- Hire someone as close to the level of the work being done as possible. If you subcontract for advertising, don't go to the head of an advertising firm. All he or she will do is tell you that his or her firm can do the advertising. If you're responsible for the advertising, make certain you talk with the people who will actually be doing the work.
- Meet the creative people one-on-one. If you have been impressed with the work of one particular firm, find out who specifically did the work. These creative people are often underpaid and change agencies frequently. Make certain that the creative person who impressed you is still with the firm, and will be there when you need him or her.
- Remember the IRS. The IRS takes a very dim view of companies that subcontract to avoid paying taxes. Read the rules about subcontracting before you sign a contract. If you don't, you could end up paying back taxes and fines — and this, as they say, will not look good on your resume.

WHAT MAKES A SMALL BUSINESS WORK

The following are some of the key factors that decide whether a small business will succeed. Even if all of these elements are handled well, you could still fail, but if even one of these is neglected, your chances of success will be slim.

Management

This is the single most important factor in any business. People make businesses successful, and it's people that cause them to fail. The better you know about managing, the better your chances of survival. If you have any questions at all, RUN to your nearest office of the Small Business Administration, and see what information and help they can give you. Often it will be free.

Staff

Finding people who are willing to work is never hard. Finding the RIGHT people is an altogether different problem. Good peple are hard to find and even harder to keep. When you find good people, pay them what you need to keep them.

Overhead

Too much overhead can kill a starting business. Don't believe people who tell you to "fake it 'till you make it." People who fake success usually don't get the chance to **really** become successful. If you're feeling nervous about having a modest office, visit clients at their office, or take them to lunch. Unless you're flush, all you need to start a business is a business license, a phone, a business card and stationery. Save the fancy furniture for later.

Collections

People and businesses don't like to pay bills at all, much less on time. If you haven't been paid by your clients, you won't be able to pay your bills. You can save yourself grief and sleepless nights by developing a collections strategy BEFORE you do your first job. Again, if you aren't sure about collection strategy, see the Small Business Administration in your area. We'll talk more about collections in just a bit.

If you're still convinced you have what it takes to start your own business, consider the following six critical rules.

THE RULE OF THE TWO-HEADED MONSTER

Every successful business venture has to have two people: a *worker* and a *hustler*. Most small businesses start out with the same person doing both jobs — the two-headed monster.

Unfortunately, unless you're *very* talented, you will have trouble doing both jobs. Every moment you spend working is one less moment you have available to hustle new clients. On the other hand, every meeting that you attend is two hours taken away from the bread-and-butter of servicing the clients you already have.

If you're considering going into business for yourself, think seriously about being a two-headed monster. Can you effectively sell your product or service to people like the ones you have worked with? At the same time, if you have been a sales or marketing person, can you service your customers without all of the computers, staff and secretarial backup you now have?

THE RULE OF COLLECTIONS

If going into business for yourself was easy, everyone would be doing it. It is not easy. Before you cut the umbilical cord at your present job, think again about collections.

No matter what you think, the hard, cruel truth of collections is that *you* will be doing most of the collections. Most people who start off in their own business don't think about people who don't pay their bills. They just assume that they will open an office, provide a quality service for which other people will be willing to pay "quite a bit of money."

Wrong! Your business will only survive if you can collect for the services you render. Period. Initially, most of your clients will be those with whom you are doing business now. Can you pick up the phone, call these people, tell them they owe $9,786.34, mention that it's 90 days late, insinuate possible legal action, *and*, at the same time, keep their friendship and business? If you can't, don't start a business of your own.

For months, a small businessman was trying to collect a debt. Finally, in desperation, he sent the debtor a tearful letter with the photo of a pathetic little girl on a sidewalk. On the photo was the caption: "The reason I need the money."

Two days later the collector received a letter back. Opening it he found a photograph of a voluptuous woman in a bikini with a beachball. On the photo were the words: "The reason I can't pay."

THE RULE OF ADVERTISING

One of the facts of life is that you must advertise. Even if you have no faith in advertising or feel you have such a grip on the market that *everyone* knows who you are, you will still have to advertise.

You will also have to keep advertising. The newer your company is, the more advertising you will have to do. A good rule of thumb is that your advertising budget should be about five percent of your expected gross income for the year. If you plan on making $100,000, you should spend at least $5,000 on advertising.

❖ ❖ ❖

Not advertising to save money is like stopping your watch to save time.

old business adage

❖ ❖ ❖

Now comes the bad news. Advertising is a very sophisticated business. If you're not in the advertising field, you have a choice of doing one of two things. You can hire a creative professional to advise you, or you throw $5,000 in cash out your office window. Don't try to do your own advertising.

If you don't have a personality that will let other people handle your advertising — from creative input to placement — do not start your own business. People who can't trust their agency don't last. They either show symptoms of cardiac arrest every time their ad shows on television or they believe that "I can do a better job than that," and end up with an advertisement so bad it drives business away.

Good advertising doesn't cost; it pays. One good advertisement will do wonders for your client base. One bad advertisement can kill your company. If you don't know this for a fact, you had better go talk to the creative people before you get your business license.

An art buyer was complaining about the cost of a painting. "After all, it's just oil and canvas," he noted.

"Well, if that's all you want," replied the painter. "I'll sell you a tube of cobalt blue and a blank canvas for fifty dollars and you can paint your own painting."

THE RULE OF PAPERWORK

One of the staggering realities of starting your own business is paperwork. Working for a company, you don't see the paperwork that is generated. You do your job and someone else handles "the details." Well, when you work for yourself, *you* handle the details. There are quite a few of them. As a good rule of thumb, figure that paperwork is going to take you about two hours a day. Since you're going to be servicing accounts or hustling clients during the traditional 9-to-5 day, this paperwork is going to have to be completed after 5 P.M. — unless you're a morning person. If you have strong personal or family commitments in the evenings, forget about being your own boss.

Worse yet, understand that running your own business is a family affair. When you hang out your shingle, your spouse and children are as much a part of that business as you are, because you're going to ask a lot of patience and understanding from them. You'll be apart a lot. Be sure you have the support at home before you start setting up an office.

THE RULE OF TIME AND TASK BENCHMARKS

Even though you finish all your "tidal" paperwork, you will still have time and task benchmarks to meet. Before you even start your business you should develop a business plan (see next chapter).

A business plan provides a direction of travel as well as time and task benchmarks to make certain that you're "on track."

These benchmarks give you an outline or guide to ensure that your business is moving in the right direction and at the pace you planned.

What does this have to do with starting a business? To be successful, a company has to make progress. Anyone can work hard. But can they work smart?

"A business that is dying on its feet is one that has a lot of motion but no movement."

old business adage

"Every businessperson has a choice: to work hard or work smart. People who work smart retire early. People who work hard also retire early. Usually on doctor's orders."

Warren Sitka, humorist

If your time and task benchmarks are unrealistic when you put together your business plan, they will be just as unrealistic when you try to meet them. Expect to meet every single time and task benchmark. This will require work above and beyond the normal, tidal flow of paperwork and business-as-usual activities.

THE RULE OF THE VALLEY OF DEATH

Don't forget the final fact of life in starting your own business. It is going to be expensive and it will remain that way for a long time. We are talking years here, not just a few tight months. You can easily identify those business owners who broke into the black at the end of their first year. Those are the people dancing in the street. If you don't see a lot of people dancing in the street, that should tell you something.

Count on breaking into the black in your third year. You're not going to be receiving a paycheck of any kind from that business for those three years, so consider your fate very carefully before burning any bridges you can't repair.

How to Invite an IRS Audit

- Fail to document your company's receipts properly. File a tax return based on guesstimations rather than receipts.
- Put business expenses on personal receipts and personal business on business receipts.

- Miss your quarterly deadlines or don't file tax returns at all.
- File a tax return that shows travel and entertainment expenses that are half of your income.
- Write off your new car as "office equipment."
- Pay twenty dollars and get a minister's certificate through the mail. Then claim that you're a minister and therefore not required to pay taxes.
- Assume that you know more than any accountant, and do your own business tax returns.
- Conduct your business solely in cash.
- Refuse to respond to letters or calls from the IRS.
- Presume that *you* know more than the IRS and make claims that you feel are fair without checking with anyone — particularly your accountant.

SELLING YOURSELF AS A PRODUCT

Regardless of what product you sell or what service you represent, the most important aspect of being in business for yourself is selling yourself. Your clients won't look at you as being separate from your product. To them, you are your product. If you can't sell yourself, you won't sell your product.

Selling yourself is more than just having the gift of gab. It is packaging yourself, and the package had best be streamlined for the target audience. For example, learn something about your clients before you approach them. The larger the client, the more time you should spend doing research. What's happening in their industry? What are some of the difficulties they're facing? What are some of the inside jokes? Let the clients know that you're aware of their needs.

Also, when you approach a client, always bring something extra. If you're selling advertising, bring a sample ad already made up. It doesn't have to be much, just enough to show the client you're making an extra effort, and that you don't think of him or her as "just another account." Don't *ever* be afraid to do more than is required. Whenever you think about starting a business, remember that *you* are on the line: personally, emotionally, and financially. Your business is worth any effort.

If you're concerned about developing new ideas and angles to sell yourself and your product, relax. That's the least of your problems. The first way, of course, is to follow the old adage, "if you don't have brains on top, get them on tap." If you're not the brightest person around, then find someone who is and hire them. If you can't hire them, sign a subcontract agreement. Bright people are hard to find and impossible to keep, but they are some of your greatest resources.

If you're bright enough to develop your own creative ideas, then you're bright enough to realize that someone better look over your ideas before you spend money on them. If you don't realize that, you're in for a very expensive lesson. In the long run, your greatest asset will not be accounting or horizon thinking or creative marketing. It will be your talent to recognize talent.

Being a Sharp Negotiator

- Be prepared. Know your own guidelines before you begin negotiating. If you're unused to negotiating, find someone to play devil's advocate.
- Recognize the differences in your position and your competitor. Put yourself is his or her place, and consider what they want.
- Avoid the "Fixed Pie Assumption," the assumption that all there is to talk about is already on the table. This necessarily means that for someone to win something, someone else has to lose something. Bring an unexpected bargaining chip to the table.
- Learn the power of silence. If you have nothing to say, don't say anything.
- Leave yourself room to wriggle. Start stingy. Refuse to make a decision if the timing isn't right. When in doubt, don't.
- Don't expect things to happen overnight. Some negotiating takes years.
- Before you negotiate, read Max H. Bazerman's article on the art of negotiating in *Psychology Today*, June 1988.

Two excellent articles on the nuts-and-bolts of negotiating are Jeffrey Winke's "Negotiating Better Deals" in *Nation's Business*, November 1985 and, if you happen to be negotiating with a difficult person, Len Leritz's "Negotiating with Problem People" in *Working Woman*, October 1988.

DISCOVERING AND DEVELOPING HIDDEN TALENTS

If you're going into business for yourself, you'll need all the talent at your disposal, whether you realize you have it right now or not. You should always be seeking out your hidden talents and putting them to good use. The best way to uncover those hidden talents is to *force* yourself to do things that you normally wouldn't do. This isn't nearly as unpleasant as it sounds. In fact, it may be the most enjoyable aspect of running your own business.

The key is to keep an open mind. Suppose that you get involved with a community theater. That doesn't mean you have to be an actor. You can make the sets, sew costumes, handle the lighting or generate the publicity. Just make sure it isn't something you ordinarily do any way for a living. That won't help you.

Local arts councils can provide you with a list of community organizations that need volunteers. This is your best source. Also check your chamber of commerce. Most will have a list of civic and nonprofit organizations, from the pet cat club to antique car collectors. Get out there and get involved.

You may be wondering what good it will do you to learn that you can, for example, be a clown for a local fundraiser. Look at the broader picture. You're really seeing that, perhaps, you have a knack for dealing with people. Maybe you like social contact. Explore that. Capitalize on it.

Maybe you're thinking you won't have time to go running around doing volunteer work. This, too, is narrow thinking. Remember, you do plan to benefit from this. Think of it as taking a course to help your business. You're improving yourself and your business.

Liability: Are You at Risk?

Regardless what your business may be, the answer to this question is *yes*. Unfortunately we are in a period of American history where law suits are as common as sidewalk cracks. Corporations with sterling records are finding themselves being sued for conditions or quality of products beyond their control. You can reduce the risk of law suit by making certain that:

- You have a safe office. Are all of your electrical cords secure? Are the electric plugs hidden by desks? While you may not have children in the office, one or your clients might bring theirs. Is your office childproof?

- A disabled person could make his or her way to any desk in the office from the street. If not, why not?
- The office is properly vented. Do you have a special smoking area? Is all of your office furniture usable? If you're responsible for your own janitorial work, how often are the floors cleaned? Do you leave those floors wet? Are there open chemicals anywhere? Is your refrigerator clean?
- The emergency equipment is working. When was the last time you checked your fire alarm? Your fire extinguisher? When was the last time your office had a fire drill? Have you ever had a fire drill? Do all of your phones work even if the power is turned off?
- You have applied the "Reasonable Person" test to your office, warehouse and workshop. Look around. Would a Reasonable Person suffer any damage or harm by being here? The "Reasonable Person" test assumes no one is going to put themselves at unreasonable risk, like swinging from rafters, or pouring flammables on the floor while lighting a cigarette.
- You have contacted local tort reform groups. Whether you favor the side of the lawyers or the tort reforms, join and make a difference.

LEGAL ASPECTS OF BEING YOUR OWN BOSS

If you have not yet been dissuaded from forming your own company, consider the legal make-up of your firm. You have four basic choices.

1. Sole Proprietorship
2. Corporation
3. Limited Partnership
4. General Partnership

Sole Proprietorship

The most common form of business in the United States is the sole proprietorship. Also known as a "dba" ("doing business as"), it is a one-person shop with one person acting as the two-headed monster. There's no legal protection for a sole proprietorship and the personal assets of the proprietor are at risk for the entire enterprise. A business failure is thus a personal failure and personal bankruptcy generally follows. On the other hand, startup costs are low and you'll never have trouble with your partners.

❖ ❖ ❖

"Every sole proprietor in America has a partner; they just don't know it. It's the IRS."

advice from sadder, but wiser, sole proprietors

❖ ❖ ❖

Corporation

A corporation is a person or group of persons who form an entity unto itself. Decisions are made in accordance with bylaws and articles of incorporation, which must be filed with, and approved by, the state where business is being conducted.

The advantages of incorporation are many. Investors and partners are shielded from suit, and stock can be sold to raise more money. Unlike a sole proprietorship, investors in a corporation cannot be held personally responsible for the corporation's debts. The corporation simply goes bankrupt. The disadvantage is that it is a large, bulky operation where you can become just as lost and impotent as you were in the job you just left.

Limited Partnership

A limited partnership is one in which you have money at risk but have no say in how the business is run. You should not look at this as a business *venture*, but as a business *investment*.

General Partnership

A general partnership is comprised of two or more individuals who run a business on at least somewhat equal footing. In essence, these individuals form a management body that is responsible, collectively and individually, for the operations and commitments of the company. Without a doubt, the greatest source of aggravation in American business comes from general partnerships.

On the plus side, the more people involved, the greater the asset base of the company. On the negative side, any member of the company can chain the company to a financial commitment. And creditors can reach into everyone's pocket, business as well as personal.

❖ ❖ ❖

"I would never belong to any club that would have someone like me as a member."

Groucho Marx

❖ ❖ ❖

A good rule of thumb for dealing with partnerships is don't. Unless you know your partners very, very well, don't go into business with anyone. If they commit to a debt, *you* have to pay it. Your business partner is going to be more than a business associate. He or she is going to be chained to you for years to come. Make sure you like the company.

❖ ❖ ❖

George was sick the day he received a call from his business partner.

"There's $5,000 missing from the safe," his partner told him. "What should I do?"

"Put it back," snapped George as he hung up the phone.

❖ ❖ ❖

Finding the Right Office Space

There are three main criteria when looking for office space:

1. Location
2. Location
3. Location

Do not be fooled into thinking that you should compare offices on the basis of lower cost per square foot alone. You can get very low cost per square foot in the industrial district, but will your clients drive for an hour to see you?

- What you're looking for *first* is a good location. *then* you can balance your options on other criteria such as:

- What are the shapes and locations of the actual rooms? This may sound basic, but you'd be surprised how many people don't take this into account.
- Is the new space compatible with your fixtures and furnishings? If not, you could find yourself paying as much for new fixtures as for the move itself.
- Will the electrical configuration be adequate? Where are the outlets? If they are only in the floor, you may not be able to move your furniture. Are you willing to leave your furniture in the same places for years?
- What condition is the building in? Do the pipes leak? Are the windows insulated? Will you be losing money in heating and cooling costs?
- Where is the storage? Is it under security? Is there enough of it?
- Can you put in new phone lines if your business expands?
- If you're leasing, when is your landlord's lease up? Who actually owns the building?
- What about esthetics? Will you have to repaint? Are there nice views? This won't be as minor as it sounds if you grow to hate the place in a little while.
- The basic rule when it comes to choosing an office location is to use your head before you reach for your wallet. Don't settle. If it isn't exactly what you want, keep looking.

CYA ADVICE FOR THOSE WHO ARE STILL INTERESTED IN A PARTNERSHIP

1. Know your partners and their financial situation *well!* Do you really need these partners? Are they financially dependable? Will they do their fair share of the work? What will you do if one of them dies? Can your spouse work with these people if you die? Does your partner pay his personal bills on time? Does your partner's current business pay its bills on time. Are you being played for a sucker? Are you sure?

2. Put *everything* in writing.

3. Carefully examine your reasons.

   If you're forming a general partnership because your business is not doing well and your potential partner is not doing well either but, "together we couldn't do worse than we are doing individually," you're in for a sad surprise. Remember that one turkey plus one turkey does not an eagle make.

The Small Business Administration

One of the best sources for information on starting a business or keeping one afloat is the Small Business Administration (SBA).

- There are SBA offices all over the country. Check your phone book for the listing nearest you.
- If you live in a remote area, you can reach the SBA toll-free at l-800-368-5855. (In Washington, D.C. call 653-7561.Or write to the SBA, Office of Business Development, Washington, D. C. 20416.
- When dealing with the SBA, ask for a copy of the Directory of Business Development Publications. This is a complete list of the pamphlets the SBA has to offer, many of them for free. The subjects run from record-keeping to creative selling.
- The SBA has recently released a series on money entitled Focus on the Facts. This series was done in conjunction with Dun & Bradstreet Information Resources. The first of the series is entitled *How to Raise Money for a Small Business.* If you're interested, ask for the whole series.
- SBA offices also provide FREE consulting services. You do not have to live in a major city to receive these services. The SBA can retain someone to help you.
- The SBA also offers classes, some of them free, on a wide variety of subjects. Make sure you're on your local SBA mailing list.

BEFORE YOU SIGN ANY PAPER

1. Who, specifically, is forming the partnership and what, specifically, will each partner bring to the partnership? Is it really worth the risk?

2. Are the percentages of ownership equivalent to the assets being brought into the partnership? If not, why not and would a person not associated with the partnership find your answer reasonable?

3. Have you done any kind of background search on your partners, even if you have known them "for years?" If not, why not?

4. Are any of the partners from out of state, from foreign countries or are they foreigners? If you answered "yes" to any one of these, have you talked with a lawyer about the legal consequences of bills incurred across state or national borders? If not, why not?

5. Are you willing to pay the bills your partners are going to incur?

6. Are there any assets your partners are shielding? Why? Why are you allowing this to happen?

7. Are all partners willing to sign the partnership papers? If not, why not? If not, why are you signing them?

8. Is there a reasonable escape clause to allow you out of the partnership if you wish?

9. Do the partnership papers allow for a limited length of time before the terms must be renegotiated?

10. What will happen if one of the partners dies?

11. Does everyone get the same fringe benefits?

12. How will new partners be added? Can you leave without financial loss if you don't like the new partner?

13. How will disputes be settled between partners?

14. What restrictions will be placed on partners with respect to obligating the company to expenses? Do you really BELIEVE your partners will abide by these restrictions?

15. Who handles cash? Why? What paperwork has to be filled out? Who is the second signature on all checks and why aren't you in that loop?

16. If the partnership is likely to be sued, what are you doing — on paper and in person — to minimize that risk?

17. Are your partners being honest with you about their health? Do they drink to excess, use illegal drugs or have a lifestyle that might make them susceptible to an untimely death?

18. In whose name will the business be listed?

19. Who will do the taxes, and can you guarantee they will be done on time?

20. Do you feel your potential partners are being honest with you?

Go back over each question and answer it again. If you feel uncomfortable about even one question, *don't sign any papers.* When you don't know what to do, don't do anything. Most importantly, have a business lawyer or financial advisor look over everything.

6

WRITING A BUSINESS PLAN

Once you have made the decision that you're deadly serious about going into business for yourself, your first job is to develop a business plan. Overall, a business plan is an assessment of what you're planning to do, how much it is going to cost you, where you expect to be financially in one, two and three years. Initially even more important, the business plan will tell you whether "the numbers are good."

A business plan forces you to think backwards. Far too often, entrepreneurs just start a business. They think the community needs another travel agency, so they open a shop. They drop $50,000 into an office, computer and furniture, and then discover that there isn't enough business to support another travel agency in town. Or they discover that their personality is such that they drive businesses away. Worse still, the economy goes into a recession and the number of people who travel drops dramatically.

Starting a business is a very delicate operation. The more time you put into thinking about it, the less trouble you will have when you do it. Your biggest problem will be, of course, money. You're going to need cash to open the door to any opportunity. Since most people will leverage (borrow) the money, the business plan is critical to make certain that investors can see *on paper* exactly what they are buying. No one is going to buy a pig in a poke. Don't assume that, just because you decide to do business, investors will be stumbling over each other to sign on the dotted line.

Even if you don't need to leverage money to start your business, you will need the business plan to keep track of your time and task benchmarks. If you don't have a target to shoot for, you will spend your time stumbling around in the dark. Worse, if you start to stray off course, you won't know until it's too late.

❖ ❖ ❖

"When a man does not know what harbor he is making for, no wind is the right wind."

Seneca

❖ ❖ ❖

Before you start writing your business plan, go to the Small Business Administration or any of the small-business development centers of the state or local governments. Many of these agencies have step-by-step instructions for generating a business plan. A good overall outline is from the Small Business Administration. This is your best source, as it has become accepted throughout the American business community as the standard outline for different sorts of small businesses.

The most important advice to remember when filling out a business plan is: Don't lie. This seems like a fairly obvious point but many business people forget it. They assume that bankers or investors would be bored by all the details. So they leave some of the details out, or they "gloss over" some of the complex mathematics. This is called lying. It's illegal.

Basically, the business plan is broken into two parts. The first section is an outline, in script *with backup* on the business. The sections for the first part are as follows:

1. Description of the Business
2. Market
3. Competition
4. Location of Business
5. Management
6 Personnel
7. Expected Effect of Loan or Investment
8. Summary

DESCRIPTION OF THE BUSINESS

This section is dedicated to a *succinct* discussion of the business. It describes the product or service being offered, identifies the owners of the rights to the product or service and names all persons involved with the enterprise as of the date of the business plan. With regard to the length of this section: be factual, be forthright, be finished.

MARKET

The next portion of the business plan is a discussion of the market. In addition to stating how your product or service will prosper, you will also discuss *all* competition and how that competition will affect your sales.

Try to forecast and discuss any impending changes. Don't just look at the next year, look forward into at least the next three. If there is a reason for your entering the market at this moment, express it. If your enterprise is in a crowded field, it would also help to have a section in your appendix for news clippings over the last year.

COMPETITION

Overall, remember the "Push/Pull" Rule: When a choice is available, you offer *two* reasons for doing it your way. You give a reason for *not* doing it someone else's way and a reason *for*R doing it your way. In your business plan, you have to show the investor or banker why your competitor *should not* be given money and you *should*.

Suppose you want to start a magazine. Further suppose that there are three magazines already in publication who will compete directly with you. When you ask for investors, you will have to show the *weaknesses* in each of your competitors. Perhaps one is too small to hire a full-time sales person, the second has a broad subscription base but no advertising and the third has quite a bit of advertising but weak editorial direction. When you discuss your competition, you must *pull* the investor away from them. After all, if your competitors have a better deal to offer, why aren't *you* investing with them?

You must then *pull* the investor toward *your* project. In the above example, your proposal should show that you expect a broad enough subscriber base to support hiring a full-time sales person *and* your editorial content will be so seductive that people will have no choice but to buy your product.

Remember, in using the "Push/Pull" rule, be sure to make your logic and script both focused and crystal clear. It's far too easy to confuse people. If your investors are confused, they'll assume that you are too.

LOCATION OF BUSINESS

When discussing the location of your business, make sure you say more than just *where* in the world your office will be located. Include a floor plan of your proposed or actual office, a discussion of the utilities already in place, improvements that have been or will be made as well as a listing of furniture. Photographs could be used as well.

Remember, any fool can say that he has a business location. Don't just say your business will be at "123 Main Street in the heart of downtown." Elaborate. If it's in the heart of a certain district, point that out. Show your business location for what it is, as well as what it could be.

MANAGEMENT

List here everyone from the Board of Directors through lower level management. Include their names, addresses, phone numbers, resumes, investment in the company and duties. Be specific. Include a management chart. Show that committees already exist. Show the flow of responsibility. Who will backup whom? If there is a problem, who will handle it? Who will be responsible for backstopping? Who will deal with the press? Who will deal with the lawyers?

PERSONNEL

Now discuss personnel. Who is going to do the work? Who will do the supervising? Who will work on which shift? Will there be subcontractors? What are the wages? What are the benefits? If possible, name names and include resumes.

EXPECTED EFFECT OF LOAN OR INVESTMENT

Then, of course, there is the question of money. Even if you have your own financing, list where the money is coming from. At what intervals will you be taking money out of the bank? For what particular expenses? Do you have a timeline for bringing that money into use? If you're investing a great amount of personal income, make certain that your business plan states the source of that money.

If you're looking for a bank loan or investment capital, state in specific terms how the money you need will enhance the project. How much do you need? What are you going to do if you get more than you anticipate? Where are you going to keep the money until it's needed? What is the interest rate there?

❖ ❖ ❖

"When I was young I thought that money was the most important thing in life; now that I am old I know that it is."

Oscar Wilde

❖ ❖ ❖

SUMMARY

The final section of the first half of the business plan is the summary. Be brief. Do *not* introduce any new aspects of the project here. Simply restate the obvious.

Simple Things to Keep in Mind When Writing a Business Plan

Neglecting these little things can seriously hurt your plan.

- Put your name, title, address and telephone number on the cover sheet

- Number the pages. If you don't number the pages how will you know if a page is missing?

- Don't include hundreds of charts and graphs under the assumption that the thicker the proposal, the better.

- Don't assume that everyone knows what you're talking about. Unless your banker or investor is an expert in the field, you had better make sure your writing would make sense to a high-school senior.

- Have at least one person not associated with the project read the plan before you distribute it. Just because you think it's a great plan doesn't mean it will make sense to someone else.

- Don't hide the source of your money. The more money you have to use, the greater the paper trail you will need to convince investors that you came by the money honestly.

- Don't display financial data in a manner or form that makes it hard to follow. If you do, it will look as though you're hiding something. Creativity is an asset in marketing and R & D, not in presenting a business plan to a potential investor.

- Don't pretend you have all the answers. If something is a problem, state it clearly. Don't let an investor or banker find an error and then listen to you try to explain something you don't understand. If you don't know, say so.

- Don't lie.

- Count the pages of every proposal you send out.

FINANCIAL DATA

The second half of the business plan includes all of the financial data. The financial statements you will need have a very specific format. If you don't know that format, don't attempt to do the spread sheets yourself. There is too much potential liability if you make mistakes.

If you have no choice but to do the spreadsheets by yourself, go immediately to your local small business development center. Ask them for help.

FINANCIAL DATA REQUIRED IN A BUSINESS PLAN

Sources and applications pending for funds—Where are you getting the money you need to start your business? If you're applying for funds, to whom have you applied, for how much and what is the status of the application at the date of your business plan?

Capital equipment—What equipment do you have at this time? What is the age and condition of this equipment? Do you own this equipment or are you making payments on it? What kind of computers and software do you have?

Balance sheet—This is a basic statement of your worth on the day the balance sheet is made. It includes your assets, your debts and the equity you have in the company. Your assets must equal your liabilities plus equity.

Break-even analysis—This is a mathematical estimate of when you will break out of the red and into the black. The bank will also want to know precisely how you arrived at that date.

Income projections (profit & loss)—First, what do you expect your earnings to be over the next three years? Then break it down by month for the next one, then two, years. Explain any fluctuations.

Pro-forma cashflow—This schedule lists all changes in your net assets. In other words, this lists not only your income, but your expenses as well. Will you be able to pay your bills every month? Prove it on paper. Detail it by month for the first year and by quarter for the second.

Historical financial reports—This is where you provide all the financial documents to show the status of your business at the time of the report. These should include balance sheets, income statements and tax returns for the past three years.

APPENDICES

Resumes, personal financial statements, cost of living budgets, credit reports, letters of reference, job descriptions, letters of intent and copies of leases, contracts, pink slips and any other document that relates to the business.

Important Tips for Writing a Business Plan

- See a banker first. Talk about your proposed project and listen very carefully to what you're told.
- Ask if that banker has a sample of a successful business plan or loan application for a business similar to yours.
- Look at the titles of the reference books that the banker keeps on his or her shelf. Those are the books that you should be looking for in the library.
- Find those books in the library. If you don't feel comfortable eyeballing someone's bookshelf, look for:

  Industry Norms and Key Business Ratios (Dun and Bradstreet)

  Almanac of Business and Industrial Financial Ratios, Leo Troy (Prentice-Hall, 1988)

  Barron's Finance and Investment Handbook, John Downes and Jordan E. Goodman (Barron's, 1986)

  Investor's Encyclopedia, Chet Currier & The Associated Press (Franklin Watts, 1985)

  The Investor's Information Sourcebook, Matthew Lesko (Harper & Row, 1988)

  Investor's Dictionary (John Wiley & Son, 1986)

  The Dow Jones-Irwin Business and Investment Almanac. (Dow Jones-Irwin)

Ask your local reference librarian for help if you cannot find these books. Also ask the reference librarian to suggest other sources you could use.

- Visit the local office of the Small Business Administration for their pamphlet on creating a business plan.
- Write the first half of the business plan first. Then, find a friend to read it and play devil's advocate. Make *sure* you have covered every aspect of your project. Don't let a banker find an obvious omission.
- Pretend you're the banker. Check and double-check the figures. Make sure your ratios are close to those in the ratio books.
- Ask yourself, "If this was not my business plan, would I invest in this project?" If your answer is not an immediate yes, you're in trouble.
- Make sure your business plan is readable and the numbers clear. Hire a typist to prepare the final copy. Turn in a quality product, not a hurriedly put together collection of paper.
- Hire a technical writer if you're looking for more than $100,000.

7

CONTINUING YOUR EDUCATION

Everything in life is a risk. Living is risky. Surviving in the corporate world is risky. Surviving in the *real* world is risky. If it isn't muggers, it's toxic waste. There are no guarantees in life. You pay your money and you take your chances.

Fortunately there are a few activities in life that are "sure things." One of them is education. There's no downside to learning. The more you learn, the more competent you are in your personal and professional life.

GOING BACK TO SCHOOL

At some point in your career you will seriously consider going back to school. Perhaps you feel that a few classes in marketing would help you advance within the corporation. Or maybe you feel that an MBA would open certain doors for you. You may even want to take a few classes in art or history just to sharpen your image of the world. Congratulations!

The Top Twenty Business Schools in the United States

If you're considering going to graduate school for an MBA, read the November 28, 1988 issue of *Business Week*. In its cover story, the magazine analyzes America's business schools and ranked them as follows (If the business school has a different name than the university, it is listed in parentheses):

1. Northwestern (Kellogg)
2. Harvard
3. Dartmouth (Amos Tuck)
4. Wharton
5. Cornell (Johnson)
6. Michigan
7. Virginia (Darden)
8. North Carolina
9. Stanford
10. Duke
11. Chicago
12. Indiana
13. Carnegie-Mellon
14. Columbia
15. MIT (Sloan)
16. UCLA
17. California (Berkeley)
18. NYU (Stern)
19. Yale
20. Rochester (Simon)

Join the ranks of thousands of American businesspeople who are discovering that education is a never-ending process.

It's important to remember that education may not necessarily mean advancement in the corporation. There are no guarantees that an advanced degree will mean a fast promotion. In the long run, an advanced degree will help you move up, but don't look at it as a quick fix solution.

A better way of looking at an advanced degree is to consider it as a key. The more keys you have, the more doors you can open. Having the key doesn't mean it will be used. But it does mean that you have the *ability* to get through doors that other people cannot.

The MBA offers two advantages to your career you may not have considered. First, of course, the MBA is not just a collection of initials or a piece of paper that says you completed thirty-six graduate units. It's a body of knowledge that you can use every day. Unlike other degrees, what you have learned in graduate school can be applied on the job immediately. Not many other graduate programs can make that claim.

Second, your fellow students are either in business or about to enter business. They, like you, understand that their key to advancement is the MBA and they are willing to make the sacrifice. These people are the country's future business leaders. They will also be sources of business contacts and networking for years to come. Many of these people you will only meet in a graduate school. In the long run, you may find that the greatest benefit to be gained from an MBA is the people you meet while you're a student.

That said, you should be aware that there are possible drawbacks to going for an MBA. It will be a large investment not only in money but in time as well. If you leave your job to go to school full time during the day, you will probably be out of the career track you have put yourself in. Also, some employers are actually put off by an MBA. They feel that workers with an MBA generally ask for more money and are more concerned with their long term goals, and less with their current job. You might even be making yourself overqualified for some lower-level jobs.

Also, if you're seriously thinking about going back to school for an advanced degree, don't automatically assume that an MBA is the best possible degree for you. Generally, in the corporate world, most people find the MBA to be the most helpful graduate degree, so we will primarily discuss continuing education in those terms. But there are alternatives you should consider before you make any decisions.

If you're planning on staying with or returning to your present company, how many of your superiors have an MBA? If they all have degrees in varying fields, an MBA might not be as helpful as a graduate degree in math, economics or even history.

If you work for a company that has a number of divisions, you may find that management prefers its workers to be generalists rather than specialists. Some companies look for employees who have degrees in unusual subjects — biology, sociology, communications. Check around to see what your employers look for for before you commit yourself. An MBA can almost never hurt, but perhaps another degree might help even more. If you're unsure as to whether you should return to school, or which degree you should get, read *Should You Get an MBA* by Albert P. Heygi (Prentice Hall, 1982).

As soon as you have made the decision as to what degree you want, start narrowing your choices of where you want to get it. Are you going back to school full-time or part-time? How much can you spend? Do you need a scholarship?

If you're not sure which college is best for you, go to the library and head for the reference section (the 370s if your local library is on the Dewey Decimal System). Some of the books you should look through include *Barron's Guide to Graduate Business Schools* by Eugene Miller (Barron's, 1988); *How to Get the Degree You Want* by John Bear (Ten Speed Press, 1982); *College Knowledge* by Michael Edelhart (Anchor, 1979) and *Barron's Profiles of American Colleges* (Barron's, 1988).

While going to school part-time at night is by far the most popular way to get an advanced business degree, do not fail to seriously consider quitting your job to spend a year in a top-notch graduate school. But be advised that the best business schools in the country are very difficult to enter and the classes are very competitive.

Before you make a final decision on any business college, comparison-shop. If you're considering taking a year's leave of absence to go to school, read the cover story in *Business Week*'s November 28, 1988 edition. The article, incidentally, also has a breakdown of highlights, cost and class size for the top twenty business schools in the United States.

FIRST STEP

Regardless of whether you're considering going back to school for your first diploma, one class or an advanced degree, you're going to have to apply for admission. Start early. Before you're finished, you will probably have spent about six months waiting for all of the paperwork to arrive. Once you have chosen what college you want to attend, you must now start the process of being accepted. This will mean filling out applications, sending in transcripts and, possibly, taking entrance exams.

Books to Review Before Choosing a College

Academic Year Abroad 1989 — 1990 (Institute of International Education, 1989)

Insider's Guide to Foreign Study, Benedict A. Leerburger (Addison Wesley, 1989)

Barron's Guide to Graduate Business Schools, Eugene Miller (Barron's, 1988)

Barron's Profiles of American Colleges (Barron's, 1988)

How to Get the Degree You Want, John Bear (Ten Speed Press, 1982)

College Knowledge, Michael Edelhart (Anchor, 1979)

The Gourman Report on Graduate and Professional Programs, Jack Gourman (National Education Standards, 1989)

College Blue Book (Macmillan, 1989)

Peterson's Guide to Graduate and Professional Programs (Peterson's Guides, 1988)

APPLICATIONS

- Be sure to apply to more than one college. While you will obviously have a first choice, you should also have a few alternatives. There are only three or four sessions of college each year. If you apply to only one college and get turned down, you might have to wait four months to try again.

  You should also be aware that each college requires different types of paperwork. Don't expect to write one application and then just copy it for other schools.

- Make arrangements to have your transcripts sent directly to the admissions office. Many colleges will not accept transcripts sent by you. There is going to be a time delay when you send out for those transcripts, so start the request process early.

- Make arrangements to take your entrance exams. If you're going to college for the first time, you will most likely be asked to take the SAT (Scholastic Aptitude Test) or the ACT (American College Test). Check with the admissions office before you sign up for either test.

  If you're going for a graduate degree you will probably be required to take the GRE (Graduate Record Exam) or the GMAT (Graduate Management Admissions Test). Law schools require the LSAT (Law School Aptitude Test).

  Apply early. Allow a six month lead time between applying to take the test and the results arriving at the college of your choice.

Educational Tests for College Entrance

Before sending for any of these tests, check with your local college or university admissions office. They may have the forms on file.

UNDERGRADUATE ENTRANCE EXAMS

ACT (American College Test): For information, write to ACT Registration, P.O. Box 414, Iowa City, Iowa 52243, and request a registration package. It is free. Please note that the ACT will probably not be required for entrance to a graduate program.

SAT (Scholastic Aptitude Test): For information, contact The College Board, 45 Columbus Avenue, New York, New York 10023. Please note that the SAT will probably not be required for entrance to a graduate program.

If you're entering college for the first time, be aware that you can substitute what you have learned on your own for undergraduate units. For more information, ask your local college or university for information on CLEP (College Level Entrance Placement). Or you can send for information to The College Board, 45 Columbus Avenue, New York, New York 10023.

GRADUATE SCHOOL ENTRANCE EXAMS

LSAT (Law School Admission Test): For information, write to LSAT Registration, Box 2001, Newton, Pennsylvania 18940-0981, and request the Law School Admission Test/ Law School Data Assembly Service Information Book. It's free.

GRE (Graduate Record Exam): For information, write to Graduate Record Examinations, P.O. Box 6004, Princeton, New Jersey 08541-6004 and ask for the Information Bulletin. It's free.

GMAT (Graduate Management Admission Test): For information, write to Graduate Management Admissions Test, Educational Testing Service, P.O. Box 6103, Princeton, New Jersey 08541-6103 and ask for a Bulletin of Information. It's free.

TIPS ON FILLING OUT YOUR APPLICATION

- There is intense competition to get into any school. The better the school, the more people you're going to have to beat out. Don't assume that you're going to get in.
- Fill out all forms completely and legibly. Use a typewriter or a computer.
- If your undergraduate grades are more than ten years old, they will probably not be weighed very heavily. This means that your post-college career is going to be very important. In the sections

on activities, list your positions, volunteer work, publications, company awards or anything "special" about you. Show the school that your experience and talent make you a *better* applicant than some young kid fresh out of school.

Some experts feel you should not list organizations or awards that give any indication of race, religion or marital status. You must decide for yourself whether you feel comfortable revealing this information.

- If you're asked for a photograph, send a good one. Don't go down to the passport picture booth at the shopping mall. A picture is worth a thousand words so make sure those words are good. Remember, you're a professional. Look like one.

- The older you are, the most backup material should be included. Look at it from the college's point of view: Why should they admit a forty-five-year-old who's forgotten everything he or she has learned twenty years ago instead of an eager twenty-two year old graduate with a high GPA? Again, play up your post-college experience. That's what puts you ahead of the pack. Make sure your letters of recommendation reflect the fact that you're a well-rounded individual. Be selective as to whom you ask to write recommendations for you.

THE HIGH COST OF EDUCATION

Next, of course, comes the question "How am I going to pay for this?" If you have been out of the academic world for a while, prepare to be shocked by the cost. A year of full-time study could cost $20,000, not including living expenses. The better the school, the higher the cost. Also, remember to take into account the loss of income that will follow if you take a year or two off from work.

How do you pay for it? That's a good question.

1. Inevitably quite a bit of money is going to have to come out your own pocket. Even if you do get a scholarship, be prepared to dig deep into your savings.

2. Surprisingly few people apply for scholarships. Even more surprising is how much money is available. Don't pay for your own education if you can get someone else to do it for you. Academic expenses will be high enough.

Almost all libraries have a listing of available scholarships in the reference section. It may take you a while to go through it, but take the time. Scholarships are based on an amazing number of criteria, not just academic achievements.

Chances are, there's at least one applicable to you. They range from fifty dollars and a pat on the back to full academic scholarship.

3. Then there is the possibility of a grant, loan or work-study opportunity. Since each state is different, contact your governor's office or the Department of Education.

4. The Federal government also has a wide variety of grants, loans and work-study programs. Write the United States Department of Education in Washington, D. C. for its booklet, *Student Guide, Financial Aide from the United States Department of Eduction: Grants, Loans and Work-study.*

    There is a hotline for questions regarding federal education grants and loans. The number is 1-800-333-INFO (from 9:00 AM to 5:30 PM EST, Monday through Friday — except holidays). If you don't know what to say, ask for specific information about Perkins Loans, Stafford Loans and PLUS/SLS Loans.

How to Use the Library

Most people use a library backwards. They go to the card catalog first, and then into the stacks. These are the people who say that research is hard and information difficult to find. These people are wrong.

Using a library is very easy. Finding information is very easy. You only have to understand how the library indexes your subject. For instance, most people walk into a library and say, "I want to know about computers." Well, there's quite a bit on file about computers. What you have to do — and what the reference librarian will do — is get you to be more specific.

If you want to save time and effort, go immediately to the *Reader's Guide to Periodical Literature* which is now on microfilm. Go to the FIRST listing in the section on computers. Underneath it will say, "see also" and then list subcategories of computers. That's your first clue. Once you have identified what subject you're looking for, the library is at your disposal.

In most libraries there are three different microfilm index readers. One is for *business* another for *newspapers* and a third for *magazines* Check all three, but check the magazines first.

If you can't find what you need in magazines, go the card catalog and look up the category that was listed on the Reader's Guide screen. Then go to that call number in the reference section. Why the reference section? Because the bulk of the quick information and directories can be found there, not in the regular stacks. If you can't locate the reference sections, ask a librarian.

Finally, after you have checked the magazines and the reference section, then you can go into the stacks.

TIPS FOR A SUCCESSFUL YEAR AT GRADUATE SCHOOL

- Remember that you're in the academic world now. This means there is a new set of performance standards. Listen to what is expected of you in each class. These are your *minimum* requirements. Don't try to get by with just the minimum.
- Keep in mind that you're being taught broad overviews. In business school, for instance, marketing classes are designed to

give you the general rules of successful marketing. This does not mean everything you're taught will be directly applicable to your present job or career.

Don't forget that these broad principle are what you will be *tested* on. Do not mix up your real-life lessons with the academic overview. In school, go for good grades. In terms of the information you learn, recognize that you're being given a universe of proven theories, opinions and facts. What you choose to do with that information outside of the classroom is up to you.

- Learn from other people's mistakes — that's the most important lesson to learn in school. The history of business in America, sadly, is the saga of companies that made bad decisions and failed to correct the error.

  What does this have to do with being successful in graduate school? Overall, your grades will depend on how well you illustrate your understanding of the history of your chosen graduate field. In business, for instance, a good marketing paper will have historically accurate scenarios of good and bad examples. Dull, generic research papers and exams get average grades.

- Don't cut classes. You're paying for your education. Make sure you get every penny's worth. It's also important to remember that who you meet in class is almost as important as what you're learning.

- Turn in all your paperwork on time. That's as much a part of education as it is of business.

- Do your assignments. Yes, they may be boring and seem a waste of time, but you never know where you're going to pick up a gem of wisdom.

- Ignore people who complain that what is being taught has no relevance to "the real world." First, there is no such thing as "the real world." Second, what you're learning now will be invaluable in a year. Third, if you want a program that deals more directly with "the real world," get an internship.

- Network with *everyone* in graduate school. These are the people you will be doing business with for the next thirty years. These are your "old school ties," so make the best possible impression. Don't risk a multi-million dollar blunder in fifteen years because of unfortunate business school behavior.

- Learn how to find information. The library is the single most underrated and overlooked asset of the business community.

Most business people seem to think everything they need to know is in their own office. These people will never be any brighter or more productive than they are right now.

- Learn to write. Don't believe people who tell you that America is strictly a visual culture. This is not true. The bulk of your quality information will come via the written word. The better you can write, the more completely your ideas will be understood. Don't kill a good idea with bad writing.

❖ ❖ ❖

"If you think education is expensive, try ignorance."

School Board election slogan

❖ ❖ ❖

Twenty-five of the Top Libraries in the U.S.

(Listed alphabetically by city)

University Library, University of Michigan, Ann Arbor, MI
The Library, University of Texas at Austin, Austin, TX
General Library, University of California at Berkley, CA
Indiana University Libraries, Bloomington, IN
Boston Public Library, Boston, MA
Harvard University Library, Cambridge, MA
Chicago Public Library, Chicago, IL
University of Chicago Libray, Chicago, IL
Detroit Public Library, Detroit, MI
Northwestern University Library, Evanston, IL
Dartmouth College Library, Hanover, NH
Cornell University Libraries, Ithaca, NY
University Library, University of California, Los Angeles, CA
William Andrews Clark Memorial Library, Los Angeles, CA
University of Minnesota Libraries, Minneapolis, MN
Yale University Library, New Haven, CT
Columbia University Libraries, New York, NY
The Pierpont Morgan Library, New York, NY
New York Public Library, New York, NY

The Library Company of Philadelphia, Philadelphia, PA
Princeton University Library, Princeton, NJ
John Carter Brown Library, Providence, RI
Stanford University Libraries, Stanford, CA
University of Illinois Library at Urbana-Champaign, Urbana, IL
Library of Congress, Washington, D.C.

Things They Will Never Tell You in School

- Many business teachers can not, could not, or will not try to make it in the business world.
- The closer your term papers and essays match the philosophy of the teacher, the higher your grade will be.
- Copying from one source is called plagiarism. Integrating information from two is called research.
- Footnotes are impressive. The longer the footnote section, the more impressive the report. Bibliographies are especially impressive if they include sources other than books.
- No matter what the instructor says, the longer the paper or test, the better your chance for a higher grade.
- In-class participation counts even if your instructor says it doesn't.
- True/false and multiple-choice tests are a lazy teacher's way of coming up with grades. Be suspicious of classes in which these tests are the sole basis for grades. In the corporate world, no one asks you to take tests. They expect a report.
- The best excuse is no excuse. If you have to come up with a reason for not finishing a project on time, any excuse, no matter how true, is suspect.
- Type everything, including take-home exams.
- Network with everyone in your graduate class. You will be doing business with these people for the rest of your life. Stay on alumni lists. Keep in touch.

NEWS YOU CAN USE

8

AMERICA'S CHANGING ECONOMIC PROFILE

❖ ❖ ❖

In the beginning, God tilted the world on edge and let all the loose pieces fall into California.

New Yorker's view of California

❖ ❖ ❖

All New Yorkers have one thing in common: They don't believe there's anything west of the Hudson River.

Californian's view of New York

❖ ❖ ❖

No matter how well you plan your life, the chances are very good that you're going to have to relocate at least once in your career. Maybe you're being transferred. If you work for a large corporation, it's more than likely that you'll have to move out of the city where you were hired. Large corporations have a tendency to move their executives around, to give them more varied experience. You could even end up living in a

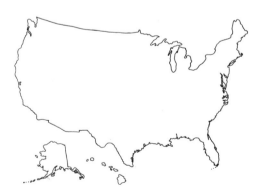

foreign country for part of your career.

On the other hand, you may choose to move on your own. Perhaps you're going to graduate school, or looking for a new job. Maybe you're tired of the smog in Los Angeles, the muggings in New York, the heat of Florida, the isolation of South Dakota or your mother-in-law living on the next block.

Whatever your reason for wanting to move, don't do it blindly. Serendipity, the unexpected discovery of one thing while looking for something else, is fine if you're a chemist. But it is too great a gamble if you're looking for a place to live.

Far too often, people don't research the city where they plan to settle. They get transferred, so they just move. They settle into a hotel for a month or two and then find a place to live permanently. Even in a case such as this, where you really don't have an option as to the city where you will live, put a lot of thought into the exact location of your house or apartment. Don't make in haste a decision you will have to live with for probably a very long time.

❖ ❖ ❖

"A fellow that owns his own home is always just coming out of a hardware store."

Kin Hubbard, American humorist

❖ ❖ ❖

CHOOSING A NEW CITY

Whether you're looking to move to a new city just to get away from your mother-in-law or are being assigned to the branch office in Deadwood, do your library work before you leave town.

Find a copy of *Money*'s annual regional profile, "The Best Places to Live in America" (often in the August edition). It compares about three hundred metropolitan areas across the country on the basis of criteria including weather, median household income, age and other factors. Why is this important? Because America is land of suburbs. Just because you work in Los Angeles does not mean you have to live in Los Angeles. There are a great number of suburbs from which you may choose your home.

Something to keep in mind when choosing your suburb is the quality of the schools where your children will be educated. Just as every man and woman is different, so is every school. While you can get in your car and drive out of your suburb to go to work, your children cannot pick and choose their school. Spend some time researching the quality of the schools. Check with your reference librarian for the latest ranking of school districts across the country. The school district you choose will dictate your child's future.

Also, when choosing a suburb, keep your eyes open for other indicators. What is the condition of the roads? Are there curbs and gutters? Find out where the nearest police and fire stations are. Keep in mind, too, that you're seeing the suburb in one part of the year. If you're looking during the summer, ask how much snow usually falls and how fast the plows clear the streets. Is there a drainage problem when it rains? If you don't feel comfortable asking neighbors, go to the town hall.

If you're interested in business information respecting your prospective community, read two or three recent issues of *Sales, Marketing & Management*. In addition to discussing the outlook for the current year, the magazine also gives regional profile information — and business projections — well into the future.

Choose your city and suburb with as much care and consideration as you do the house you buy. Quite a bit of your life is riding on that decision: possibly the rest of it.

The Hottest Cities for Jobs in the 1990s

(in alphabetical order)

Atlanta
Boston
Dallas
Houston
Los Angeles
New York
Phoenix
San Diego
San Francisco
Washington D.C.
(Source: U.S. Office of Management and Budget, 1987)

❖ ❖ ❖

"The business of America is business."

Calvin Coolidge

❖ ❖ ❖

GENERAL GEOGRAPHIC
TRENDS

❖ ❖ ❖

"The American economy is dominated by a small group of
'superstates' that to an increasing degree consists of those on the
Atlantic, Pacific and Gulf coasts."

Robert D. Hershey, Jr., American author and demographer

❖ ❖ ❖

If you haven't been following socioeconomic trends lately, you're in for a
surprise. The demographic and economic profile of America has changed
radically over the past decade. A decade ago, as energy prices moved up,
there was a flood to the sunbelt. Recently, with the stabilization of energy
prices, the decline of American industrial output and the growth of high-
tech industries, there has been a movement back to the coasts.

Today, America is becoming a bi-coastal nation. Over the last decade,
the greatest growth has occurred in California and the Atlantic seaboard.
Inland America has stagnated. But this growth of the "superstates" has
been more than just in terms of population. The sixteen "superstates" —
which now account for just over forty percent of the nation's population
— have seen personal income rise three to four times faster than the rest
of the country.

The bi-coastal emphasis has been determined partly by the increase in
size and strength of service industries such as banking, insurance and
advertising. The economy of the inland states continues to be based on
industries that have seen better days: agriculture, oil and smokestack
industries.

This does not mean that inland America is dead. What it does mean is
that, for the moment, the growth factor appears to favor a bi-coastal
economy. This is hardly a stable circumstance. Those factors mitigating
against inland America are transitory. The trade deficit has hurt
American production industries — many of them located in the thirty-
four states not benefiting from the service boom. Defense spending has
also benefited California and the fifteen Atlantic seaboard states more
than inland areas. When the world market price of oil fell there was a
loss of revenue in the "energy belt," (Alaska and the states from
Louisiana to Colorado) while, at the same time, lower energy prices
decreased production expenses on both coasts.

As far as the long term is concerned, America is moving toward an economy that will be primarily service-oriented. According to predictions from the Bureau of Labor Statistics, by 1990 an estimated seventy-one percent of the American workforce will be in service industries. Third World countries, with their supply of cheap labor, will continue to pressure the American manufacturing industry.

There are also other factors which are affecting American industry. The increase in lawsuits has fostered a rethinking of responsibility of American business. The growth of the Pacific as a focus of the world's economic interest is also reshaping American industry's view of the world. The recent budget deficit has affected the strength of the American dollar worldwide, and Japan's intransigence in allowing American firms to compete in its domestic market has denied American industries a lucrative market.

❖ ❖ ❖

"An economist is an expert who will know tomorrow why the things he predicted yesterday didn't happen today."

L. J. Peters

❖ ❖ ❖

There are other factors affecting America's businesses. By the year 2000, the median age in America is expected to be just over thirty-six years. The gap between birth and death rates will narrow to less than one-half of one percent by the year 2000. The death rate is expected to overtake the birth rate by the middle of the next century. As the baby boomers reach sixty-five, there will be a mass exodus from the workplace each year, probably making America more amenable to immigrants.

The Richest and Poorest Areas in the U.S.

Based on per capita 1987 income

RICHEST:

Stamford, CT	$26,316
San Francisco, CA	$24,593
Bergen-Passaic, NJ	$23,040
Middlesex-Somerset, NJ	$22,783
Nassau-Suffolk, NY	$22,001
Washington, D.C.	$21,539
San Jose, CA	$21,510
Anaheim, CA	$21,444
Lake County, IL	$21,432
West Palm Beach, FL	$21,246

POOREST:

McAllen, TX	$7,001
Laredo, TX	$7,035
Brownsville, TX	$7,409
Provo, UT	$8,870
El Paso, TX	$9,484
Las Cruces, NM	$9,578
Pascagoula, MS	$10,231
Houma, LA	$10,582
Jacksonville, NC	$10,668
Bryan, TX	$10,688

(Source: U.S. Department of Commerce, 1989)

REGIONAL ECONOMICS

Since 1980, the population of the United States has grown a bit more than six percent. But this population increase was not distributed evenly. New Hampshire, North Dakota, Florida and Arizona saw substantial increases in their populations, while Pennsylvania, Idaho, Washington, D. C. and Oregon saw the least growth.

The leader in the early part of the 1980s, incidentally, was Alaska. Between 1980 and 1986, the population of the forty-ninth state increased by more than a third. However, with the deterioration of the price of oil in world markets, the population of Alaska again declined substantially.

Gains in household income were strong in New Hampshire as well as Missouri, Virginia and Colorado. Weakest in the 1980s were Pennsylvania, Iowa, West Virginia, and Montana. Virginia led the nation with a 51.8 percent increase in household income. Iowa, at the bottom of the rankings, only had an 11.8 percent increase.

Average Annual Pay by State

(US average: $20,855)

AL	$18,318	KY	$18,008	ND	$16,157
AK	28,008	LA	18,707	OH	20,568
AZ	19,610	ME	17,447	OK	18,615
AR	16,529	MD	21,324	OR	18,888
CA	23,100	MA	22,486	PA	20,408
CO	20,736	MI	23,081	RI	18,858
CT	24,322	MN	20,450	SC	17,279
DE	20,764	MS	15,938	SD	14,963
DC	28,477	MO	19,601	TN	18,501
FL	18,674	MT	16,438	TX	20,463
GA	19,651	NE	16,526	UT	18,303
HI	19,091	NV	19,521	VT	17,703
ID	17,062	NH	19,414	VA	19,963
IL	22,250	NJ	23,842	WA	20,110
IN	19,692	NM	17,767	WV	18,820
IA	17,292	NY	24,634	WI	18,890
KS	18,424	NC	17,861	WY	18,817

(Source: U.S. Department of Labor, 1987)

The Northeast

The outlook for the Northeast "superstates" is good. High-tech and service industries offer sustained economic growth. Household income is high, offering local fiscal stability.

However, the Northeast can expect problems with its transportation corridors over the next decade. Bridges, roads and tunnels, many of them constructed in the early years of this century, will have to be repaired or replaced. This will place a increasing tax burden on property owners there.

The South and Southeast

The South and Southeast will show mixed growth in the next decade. While the Southeast will see sustained growth because of the service industries, the agricultural South may well see a further erosion of its economic base. Tourism will continue to be a mainstay of the region.

Experts say many places in the South may see an unexpected land boom. As agricultural land lays fallow, speculators may see this as an opportunity to buy. Additionally, as property taxes rise in the Northeast, there may be a migration of businesses to the South where land is inexpensive and property taxes low.

The Midwest

The Midwest will not see much improvement in the next five years. With the "greenhouse effect" changing from theory to reality, there is every reason to believe that harsh growing seasons will be more and more common.

There are, however, some bright spots for the Midwest. Americans, conscious of the danger of a large deficit, are becoming more attuned to "buying American." This is good news for the American automobile industry. Further, it is only a matter of time before the Japanese market opens to American products. That will put a premium on farm goods and this, in turn, will stimulate the agricultural industry.

The Far West

With California dominating the Far West, the average income looks good. But this is deceptive. Alaska slipped into a depression with the slide in oil prices. Oregon and Washington are slowly pulling themselves out of an economic downturn, but the short term outlook is still not positive.

Resource development projects such as oil, timber, fish, coal, gas and strategic metals has been stimulated, but environmental restrictions still limit exploration and development of the transportation and production infrastructure. Regulatory and civil lawsuits cause delays in production, and outright sabotage, particularly in the timber industry, creating friction between environmentalists and developers.

The bright spot for the Far West is that it is on the cutting edge of the Pacific Rim. With the shift in emphasis from the Atlantic to the Pacific, there will be a corresponding increase in shipping and transportation. West-coast cities such as Portland, Seattle, San Francisco and Los Angeles will see a corresponding increase in foreign attention. Tourism will continue to be a mainstay of the region.

The Southwest

Tourism will also boost the economy of the Southwest. Americans fleeing the frigid winters of northern climates will continue to move to the Southwest. This trend is not expected to abate over the next decade.

The Southwest can also expect an increase in the number of businesses moving from the Northeast. Just as California's sunny climate acted as a magnet to companies in colder parts of the country, so will Arizona and New Mexico attract businesses from the same areas of the country. Further, with baby boomers reaching the age when a second home is considered a well-earned perk, the Southwest is going to see an increase in absentee home-owners.

Alaska and Hawaii

Though both Alaska and Hawaii have different economic bases, both depend on the Pacific Rim for their livelihood. Hawaii will see a continued growth in tourism and trade. One of the foreseeable difficulties, however, will be land prices.

Alaska, in the midst of a depression at the end of the 1980s, will have a difficult time recovering. With ninety-five percent of its income coming from a single oil field which is expected to go into decline in the early 1990s, the oil frontier is quickly coming to a close.

However, being on the air crossroads of the world, Alaska can take advantage of its unique geographic position in the marketing of its natural resources: fish, oil, timber and strategic minerals. Further, any boycott of South African minerals will mean a corresponding burst of enthusiasm for the opening of Alaska's mineral fields.

9

THE GOOD, THE BAD AND THE UGLY

❖ ❖ ❖

Biography — the literary tribute that a little man pays to a big one.

Ambrose Bierce

❖ ❖ ❖

The best examples, the old saying goes, are from real life. That's true. So are the worst examples. This chapter is dedicated to the good, the bad and the ugly of corporate America: men and women who have shaped, or twisted, American business as we know it today. In their lives, we can all find a standard of excellence to model ourselves after — or an example of vice to avoid. In either case, here are the giants, the ones who have made the greatest difference in corporate America.

THE ERA OF THE ROBBER BARONS

Let's start at the beginning. Unfortunately, the men who founded corporate America are the very men who have come to personify all that's corrupt about it. The "robber barons," as they were called, were ruthless entrepreneurs who thought only of themselves, with little regard for the law or ethics. The term "robber barons" comes from the classic work of the same name by Matthew Josephson. One of the "muckrakers," called "investigative journalists" today, Josephson ripped back the veil on how business was really done in the days before governmental regulation. The picture was not pretty.

Published in 1934, *The Robber Barons* outlined the history of greed and deceit that went into the making of corporate America between 1861 and 1900. Written in the depths of the Depression, the book outlines the careers of some notable American icons as Jay Cooke, Jay Gould, Andrew Carnegie, J. Pierpont Morgan, John D. Rockefeller, Cornelius Vanderbilt, Henry Clay Frick and others. The portraits are not pleasant, and certainly not comforting. The key point of the book is a credo uttered by Vanderbilt, "The public be damned." That statement got as much play then as Ivan Boesky's "Greed is good" is getting today. Both statements symbolized their age.

J. Pierpont Morgan

J. Pierpont Morgan, born in 1837, created a financial empire without parallel today. At twenty years of age he was installed as an accountant in his father's banking firm. He eventually formed his own company, J. P. Morgan & Co., in 1895.

Morgan is unusual in the annals of the robber barons because he did not monopolize a product or service in the traditional fiscal sense of the word. He controlled money, and through his often questionable practice of lending and financial pressure, he built an empire. He grew so powerful he could personally adjust the economy of the United States. He proved this in 1907 when he mobilized his forces to stall a wide-spread collapse. His success inevitably led to government regulation.

Leland Stanford, Sr.

Leland Stanford, Sr., also gained his wealth in an era when there were no regulations to stall his climb to fame and fortune. A lawyer turned general-store owner, Stanford was elected governor of California and kept the new state on the side of the Union during the Civil War. After the war, he joined with four others — Theodore Judah, Mark Hopkins, Collis P. Huntington and Charles Crocker — in the building of the western portion of the transcontinental railway. However, four of the five were so rapacious that Theodore Judah, the brains behind the plan, left for Washington to find new, more honorable partners. (Judah died "mysteriously" in Panama on his way to Washington, D. C.) The four that were left, known in California history as "The Big Four," eventually sold out. Crocker sank his money in banks and an art gallery in Sacramento. Mark Hopkins built an exquisite home that is now a hotel named after him in San Francisco. Huntington moved to southern California where his money bought what is now Huntington Beach and the Huntington Library. Leland Stanford used his millions to start a university that is named for his son, a lad of sixteen who died of dissipation.

THE FINANCIAL TITANS

❖ ❖ ❖

"Advertising has done more to cause the social unrest of the twentieth century than any other single factor."

Clare Barnes, Jr.

❖ ❖ ❖

"Advertising is the rattling of a stick inside a swill bucket."

George Orwell

❖ ❖ ❖

David Ogilvy

Like many self-made people, David Ogilvy had a rather rocky start. As a young man he flunked out of Oxford and made his living in a variety of jobs, including selling stoves in England, working as a chef in Paris, farming tobacco in Pennsylvania and serving with British Intelligence during the Second World War. Then, in 1949, at the age of thirty-seven, he opened an advertising firm, Ogilvy-Mather. Today that firm is one of the largest in the world.

Most up-and-coming advertising executives of today know Ogilvy as the author of *Confessions of an Advertising Man* (Atheneum), which was a best seller in 1963 and is still the bible of the advertising industry. What makes Ogilvy's writing so memorable is its crystal clear, readable style. Additionally, Ogilvy finds unique ways to personalize his message. Once, in a board meeting on the hiring of new staff, for instance, he distributed nesting wooden Russian dolls to his executives. Each person opened his or her doll and, of course, found a smaller wooden doll inside. The executives opened doll after doll until, in the smallest one, was a short memo. In the memo, Ogilvy stated that, if the firm always hired people "smaller" than the person doing the hiring, the agency would inevitably shrink. But hiring people that were "larger" than yourself would make the agency grow. His executives must have taken that message to heart, given the worldwide dominance of Ogilvy & Mather today.

Thomas Alva Edison

❖ ❖ ❖

"The inventor tries to meet the demand of the crazy civilization."

Thomas Alva Edison

❖ ❖ ❖

American inventor and pioneer industrialist, Thomas Alva Edison was born poor. Self-educated, he became one of the most prolific inventors in American history. Three of his inventions, the incandescent light bulb, the phonograph and the moving picture camera, changed the world forever.

As a young boy, Edison sold candy and newspapers to raise money for his experiments. His first invention to be patented was the electric vote recorder. However, he could find no buyer for the invention. He resolved then never to invent anything that did not have a commercial application. His next invention was a stock market ticker — for which he received less than it cost him to build.

Edison, however, was more successful repairing gold-price tickers and worked his way up the business ladder at the Laws Gold Indicator Company. At twenty-nine, he resolved to become an inventor and moved to Menlo Park, New Jersey, where he set about investigating the world of science. There he developed the carbon telephone transmitter, the phonograph, the dictating machine, the fluoroscope, the motion picture camera, the incandescent bulb and the iron-alkaline storage battery among others.

As a businessman, Edison understood the need to market his own inventions. Though his experiments did not earn him wealth, his business sense did. Edison organized numerous companies to market his products, and in 1892, after a series of mergers, formed General Electric, today one of America's largest corporations.

However, one of Edison's greatest shortcomings was his inability to grasp the importance of alternating current. Edison designed his electric inventions for direct current and pushed hard for that concept. Eventually a one-time employee of his, Nicholas Tesla, and George Westinghouse proved that alternating current was feasible, economical and safer than direct power.

"Invention is the combination of brains and materials. The more brains you use, the less material you need."

Charles F. Kettering, American engineer and inventor

❖ ❖ ❖

Nicholas Tesla

One of the most underrated personalities in American history is Nicholas Tesla. He was born in Smiljan, Croatia in July of 1856, received a technical education in Europe, and a degree at the University of Prague. He went to work for the Continental Edison Company in Paris in 1882, but was distressed when the engineers there would not listen to his ideas concerning alternating current. He came to the United States, still convinced that alternating current was more feasible than direct current, and worked for Thomas Edison until 1887. Then he left to establish his own laboratory.

There, Tesla designed a machine that would create alternating current. This single design reshaped the world's use of electricity. Suddenly great amounts of electricity could be transmitted over great distances with less loss than with direct current. Tesla was able to put his theory into practice in 1895 when he and George Westinghouse tapped the power of Niagara Falls for New York City. The project took eight years to complete and made Tesla as famous as Edison. Today, almost all the electrical power in the world is transmitted using Tesla's invention.

Tesla was always a man ahead of his time. In 1898, to hoots of derision, he predicted radio-guided missiles and aircraft — and actually developed torpedoes and ships guided by radio waves. There is evidence that he took the first X-ray picture, and even designed a flying saucer that actually flew. He predicted radar and wireless transmissions. In 1900 he presented a theory to surround the earth with a layer of electrical energy. This energy field, said Tesla, could be used to transmit personal messages, pictures, weather reports and other data anywhere in the world. Today we call this dream broadcasting.

In his declining years, Tesla was a recluse, only appearing on his birthday to stagger newspaper reporters with predictions. At one of these dinners he claimed that he was working on a "death ray." Within hours of Tesla's death in 1943, his safe was rifled and documents stolen. The culprits were assumed by many to be agents of the United States government.

Robert Vesco

To many American businesspeople, Robert Vesco is evil incarnate. He first gained notoriety in the 1970s when he took over the management of a struggling international mutual fund empire by the name of Investors Overseas Services (IOS). Considered a white knight when he took the reins of power, it soon became apparent that he was anything but a fiscal savior. Within a few years he had skimmed off more than $224 million.

Vesco reappeared in the press in 1973 when he was indicted for fraud and making an illegal contribution of $200,000 to the re-election campaign of Richard M. Nixon. If he thought the contribution might convince the Securities and Exchange Commission to forgive his transgressions with IOS, he was greatly mistaken. Fearing indictment — with good reason — he fled to Costa Rica where he had bought the protection of President Jose Figueres. Thereafter, liberally plying the politicos of Costa Rica with cash, Vesco was able to continue his lavish lifestyle. The good times were not to last. Eventually he became too much of an embarrassment. Evicted from Costa Rica, he fled to the Bahamas.

Vesco next reappeared in the American press when he tried to bribe members of the newly-elected Carter administration with ten million dollars. The Carter administration was unimpressed with the offer and urged the government of the Bahamas to extradite Vesco back to the United States. Apparently Vesco was an embarrassment to the government of the Bahamas as well, for deportation proceedings were instigated.

One step ahead of the deportation writ — and an alleged CIA plot to kidnap the fugitive financier and return him to the United States — Vesco hopped a plane to Antigua before going to Nicaragua and, finally, Cuba. There he is said to have masterminded the smuggling of American-made machinery into Cuba in violation of American law, and negotiated the use of Cuban air space by Carlos Lehder Rivas, a Colombian cocaine kingpin now on trial in the United States.

Today, his ill-gotten fortune almost gone, Vesco lives a modest lifestyle in Havana where he's suspected of organizing multi-million-dollar drug deals between the cocaine lords of Columbia and a distribution network in the United States. He is only fifty-four years old. In an age when a man of his age can reasonably expect to live another thirty years, Vesco must wake each day worrying that Cuba and the United States will come to some diplomatic understanding. He is a man whose days are numbered, for he has no place left to go but home, to a long-delayed day in court. "The wheels of justice turn slowly," as the saying goes, "but they do turn."

Hugh Hefner

Hugh Hefner was the boy next door who made his millions undressing the girl next door. Hefner began his publishing empire with the appearance of *Playboy* in 1953, a magazine based on the precept that nice girls like sex, too. Over the next three decades, he has made that point clear twelve times a year.

Hefner's business strength was his ability to translate his own aspirations — and fantasies — into a money-making proposition. He has been very successful; *Playboy* is still a profitable enterprise, in spite of the fact that sexual mores have changed significantly since the early 1950s, and that magazines like *Penthouse* have taken a chunk of the market that *Playboy* once held exclusively. Today, at sixty, Hefner is still living the life he has personified for more than thirty-five years. He has proven that it is possible to have your cake and eat it too.

❖ ❖ ❖

"The only question with wealth is what to do with it."

John D. Rockefeller, Jr.

❖ ❖ ❖

The Guggenheim Family

In the United States there are very few families which can truly be called *dynasties*. Like the Rockefellers and the Fords, the Guggenheims seized the opportunities of the moment. The family has pumped millions of dollars into charities through a foundation which provides financial support for a wide range of projects — some of them so unusual that it is doubtful whether any of the original Guggenheims would have approved.

The patriarch of the family was Meyer Guggenheim, born in Langnau, Switzerland in 1828. He immigrated to the United States in 1847 and settled in Philadelphia, where he made his living selling Swiss embroidery. Forty years later, he acquired an interest in two mines in Colorado and soon made a fortune in the processing of metals. His seven sons assisted him, and kept the business alive after his death in 1905.

The second son of Meyer Guggenheim was Daniel. He, too, began in the family's embroidery business but soon joined his father in the metallurgy business. For more than forty years he was the dominant force of the Guggenheim empire. He built smelters and refineries around the world and initiated the search for new sources of minerals. Eventually that search resulted in nitrate fields in Chile, tin mines in Bolivia, gold in the Yukon, coal in the Alaska territory and diamonds in Zaire and Angola. Shortly before his death in 1930, Daniel and his wife Florence established the Guggenheim Foundation. Providing money for musical, scientific, scholarly, medical, civic and educational projects, the Foundation is one of the largest philanthropic enterprises in the United States.

Solomon R. Guggenheim, the sixth son of Meyer, worked in the family metallurgy industry and also served as U.S. senator from Colorado from 1907 to 1912. He is best known today for the establishment of the Solomon R. Guggenheim Museum in New York City. Established in 1937, the Museum began with Solomon's private art collection. Frank Lloyd Wright was commissioned to design the current structure, completed in 1959.

If there is any one item for which the Guggenheims should be remembered it is their understanding that there is a strong, nourishing link between business, academia and culture.

H. Ross Perot

H. Ross Perot is one of the few truly self-made men in the latter half of the twentieth century. The son of a horse-trader and cotton farmer, Perot began a company by the name of Electronic Data Systems in 1962 with one thousand dollars. He was thirty-two years old at the time and started his company because he had become frustrated trying to convince his employer, IBM, that it should be providing computer service. IBM should have listened. In 1984, Perot sold EDS to the General Motors Corporation for $2.5 billion.

Perot has become a cult hero. A man who speaks his mind is rare in any culture, and Perot is not afraid of expressing his opinion even when that opinion is bound to enflame passions. In 1984, for instance, when he was the chairman of an education-reform committee, Perot pressed for a law which would have prohibited high-school students with poor grades from competing in football. It should be pointed out that he did this in Texas, a state where football is as sacred as motherhood, the American flag and apple pie. Perot wasn't interested in being a moderating influence; he wanted to do what was right.

When Perot began pushing for education reform, a local columnist wrote that he "went seven bubbles off plumb, crazy as a peach-orchard boar," but Perot is not afraid of controversy.

When two of his employees were kidnapped in Iran during the reign of Khomeini, he hired a mercenary to free them and get them out of the country. The escape was a stunning success, and inspired the 1983 book, *On the Wings of Eagles* by Ken Follett.

Perot also came to blows in the business arena, this time with another entrepreneur of note, Roger Smith, CEO of General Motors. GM had bought out EDS in 1984, but part of the deal was that Perot would sit on the board of GM. Things did not go well from the start. Perot was used to speaking his mind, and grew increasingly vocal in board meetings. Eventually he was bought out and ejected from the board. Perot, referring to the board of directors as "pet rocks" of Roger Smith, went on the road talking about what GM should have done to stay competitive.

In the February 15, 1988 issue of *Fortune*, Perot launched a double-barrelled attack on GM. First he advocated changing the structure of the board, as many of the directors had virtually no stock. Second, Perot came out swinging on the quality of GM cars. The problem, he noted, was that the factory was not listening to the car dealers. This lack of communication was financially disastrous. Smith was not pleased and tried to rebut Perot's statements, but to no avail. Basically, Smith stated that it was a difference of style. Perot agreed, "I come from an environment where, if you see a snake, you kill it. At GM, the first thing you do is go hire a consultant on snakes."

Perot now spends much of his time encouraging education. In 1984, he bought a copy of the Magna Carta for $1.5 million and donated it to the National Archives. Two years later he spent $15 million to buy "a mother lode of English literature" from the New York-based Carl H. Pforzheimer Library of English Literature. He donated the entire collection — 1105 books and 250 manuscripts — to the University of Texas.

The lesson in the life of H. Ross Perot is two-fold. First, if you have an idea that you believe in, develop it. Second, education is a lifelong process. Advanced technology won't make Americans smarter. That's a job we have to do ourselves.

Andrew Carnegie

❖ ❖ ❖

"As I grow older, I pay less attention to what men say. I just watch what they do."

Andrew Carnegie

❖ ❖ ❖

One of the most roundly cursed, yet underrated businessmen in the history of the United States is Andrew Carnegie. Born in Dunfermline, Scotland in 1835, the son of a handloom weaver, Carnegie learned early the privileges of wealth. Following a depression in Scotland, he emigrated with his father to what is now Pittsburgh, where he worked in a cotton factory for $1.20 a week.

Working by day as a clerk and attending school at night, Carnegie became a messenger boy and subsequently worked his way up the ladder of success. He enhanced his success by taking advantage of every opportunity that presented itself, the epitome of the American success story.

Like many other industrialists, Carnegie profited from the Civil War. He saved his money and, after hostilities had ceased, became involved in the expanding iron industry. Within three years he was earning $50,000 a year. Shrewd enough to understand vertical integration and rich enough to capitalize on business opportunities, Carnegie secured his grip on the iron industry when he won a favorable lease on iron-rich Mesabi, Minnesota in 1898. At that time iron ore from Carnegie holdings traveled on Carnegie steamers and trains to Carnegie smelters in Pittsburgh.

By July of 1900, Carnegie and his company were more than profitable. In that year the company made a $40 million profit; $25 million going to Carnegie. The next year, as competitors began to hungrily eye his iron business, Carnegie sold out to J. P. Morgan for $250 million. Later the Carnegie Steel Company became the United States Steel Corporation.

For the balance of his life, Carnegie dedicated himself to giving away his wealth. He established a number of endowments, some of which are still in existence today, and became best known for his liberal gifts of funds for the establishment of public libraries across the country. Many modern yuppies started their education in public libraries funded by the Carnegie largesse.

Though he was deeply rooted in the school of hard knocks, Andrew Carnegie was well aware of the necessity of an education. Hard work and ruthless tactics, coupled with a keen market sense took him from poverty to the pinnacle of success. Carnegie's reputation has mellowed somewhat over the years — except among labor historians — but it remains to be seen how the next generation will judge him.

Herbert Hoover

One of the most unlikely entrepreneurs in American history is Herbert Hoover. Although he has a negative financial image due to his failure to stop the Depression of the 1930s, Hoover was hardly the failure that many historians would have us believe.

Born the second of three children in a Quaker household in 1874, Hoover grew up in Iowa and Oregon. He went to night school in Oregon and eventually entered Stanford. He graduated with a degree in engineering in 1895.

From 1895 until the end of the First World War, Herbert Hoover traveled the world as an engineer. By the time he was thirty-four, he was a millionaire. His reputation as an organizer was so noted that the President of the United States, Woodrow Wilson, asked him to undertake the greatest task facing the world at the end of the First World War, to feed the starving of Europe. Over the next four years, Hoover ran the effort to feed and clothe over 200 million people in Europe. His budget was $1.5 billion, a staggering figure in those days.

Herbert Hoover was able to use his skills as an engineer to feed the world. Far too often businesspeople feel that what they learn in business has no connection with real life. "Business is business," they say. "Leave the social work to social workers." Herbert Hoover proved them wrong.

Steven Jobs

He is the enfant terrible of the computer age, the brain behind the Macintosh and the Apple. He is the entrepreneur who canvased Silicon Valley — successfully — for millions of investment dollars. On the flip side, he is a hippie whose personal habits are more than eccentric. He is Steven Jobs, and his saga is far from over.

In 1976 — at twenty-one — Steven Jobs established Apple Company. The company grew at a breakneck speed as did Jobs' reputation. Then, in May 1985, in a very open and bitter corporate bloodbath, Jobs lost the power struggle at Apple to John Sculley, formerly a very close personal friend. Four months later he left the company altogether.

But the world had not seen the last of Steven Jobs. In October 1988, Jobs reappeared on the front pages of newspapers across the country with his next project, appropriately called NeXT. The NeXT computer was called by *U. S. News & World Report* a mixture of "brains, brawn, beauty and Beethoven." Rather than simply designing a computer that was one-step-better than the rest, Jobs made a quantum leap. NeXT is more than a computer, it is a multi-media package with stereo sound and a high-resolution screen. It places data on a removable disk which has more storage capacity than seven hundred of the old floppy disks. NeXT can create "living textbooks" with recorded speeches and pictures alongside the text. Musicians can compose and hear their symphony played back at the touch of a button.

Jobs is the Nicholas Tesla of the computer age. He has opened the door to a new era. What is worthy of note, however, is that Jobs understands that there is more to progress than just technology. After all, with each NeXT computer, Jobs includes the entire works of Shakespeare on disc, a little something to take with us through the door he has opened to the future.

Henry Ford

❖ ❖ ❖

"It's not the employer who pays wages — he only handles the money. It is the product that pays wages."

Henry Ford

❖ ❖ ❖

Another of the industrial giants of the twentieth century is Henry Ford, the patriarch of the Ford dynasty and innovator of the internal combustion engine. Oddly enough, Ford, like Nicholas Tesla, worked for Thomas Edison as a young man.

Fascinated with the internal combustion engine and its commercial applications, Ford constructed a one-cylinder gasoline engine in 1893. Constantly tinkering with the mechanism, he advanced to a two-cylinder model in 1896. Convinced he could make an automobile, Ford left the Edison company in 1899 and established the Detroit Automobile Company.

At first Ford failed. His company went into bankruptcy. Rather than give up his idea of a car, however, he turned to automobile racers. In October of 1901, on the frozen surface of Lake St. Clair, Henry Ford was able to cover a mile in an amazing 39.4 seconds.

With credibility as a racecar maker — and some investors — Henry Ford reorganized his motor car company in 1902. He became president and majority stockholder in 1906. His goal was to produce a car for the average consumer, one that was inexpensive yet well-made. His product was the Model T, a four-cylinder, twenty-horsepower "horseless carriage" that came in any color you wanted as long as that color was black. The Model T sold for $825 and by 1914 there were 250,000 of them on the road.

But Henry Ford is remembered for more than just being the popularizer of the automobile. He is also the inventor of the assembly line. With the standardization of the Model T, Ford was able to accelerate the building of cars by making the assembly process simpler. Rather than having each group of workers put an entire car together by themselves, Ford was the first to design a line in which the making of the automobile was broken into functional tasks. This sped up the making of cars and also reduced the cost.

Henry Ford should of course be recognized for his contribution to American business, but, like some of the other entrepreneurs we have seen, he should also be credited with the understanding that with great wealth comes great responsibility. To this end he established the Ford Foundation, a philanthropic association still in existence today which grants money to academic institutions, nonprofit organizations, and individuals for a wide variety of projects. He also established the Henry Ford Museum, and collected early motion pictures which he donated to the National Archives.

The Harriman Family

Another father-son combination of note was Edward Henry Harriman (1848-1909) and his son Averell. Edward left school at fourteen to work as an office boy on Wall Street. He bought his seat on the exchange at the age of twenty-two with some family help, and began reorganizing bankrupt railroad companies. At thirty-five he became a director of the Illinois Central Railroad and began a long and distinguished career as a railroad magnate.

His big break came in 1897 when he was appointed to the board of the bankrupt Union Pacific Railroad. Assisting in the reorganization, he became Chairman of the Executive Committee the next year and president in 1903. In his tenure as president, Edward was the moving force behind the Union Pacific. By the time of the elder Harriman's death in 1909, the UP had bought out the Southern Pacific line and owned rails extending from Chicago to San Francisco and Los Angeles.

Late in his life, however, Harriman cared little for public relations and his imbroglio with James J. Hill led to what is known as the Northern Securities Company scandal. Rather than compete for a small railway — and thus drive up the price of its stock — Harriman and Hill formed a holding company to own the railway. Thus, both of them controlled the company, though neither of them owned it. President Theodore Roosevelt felt that this was a violation of federal law and took it to court. In 1904, the United States Supreme court declared the company in violation of the law and ordered it disbanded. In the end, Hill acquired the railway line and Harriman lived out his life as a symbol of corporate greed.

Harriman's son Averell was well suited to wealth. After serving as vice president of the Union Pacific at twenty-four, he established his own banking firm at twenty-nine.

When he had achieved financial independence for himself, Averell moved into politics. He served as an administrator for Franklin Roosevelt's National Recovery Administration in 1934 and 1935, and as member (1933-1937) and finally Chairman (1937-1940) of the U. S. Department of Commerce's Business Advisory Council. FDR then sent Averell to Europe to work out the logistics of lend-lease and, impressed by his work and contacts, named him as ambassador to Moscow during the Second World War. Harriman later became FDR's Secretary of Commerce, then governor of New York in 1954. He was defeated by Nelson Rockefeller in 1958. In 1964, Lyndon Johnson appointed him ambassador-at-large, and he finished his service for Johnson as the U. S. negotiator during the Paris peace talks with the North Vietnamese

Ivan Boesky

Ivan Boesky, one of the richest men in America, lived up to his infamous slogan, "Greed is good." An investment banker of unquestionable talent, Boesky ran afoul of the law when he used inside information to make millions. Eventually caught, he was forced to pay a fine of $100 million, and spend some time in jail. Greed may be good, but it, in the long run, it's not profitable.

John De Lorean

One of the brains of the automotive industry, De Lorean, left the traditional confines of the board room to start his own company. Making a car he modestly named after himself, he soon ran into financial as well as political difficulties. To avoid U.S. governmental regulations, De Lorean established his factory in Northern Ireland. It is alleged that he was eventually forced to sell drugs to keep his company solvent. Later acquitted, De Lorean is now best known for being the maker of the car that was used in the popular movie *Back to the Future*.

Francisco A. "Frank" Lorenzo

Frank Lorenzo is another man who people love to hate. Ten years ago Lorenzo ran a small airline in Texas. He was opposed to rapid deregulation because he could see the disastrous effect it would have on small airlines. But when the disaster struck, rather than wring his hands and lament, he took advantage of the business opportunity. Through shrewd acquisition, he expanded Texas Air into one of the largest airline conglomerates in the world. He bought Continental, People Express, and Eastern. By 1986 it was estimated that one in every five air passengers in the United States was flying on a Lorenzo-owned carrier.

But being large means having large problems. When talks with Eastern employees broke down, a strike erupted which eventually forced the company into bankruptcy. Though Lorenzo's operations are not as large as they once were, he is still a power to be reckoned with in the airline industry.

Donald Trump

Then there is Donald Trump, a man whose name is synonymous with wealth. A New York developer and entrepreneur, he is known as an astute businessman and fierce competitor. Born in 1946, he has rapidly parlayed his family's real-estate wealth into a veritable empire. He now divides his time between entrepreneurial projects and philanthropy. What makes Trump so unusual is his willingness to maintain an extremely high profile. In many cases, men and women of great wealth prefer to avoid the limelight. Trump, on the other hand, savors it. Seemingly obsessed with keeping his name before the public, Trump, like Carnegie before him, has left a wake of projects and properties behind him, all named after himself.

Steven Spielberg

Born in 1947, Steven Spielberg has acquired a sterling reputation as a creative filmmaker. His projects are a hallmark of our era, and include *ET: the Extra Terrestrial, Jaws, Close Encounters of the Third Kind, An American Tale, The Color Purple,* and *Raiders of the Lost Ark* and its sequels. A millionaire many times over, Spielberg has proven that you can make money from your dreams.

Laurence Tisch

In September of 1986, the aging William Paley came out of retirement to retake control of CBS, the company he founded. It was turbulent week, and when it was over a previously little-known man by the name of Laurence Tisch, age 63, emerged as the head of the company.

An astute businessman, Tisch bought into CBS with about twenty-five percent of its stock, and was assigned by Paley to clean up the network's financial turmoil. The problem that Tisch faces is balancing the interests of a news and entertainment network with the hard-nosed business realities of turning a profit. It will not be a pleasant task. How profitable it will be is something else again.

Ray Kroc

In 1954, at age fifty-two, Kroc bought a hamburger stand called McDonald's in Des Planes, Illinois. Two decades later, in 1976, his corporation grossed more than $1 billion in revenues. In the process, he revolutionized the fast-food industry.

Perhaps the most significant lesson to be learned from Ray Kroc, made clear in his autobiography, *Grinding it Out, the Making of McDonald's*, is that it is still possible for a man armed with an idea to become rich and famous. There is always room at the top.

THE ECONOMISTS

The last group of business giants in these closing years of the Twentieth Century is the economists. With technology interlocking with advanced communications, there is no longer such a thing as an "isolated incident." Riots in South Africa can cause gasoline lines in Des Moines. There is no escaping the global community.

Paul Samuelson

A good look at the economists should include Paul Samuelson, the co-author (with William D Nordhaus) of the text most college students read, *Economics* (13 ed., McGraw-Hill, 1989). Samuelson believes that a little bit of a deficit is a good thing.

Arthur Laffer

From a different perspective, Arthur Laffer is a supply-side economist. He believes that massive government spending will produce a healthy private sector that can stand on its own and eventually attract workers from the public sector. This is eventually supposed to reduce government personnel while, at the same time, increasing tax revenues from the thriving private sector to pay off the deficit.

Louis Rukeyser

Yet another perspective is shown by the noted economic columnist Louis Richard Rukeyser. Rukeyser's most frequently-voiced theory is that of free trade. By reducing the barriers to trade, he says, all goods will be able to compete equally on the world market. In the long run, as Charles Darwin was often misquoted as saying, "only the strong will survive."

Milton Friedman

Then, of course, there is Milton Friedman, the monetarist. A monetarist believes that inflation, deflation and other economic ills can be adjusted by the supply of money. To reduce inflation, for instance, actual dollars would be withheld from circulation. Since there is less cash in circulation, there is less spending. This causes the economy to slow down, thus reducing inflation.

Paul Volcker

But the economist who has done the most to structure American thinking is Paul Volcker, the former chairman of the board of the Federal Reserve. He was more than *just* the Chairman. *Newsweek* accurately described him as "America's Money Master." He was the man who controlled the purse strings of a $4 trillion economy.

What makes Volcker so noteworthy is that from 1979 to 1986, the bulk of the Reagan boom years, Volcker made the transition from an academic dealing in theories to an economist in the real world. Using his power to control inflation by the adjustment of the prime interest lending rate, Volcker effectively stabilized the economy. Volcker's shoes will be hard to fill.

Academics should not be left out of the list of those shaping the future of business. Two of the best known academics are Paul Kennedy, author of *The Rise and Fall of the Great Powers* (Vintage, 1989) and a Canadian, L. J. Peter, most known for *The Peter Principle* (Bantam, 1984). What makes these two men unique is that their work has profoundly effected the way businesspeople view themselves and their careers.

Paul Kennedy

In *The Rise and Fall of the Great Powers*, Kennedy chronicles how nations overextend themselves militarily and in turn financially. The logical extension of this is massive deficit spending financed by foreign investors. Inevitably this leads to a decline of that civilization. For many Americans, it is as if Kennedy has taken his book from the front pages of America's newspapers.

L.J. Peter

In a more humorous vein, L. J. Peter invented the term the "Peter Principle," describing how workers are promoted to their "level of incompetency." In other words, a worker will continue to be promoted until he can no longer do the job to which he was promoted. This person is at his or her level of incompetency and will not be promoted further. Once in this "final placement," this person will most likely retire on the job.

The list of entrepreneurial giants, economists and thinkers in American corporate history could go on and on. Every industry has its standouts, its unsung heros, its silent, strong leaders. These are the men and women who move America forward, the horizon thinkers who believe that R & D is just as important as marketing. They understand that the future of their corporation depends on innovation, bold steps and agonizing attention to detail. In a nutshell, this is the history of America's corporate success. It is also a prescription for the future.

Recommended Business Biographies

Grinding it Out; The Making of McDonald's, Ray Kroc (St. Martin's Press, 1987)

Trump: The Art of the Deal, Donald J. Trump (Warner, 1988)

The Robber Barons, Matthew Josephson (Harcourt, Brace, Jovanovich, 1962)

Irreconcilable Differences; Ross Perot Versus GM, Doron Levin (Little, Brown, 1989)

The Rockefellers: An American Dynasty, Peter Collier and David Horowitz (New American Library, 1977)

Certain Rich Men, Meade Minnigerode (Ayer, 1927)

E. H. Harriman, George Kennan (Ayer, 1922)

Steven Spielberg, Donald R. Mott and Cheryl M. Saunders (G. K. Hall, 1986)

The Big Four, Oscar Lewis (Comstock, 1982)

Going for It: How to Succeed as an Entrepreneur, Victor Kiam (New American Library, 1987)

The House of Morgan, Lewis Corey (AMS, 1930)

Iacocca, David J. Abodaher (Zebra, 1985)

Steve Jobs: The Journey is the Reward, Jeffrey S. Young (Lynx, 1988)

De Lorean, John Z. De Lorean and Ted Schwartz (Zondervan, 1985)

Andrew Carnegie, Joseph Frazier Wall (Univ. of Pittsburgh, 1989)

Not So Free to Choose: The Political Economy of Milton Friedman and Ronald Reagan, Elton Raynack (Praeger, 1986)

Volcker: Portrait of the Money Man, William R. Neikirk (Congdon & Weed, 1987)

The Gold Ring: Jim Fisk, Jay Gould and "Black Friday," 1869, Kenneth D. Ackerman (Dodd, Mead, 1988)

Paul Samuelson and Modern Economic Theory, E. Carey Brown and Robert Solow (McGraw-Hill, 1983)

10

HANDLING YOUR MONEY

❖ ❖ ❖

Shortly after President John F. Kennedy had forced the steel industry to forgo a price increase, he was talking with a businessman who expressed uneasiness about the American economy. "Things look great," said the President enthusiastically. "Why, if I wasn't president, I'd be buying stock myself."

"If you weren't president," replied the businessman, "so would I."

❖ ❖ ❖

"'Invest' is a word that comes before investigate in the dictionary, but the action of both words should be done in the reverse."

Warren Sitka, humorist

❖ ❖ ❖

Everyone wants to be rich and famous. But those who are rich will tell you that *getting* rich is only half as hard as *staying* rich. The key to staying rich is knowing what to do with your money *befrore* you earn it.

Investing is not a game for the amateur. The mistake most people make is that they start their investment research after they have money to invest. They spend years accumulating money and then invest on the basis of a few days of casual research. This is like choosing a car on the basis of a test drive, or a spouse on the basis of the first two dates.

Long before you have money to invest, you should be researching available options. You should be hungering for investments long before you have the money to take advantage of what you see. If you can see all kinds of financial opportunities just inches beyond your financial fingertips, then you're doing your research correctly.

The first step in research is reading. Subscribe to magazines like *Money* and *Inc*. Attend business management classes. Join neighborhood investment groups. Buy a handful of penny stocks. Talk to stockbrokers and financial counselors. Start reading the stock market reports each day. Learn the lingo of the investment community. Study hard, because if you think the street is a jungle, wait until you get into the investment world.

For basic information on a wide range of investments, written in a language that a layman can understand:

Consumer Guide Investment Series, 5615 West Cermak Road, Cicero, Illinois, 60650.

The Only Investment Guide You'll Ever Need, Andrew Tobias (Bantam, 1983)

Marshall Loeb's Money Guide, Marshall Loeb (Little, Brown, 1989)

It is important to understand that all investments are risks. There is no such thing as a sure thing, just as there is no such thing as a free lunch. Over the long run you will learn that many of your best leads resulted in garbage investment while some of your long shots eventually paid off handsomely.

How you invest your resources depends on your willingness to take risks. High profits come only with high risks. Low profits come from low risk. Some people prefer the fast track with high risk and potentially high return, while others are more than happy to have money sit for years in an IRA.

As a general rule of thumb, financial advisors suggest that you should invest in low-risk enterprises in the same percentage as your age. In other words, if you're forty years old, you should have forty percent of your assets in low risk enterprises. The logic behind this advice is simple yet sobering. If you're forty and lose all your high-risk assets, you have the time to recoup the lost sixty percent of your money while you're living on the forty percent you were intelligent enough to have in low-risk investments.

❖ ❖ ❖

"Put not your trust in money, but your money in trust."

Oliver Wendell Holmes

❖ ❖ ❖

Another bit of general advice that every investor should heed is "spread your money around." It is not a good idea to sink all your money into any one investment. If you invest all your money in stocks and there's a crash, you're broke. But if you have some money in stocks, some in bonds, some in real estate, some in long term paper and some in gold, the stock market crash will affect only one portion of your portfolio.

❖ ❖ ❖

"Money is like fertilizer, it doesn't do any good unless you spread it around."

old adage

❖ ❖ ❖

Finally, don't become enamored with your percentage return on investment. If you invest ten dollars and get a 100% rate of return, you have still made only ten dollars. If you invest one thousand dollars and only get a five percent return, you've made fifty dollars. Don't judge an investment on the basis of its rate of return only.

REAL ESTATE

Traditionally, the single largest investment the average American makes is a home. In fact, the American success story revolves around the typical talented American, hungry for fame and fortune, starving in a basement apartment with a clunker for transportation. Dollar by dollar, he or she squirrels away a portion of his or her meager wage while struggling up the ladder of success. Gradually the hard work pays off. The hero eats better, drives a better car and finally buys a home in the suburbs. Ideally that home has a white picket fence enclosing the front yard.

The purchase of a home is considered the turning point for the economic portfolio. The home offers two investment packages for the price of one. First, since the interest on the home loan is deductible, the homeowner's tax liability is lowered. State and local property taxes are also deductible against the homeowner's federal income tax.

The second advantage is the increase in value of the home. If a house was bought for $100,000 and sold for $150,000 six years later, the home owner would have realized a $50,000 profit in six years, an annual return on investment of roughly 8.3 percent a year. The beauty of this investment increase is that the homeowner was *living* in the investment at the time. He or she acquired the luxury of living in the house, received the tax advantages of buying a home, and still saw an increase in the value of the property.

But before you dash off and buy a home, there are some downsides to home ownership. Two of the problems are finding the right place to buy, and choosing the right time to make the purchase. Remembering that when you buy a home you will probably be living in that home for years to come, choose your local community carefully. All neighborhoods change over the years. If you buy a house in a neighborhood where the residents care about the upkeep of their homes, take an active role in the local school, know their city council representative and school board seatholder, your property will probably increase in value.

If, on the other hand, you choose to live in a neighborhood where no one cares about taking care of their property, drugs are being sold openly at the local

Real Estate Investment Books

Marketing Investment Real Estate, Stephen Messner, Irving Schreiber and Victor Lyon (Realtor's National Marketing Institute, 1985)

How to Profit from Real Estate, Robert C. Kyle and Jeffrey S. Perry (Financial Services Institute, 1987)

How to Find Hidden Real Estate Bargains, Robert Irwin (McGraw-Hill, 1986)

How to Profitably Buy and Sell Land, Rene A. Henry, Jr. (Books on Demand, 1977)

How to Go from Rags to Riches in Real Estate, William Donner and William Proctor (William Morrow, 1982)

How to Make Money in Real Estate with Government Loans and Programs, Albert J. Lowry (Simon and Schuster, 1985)

Successful Real Estate Investing, Peter G. Miller (Harper & Row, 1989)

How to Build a Real Estate Money Machine, Wade B. Cook (Regency, 1986)

From Main Street to Wall Street, Frank Cappiello and Karel McClellan (John Wiley & Sons, 1988)

school, the city council representative is under indictment for bribery and the area school board seatholder doesn't recognize the name of your subdivision, you will probably not make a profit when you sell. Be aware, though, that if enough investors get involved in an area, no matter how bad the area seems, it will eventually become "yuppified" and "up-and-coming." Then, of course, real estate values will rise.

There is also a right time to buy a home. Before you sink your hard-earned money into a home, study your community's economy. Are economic conditions getting better or worse? Has the value of homes gone up or down? What caused that rise or fall? Is this an ongoing circumstance? Don't find yourself buying high and selling low; leave that privilege to HUD.

If you're considering buying a condominium, keep in mind that in many ways condo living is like apartment living. You will probably have neighbors on three sides of you as well as above and below. You're still going to have to fight for a parking space and a washing machine in the laundry room.

From a financial point of view, your condo association fee is not tax deductible, and appreciation is often not as high as with a house. But on the plus side, some of the headaches of home ownership may be eased by the condo association — such as cutting the grass, paying water and sewerage bills, plowing the parking lot during the winter and providing security while you're out of town on vacation. And, most importantly, condos are often less expensive than houses.

Whether you buy a condo or a house, it's important to remember that you're your own landlord. When you were a tenant, the landlord unclogged the toilet, fixed the broken window and replaced the refrigerator. When you buy a home, you get the honors.

Before you put any money down, consider the expense of upkeep. While repair and replacement may seem a small expense, investigate the cost of a new refrigerator, carpeting the living room or curtains for the entire house. Then there are the unexpected expenses: plumbing, wiring, phone installation, insulation, pest control and wall damage caused by drunk in-laws. Do not believe that you will be saving money by doing your own work, particularly if you're working overtime at your regular job. Inevitably you will do what you have time for and contract out the rest.

REAL ESTATE TERMINOLOGY

two story house — the realtor's story and the truth

windshield appraisal — an appraisal made by a realtor as he or she drives by the property in question

taillight guarantee — a guarantee by a realtor that is good so long as you can see taillights of the realtor's car

motto — "Buyers are liars and sellers are worse."

wildlife — cockroaches and mice

Real-estate investment, however, means more than just buying your own home. You could invest in vacant lots, warehouses, apartment buildings, time-share condos, office space or join with others to form a corporation for real-estate ownership.

While it would take an entire book to cover all the details of real-estate ownership, there are four aspects you should consider before getting involved in any transaction.

Long term financial commitment — You should understand that the financial reward from real estate comes over the long term. Do not put money into real estate if you're unwilling or unable to wait a number of years for a return on your investment.

You should also be aware that real-estate investment often means putting money into the property every month. This amount will vary with the number of vacancies you have. If you cannot afford that kind of financial commitment, do not look to real estate as a long term investment.

Time commitment — Any real estate investment will require much of your personal time. Even with vacant land, you'll have to visit it occasionally to make sure no one is squatting on it. If you invest in an apartment building, you'll have to spend time doing landlord-like duties even if you've hired someone to manage the property. If you don't have the time to look after your own investment, don't make the commitment.

Liability — There's always the chance you'll be sued. Even if you win a liability suit, the legal costs can be astronomical. Before you take on the responsibility of property, understand your legal risks.

Taxes and regulations — Do not assume that the tax structure and government regulation will remain unchanged.

❖ ❖ ❖

"Debt — an ingenious substitute for the chain and whip of the slave-driver."

Ambrose Bierce

❖ ❖ ❖

"The safest way to double your money is to fold it over once and put it in your pocket."

Kin Hubbard

❖ ❖ ❖

SHORT- VS. LONG-TERM PAPER

If you're not thrilled by the prospect of being a landlord, another avenue of investment is long- and short-term paper. "Paper," is nothing more than a certificate of investment. Suppose, for instance, you didn't know where you wanted to invest your money. You've left your money sitting in a checking account, probably earning little or no interest. In a savings account, it might earn about three percent. But invested in short- or long-term paper, your interest rate could be two or three times as high.

Short-term paper is specifically designed for the investor who wants his or her money to earn a reasonable rate of return but does not want the money tied up for years. Short-term paper is issued for as little as one month.

❖ ❖ ❖

"Never invest your money in anything that eats or needs repairing."

Billy Rose, American songwriter and producer,
best known for his song "Me and My Shadow"

❖ ❖ ❖

"Money is a terrible master but an excellent servant."

P. T. Barnum

❖ ❖ ❖

Long-term paper is defined as any cash investment committed to a year or longer. Long-term paper usually pays a higher rate of interest than short-term paper, but the money is inaccessible for a longer period of time. Long-term paper is specifically designed for people who are interested in putting their money into an investment they don't have to watch.

Two of the most common forms of paper are certificates of deposit (CDs) and treasury bills (TBs). Both of these financial instruments are federally insured and can be purchased at most banks or financial institutions. The downside to CDs and TBs, however, is that you cannot withdraw your cash early without a substantial penalty.

Another long-term financial instrument is a bond. A bond is an investment offered by a government agency. There are two kinds of bonds, both of them considered long-term paper. The first, and safest, is the general-obligation, or GO, bond. It is guaranteed by the full faith and credit of the body that issued the bond. For instance, municipal general-obligation bonds are voted into existence by the people of the municipality seeking the money. Part of that acceptance is a guarantee that, if the obligations of the bond cannot be met, municipal taxes will be raised to cover those obligations. If the municipality cannot raise enough money to pay off the bonds, the state is liable.

A second kind of bond is a revenue bond. In this case, money is bonded for the development of a specific, income-producing project. Then the revenue from that project is used to repay the bond holders.

The key difference between a GO and revenue bond is that with the GO bond, full faith and credit of the government backs the bond. With the revenue bond, there is no such guarantee. If the project goes under, so does your investment. And a GO bond is tax deductible while a revenue bond is usually not.

MONEY-MARKET ACCOUNTS

For the investor who wants his or her money earning a high rate of interest but does not want to be tied down with "substantial penalties for early withdrawal," there are money-market funds. Money markets were specifically formed to offer investors the advantages of short- and long-term investment at the same time. Using dollars from a large number of clients, money-market managers invest in a wide range of financial options. With thousands of clients, the money market managers have hundreds of thousands of dollars to truly diversify their assets. The clients of the money markets are thus able to take advantage of a wider range of investment options than individuals. Since many money-market funds allow for withdrawal, there is usually no penalty. Interest on the entire account is based on the average return from all of the investments.

There are thousands of money markets available. Some specialize in tax-exempt investments, others in government securities, and others in retirement accounts only. Most financial institutions have some kind of a money market. Money markets are also relatively secure; to date, there has not been a single failure.

But of course there is a downside to money-market accounts as well. Though some of their investments are insured, the money markets themselves are not. If the managers make bad choices, you could lose your money.

PRECIOUS METALS

Over the centuries, gold and silver have been the standards for wealth due to their consistent value even in the worst of times. When paper money is worthless — even if backed by gold — gold itself has a value. Gold can always be bartered. It is a universal medium of exchange and good in any country of the world. Its value is generally inversely proportional to the American dollar; as the value of the American dollar goes down, gold goes up proportionately. Silver is affected by the rise and fall of the dollar similarly.

Alas, there is a negative side as well. First, you're going to have to store your gold someplace — and under the mattress is not a good idea. This usually means a safe-deposit box. If you're only buying $500 worth of gold and paying seventy-five dollars a year in box-rental charges, you're losing any financial advantage you may have had by buying gold in the first place. An alternative is to buy gold certificates, and allow the brokerage house to store your gold. This is very risky, however. If anything goes wrong at the brokerage, you can end up with a worthless piece of paper while someone else absconds with your investment.

Second, you will have to pay a commission to buy the gold, and another to sell it. That can get expensive. Worse, however, by buying gold you're betting against the American dollar. If you earn $40,000 a year and buy $10,000 in gold you're, in essence, hoping that $10,000 of your investment portfolio will increase at the expense of your $40,000 salary.

Investment Guides

The Women's Financial Survival Handbook, Gail Perkins and Judith Rhoades (New American Library, 1980)

The Retirement Money Book, Ferd Hauheim (Acropolis, 1982)

Planning your Financial Future, H. Stanley Jones (John Wiley & Sons, 1988)

Be Your Own Financial Advisor, Robert E. Pritchard, Gregory C. Potter and Larry C. Howe (Prentice Hall, 1988)

Money Management Information Source Book, Alan Rees, Jodith James (R. R. Bowker, 1988)

IRA AND KEOGH PLANS

If you happen to be working for yourself, or at a corporation which does not have an retirement program, you might consider an Individual Retirement Account (IRA) or a KEOGH plan. Both of these are tax-free investments until you withdraw the money. Though the difference between the two is simply a matter of amounts of dollars that can be covered, check with an accountant before you make any financial commitments.

STOCKS

❖ ❖ ❖

"October. This is one of the peculiarly dangerous months to speculate in stock. The others are November, December, January, February, March, April, May, June, July, August and September."

Mark Twain

❖ ❖ ❖

If you're looking for an investment with excitement, try stocks. In essence, a stock is a share in a corporation. As businesses expand, they need money to sustain their growth. While they could pull it out of their retained earnings, often they sell shares of their company.

What make stocks so exciting is that their value fluctuates each trading day *throughout* each trading day. Since the wise investor has scattered his or her money across the board, each day is one of thrills and chills. Some stocks will rise, others will fall. Day by day, the financial picture changes. The trick is to make sure that you have more stocks that increase in value than those that fall.

Once you become familiar with the turbulent world of the stock market, you will discover that there are quite a few more investment possibilities than just buying a selling stock. If you have the heart for gambling and are immune to ulcers, there are options, futures, buying on the margin and selling short.

PENNY STOCKS

For a wild fling at speculation, you may want to invest in a penny stock. A penny stock, quite literally, is a stock that can sometimes be bought for pennies a share. (Actually, a penny stock is roughly defined as a stock selling for less than ten dollars a share). While penny stocks are fun to play with, particularly when you have thousands of shares, they're not the best investment you can make. If you buy your stock through a regular broker you will have to pay an expensive commission, as well as ongoing account charges. If you're not careful, you can end up paying more in fees than you've invested.

On the other hand, if a penny stock goes from one cent a share to four cents, you've made a 300% profit. That's a better rate of return than if you had bought GM. Of course, with one hundred dollars originally invested, you're really not earning that much.

DEALING WITH FINANCIAL PROFESSIONALS

Finding the right financial professional is like finding the right house. Anyone can call themselves a professional. All they have to do is pay twenty-five dollars for a business license. Even if they have to go to school to earn a certificate, that piece of paper does not make anyone an expert — it just means they can't be arrested for giving bad advice.

When it comes to choosing a financial advisor, be mindful of the Latin expression, *caveat emptor*, or "let the buyer beware." The money being discussed is yours. Don't take unnecessary chances. If you choose poorly, you could end up paying for that mistake for years to come.

Here is some advice for dealing with financial professionals:

1. Do not let one financial counselor handle all of your money. Buy your investments through two or three brokers. If you only use one broker and he or she happens to be incompetent, you could lose all your money.

2. Make sure all of your financial counselors see each other's work. This is a great way of making sure that no one is giving bad advice.

3. Keep records of all your transactions. Don't depend on the brokers to do it for you. If *they* make a mistake, *you're* going to have to explain it to the IRS.

4. A discount broker will buy or sell at your command, but will not offer advice. Seriously consider using a discount broker if you usually buy the stock *you* want anyway.

5. Be wary of people with inside information, or what appears to be inside information. Trading on inside information is illegal.

6. Don't get involved with investment options in which a participant has a questionable reputation. It will sully your own reputation and put you at risk with the IRS.

7. Be wary of unexpected calls for investments, even from your broker.

8. If you buy precious metals, ask for the metal, not certificates. Too often an investor will be told that a certificate is "just as good as the real thing." That's not true. An ounce of gold in your hand is an ounce of gold in your hand. A certificate for an ounce of gold is only as good as the business that issued it.

9. Research your investment potential. Ask your broker for all the pamphlets and general information his firm offers. Get on as many financial mailing lists as possible. Read books like *Martin Zweig's Winning On Wall Street* by Martin Zweig (Warner, 1989) and subscribe to investor newsletters.

10. Think for yourself.

DEALING WITH YOUR ACCOUNTANT

1. Structure your receipts functionally into categories established by your accountant. This makes it easy for him or her to assess your tax filing. The less time your accountant takes, the less you get charged. This also makes it easier to spot any legitimate deductions you may have missed.

2. Meet all time and task benchmarks set by your accountant. When he or she needs more information, provide it quickly and completely.

3. Be ready to provide your accountant with copies of all legal documents pertaining to stock gains, interest paid or received and documents relating to sale or acquisition of property.

4. Never try to fool your accountant. He or she works for you. If you want to do something that's not legitimate, your accountant will tell you.

5. Expect a high level of compe-tence from your accountant, and be prepared to have the same asked of you. After all, the IRS will be looking over both his or her work and your receipts.

HANDLING AN IRS AUDIT WITHOUT GETTING AN ULCER

Sooner or later, even the best of investors will face an IRS audit. That's a fact of life. It's a fact of life even if you're not rich, famous or sleazy. Be prepared.

Here are some common sense tips for dealing with an IRS audit:

1. Maintain your own financial records as if you expected an audit.

2. Don't mix business receipts with personal expenses. Keep your accounting records straight.

3. Don't miss deadlines.

4. Don't guess as to what is and what is not deductible.

5. Double-check your arithmetic.

6. Be an informed taxpayer. Read up on all changes in the tax law. Read Sandor Frankel and Robert Ink's *How to Defend Yourself Against the IRS*, (Simon & Schuster, 1986) and Jack Warren Wade, Jr.'s *Audit Proof Your Tax Return* (New American Library, 1988).

7. Get an accountant.

INVESTING IN YOUR FRIEND'S BUSINESS

Mixing friendship and business is rarely a good idea. Unless you have the rare ability to separate friendship concerns and business realities, stay away from investing in a friend's business.

If you do decide to become involved, make it clear at the very beginning of the financial relationship that you intend to make business decisions based on business realities. Try not to let business interfere with your friendship. Also, be absolutely certain that you're not making business decisions for friendship reasons or friendships for business reasons. Finally, write up a contract that clearly states your obligations, powers, amount of investment, etc. In short, get it all in writing.

BUYING A BUSINESS

Another means of investing your money in business is by simply buying a business. While the ins-and-outs of this decision would require a series of books, there are some questions you should be able to answer before even looking into it. (Also, see the section in this book on running your own business.)

1. If this company is successful, *who* specifically is making it successful? Will these people stay if the company is bought?

2. What is the long-term market for the product or service? Since you will probably be amortizing your buyout over ten years, you want to make sure that the market will be stable enough for you to at least recover your initial investment.

3. How old is the machinery? How old is the staff? How old is the market niche that has allowed this business to survive? Remember, a business may be successful in spite of the incompetence of its management.

4. How strong is the competition? If it's weak, have you considered buying out the competitor as well?

5. Are there IRS problems, liens, missed payments, debts in arrears or unpaid staff? If there are, you could be looking at a company that is pouring debt money into a "face lift" just to get someone to buy the company.

6. Who started the company? Has he or she left? Why?

7. Is the company advertising its product? How? If not, why not?

8. Who is the average customer? Demographically, is this chunk of the population increasing?

9. How much liability insurance does this business carry? Is it at the maximum level? If so, why?

10. Are there any lawsuits pending?

CAVEAT EMPTOR

It's important to remember that the financial world is spooky. As circumstances change, so do investment risks. If inflation is rising, for instance, real estate is a good investment. If there is deflation, real estate is *not* a good investment. Sooner or later, *anything* can be a good buy. It's just a question of the circumstances when you buy and sell the investment.

Finally, it's important to remember that the financial world is replete with charlatans, incompetents, cheats, boobs and the kind of lawyers who give the profession a bad name. What's at stake here is not principle, it's your money. Money, as you know, is hard to get and easy to lose. Regardless of how well you think you know your financial counselor or how intimate you're with your investments, follow the guideline of *caveat emptor.* If you aren't sure of what you're doing, don't do it.

IV

DATABANK

STAY INFORMED!

How to Read a Newspaper Article

Any time the subject of "staying informed" comes up, one of the first bits of advice that gets passed along is, "Read your local newspaper." While this is very useful advice, what no one bothers to tell you is *how* to read the newspaper. Most people just pick up the newspaper, whip through the business and city sections, reading the first few paragraphs of each story. Since they're reading more stories, they have the feeling that they are more informed.

Wrong! If that's how you read, you've been hoodwinked by your local press.

First, you have to understand that there is no such thing as a unbiased story. Every story has an angle. Combined, all stories give the newspaper its flavor. Be it liberal or conservative, the newspaper has an audience to which it plays.

This does not mean you should cancel your subscription because your local paper is conservative and you happen to be liberal. You can still get the facts; you just have to spend more time digging for them.

Understand that the first handful of paragraphs are specifically designed to give you a feel for the story — and the angle of the paper — in as short a time as possible. Then, starting at about paragraph five or six, the story will begin to broaden its scope, add some history, tie in some other facts and add some obligatory quotes.

Also, remember that just because it's in the newspaper doesn't mean it's true. Newspaper articles are often written by a number of people looking at different aspects of the same story. In many cases they are pressured for time. Many times, a story is written by someone sitting in an office who puts the pieces together over the phone. Don't form an opinion based solely on what one newspaper says. Read more than one paper to get more than one perspective. Watch local and national television news and listen to your local radio stations — public and private.

Journalists make mistakes just like everyone else. Note that your newspaper has a place for corrections. Check it occasionally to make sure that what you *thought* you read was indeed what was meant.

Be very careful when reading quotes. Think about what they're saying. When the mayor says he is cutting positions to bring the budget under control, this does not necessarily mean that people are going to be laid off. It just means that "positions" are going to be eliminated. This is particularly true of polls. If the newspaper quotes poll results, make sure you read the questions very carefully before you believe the numbers.

Newspaper stories change every day. There are follow ups and continuations. New developments and facts come to light. Be wary of the attitude that "all of the important facts have been brought out, so I don't need to read this story." In an ongoing story, the drama is in watching the principle characters change their positions. It's like an ongoing chess game; with each new move there is a new picture. Newspapers stories are designed to show the reader the ongoing drama of the news. Don't miss it.

Finally, get a big-city newspaper if possible. Local papers print local news and use the wire services for their national stories. This makes their national and international pages generic. Big-city newspapers have their reporters on the site of the story. That makes a difference.

How to Read a Magazine Article

Far too often, readers view a magazine as a fat weekly or monthly newspaper. Thus they do the same thing with the magazine that they do with the newspaper: whip through the pages looking at the first few paragraphs of each story. This is a mistake. While newspapers are designed to give you as much information as possible — plus the slant of the paper — in the first few paragraphs, the magazine article is meant to grab your attention with what is known as the lead. This may be a juicy detail, an interesting opinion or a scintillating quote, but it's usually *not* succinct summary.

Further, while a newspaper article is ideally *supposed* to be unbiased, a magazine article is under no such obligation. It is, in fact, exactly the opposite. It's meant to convince you of a point of view, or to coax you to a conclusion.

If the subject you're reading is important to you, read the last part of the article first. Find out where the author's going before starting to read his point of view. Don't get hooked too easily.

If you really like what you read in a magazine, learn more about the author. Check *Who's Who* and *Current Biography*, both in the reference section of your library. If you like the writer's style or knowledge base, follow up your lead. What else did this person write on the same subject? In what other magazines has he or she appeared? Check your *Reader's Guide to Periodical Literature*. You might even find a book he or she has written on a subject that is near and dear to your heart.Here's a list of some of the best magazines — as well as some more unusual sources — for staying informed.

Magazines

Time, Time/Life Building, Rockefeller Center, New York 10020

Newsweek, 444 Madison Avenue, New York, New York 10022

Barron's, Dow Jones and Company, 200 Liberty Street, New York, New York 10028

U. S. News & World Report, 2400 N Street NW, Washington, D.C. 20037-1196

INC., 38 Commercial Wharf, Boston, Massachusetts 02110

Forbes, 60 5th Avenue, New York, New York 10011

Changing Times, The Kiplinger Magazine, 1729 H Street NW, Washington, D.C. 20006

Nation's Business, 1615 H Street NW, Washington, D.C. 20062

Business Age: The Magazine For Small Business, Business Trends Communication Corporation, Box 11597, Milwaukee, Wisconsin 53211

Consumer's Digest Magazine, 5705 North Lincoln Avenue, Chicago, Illinois 60659

MBA, 18 North Main Street, Box 8001, Chagrin Falls, Ohio 44022-8001

Washington Monthly, 1711 Connecticut Avenue, Washington, D.C. 20009

Entrepreneur Magazine, 2311 Pontius Avenue, Los Angeles, California 90064

Black Enterprise, 130 Fifth Avenue, New York, New York 10011

Venture, 521 Fifth Avenue, New York, New York 10175

Smithsonian, 900 Jefferson Drive, Washington D.C., 20560

Other Sources

Better Business, National Minority Business Council, Inc., 235 E. 42nd, New York, New York 10017

Executive Female, NAFE, 1041 Third Avenue, New York, New York 10021

The NCFE Motivator, National Center for Financial Education, Suite 3100 West, 50 Fremont Street, San Francisco 94105

Travel Smart For Business, Communications House, 40 Beachdale Road, Dobbs Ferry, New York 10522

What Makes People Successful, The National Research Bureau, Inc., 424 N 3rd, Burlington, Iowa 52601. This firm also publishes *Economics Facts*.

REGIONAL BUSINESS MAGAZINES

Alaska Business Monthly, 400 D Street, Suite 200, Anchorage, Alaska 99501

Alaska Journal of Commerce, 900 West 5th, Suite 510, Anchorage, Alaska 99501

BC Business, Canasus Communications, 200-500 Burrard Street, Vancouver, British Columbia, V6 2J6, Canada

Boston Business Journal, P & L Publications, 393 D Street, Boston, Massachusetts 02210-1907

Boulder Country Business Report, Box 8005-265, Boulder, Colorado 80306

Business Atlanta, Communication Channels Inc., 6255 Barfield Road, Atlanta 30328

The Business Times for Connecticut Executives, 544 Tolland Street East, Hartford, Connecticut 06108

Business to Business: North Florida's Business Magazine. Box 6085, Tallahassee, Florida 32314

Business View, Florida Business Publications, Box 9859, Naples, Florida 33941

Crain's Cleveland Business, 140 Public Square, Cleveland, Ohio 44114

Crain's Detroit Business, 1400 Woodbridge, Detroit, Michigan 48207

Dallas Magazine, 1507 Pacific Avenue, Dallas, Texas 75201

Indiana Business, 1000 Waterway Blvd., Indianapolis, Indiana 46202

La Crosse City Business, MCP Inc., Suite 217, 505 King Street, LaCrosse, Wisconsin 54601

Memphis Business Journal, Mid-South Communications, Suite 102, 88 Union, Memphis, Tennessee 38103

Nevada Business Journal, H & M Publications, Suite 270, 2375 E. Tropicana, Las Vegas, Nevada 89109

New Business Magazine, Clubhouse Publishing, Box 3312, Sarasota, Florida 33581

New Jersey Business, 310 Passaic Avenue, Fairfield, New Jersey 07006

Ohio Business, 3rd Floor, 1720 Euclid, Cleveland, Ohio 44115

Orange County Business Journal, Scott Publishing, 1112 E. Chestnut, Santa Ana, California 92701

Oregon Business, MIF Publications, Suite 500, 208 W Stark, Portland, Oregon 97204

Orlando Magazine, Box 2207, Orlando, Florida 32802

Profit, Making It in Broward, Ft. Lauderdale/Broward County Chamber of Commerce, 208 SE 3rd, Ft. Lauderdale, Florida 33301

Regardies: The Magazine of Washington Business, 1010 Wisconsin Avenue NW, Washington, D.C. 20007

Tidewater Virginian, 711 West 21st Street, Norfolk, Virginia 23517

Western Investor, Suite 1115, 400 SW 6th Avenue, Portland, Oregon 97204

Western New York Magazine, Greater Buffalo Chamber of Commerce, 107 Delaware Avenue, Buffalo, New York 14202

For a current listing of regional publications in your part of the United States or Canada, find a copy of the most recent *Writer's Market 1990* (Glenda T. Neff, Writer's Digest Books) and check the section entitled "Regional Magazines."

For a current listing of professional publications in your own field, find a copy of the most recent *Writer's Market* and check the section entitled "Trade, Technical and Professional Journals."

How to Tell if Your Representative Is Lying to You

With the low esteem in which most Americans hold legislators, it's no wonder that you don't listen when your representative speaks.

That, however, is an error. If you make the assumption that what you're going to hear is a lie, you will miss what is being said. There is nothing wrong with being skeptical; but there is something very wrong with refusing to think about what is being said. Whether you believe what is being said or not, your representative may be talking about bills that may come to pass, and effect your life.

How do you tell if your representative is lying to you?

1. Is what he or she says logical?

2. Is what he or she says practical?

3. Who will make money from it?

4. Does your representative have any backup for what is being said? Just because you're told something is true doesn't mean that it is. If a legislator proposes an idea, look for the backup. That's your right. If you don't find any backup, don't put much credence in the idea.

    If there is backup, look at it VERY carefully. Who put it together? If it was not the legislator's staff, then who? Does that person or organization have a stake in the idea? How much?

Once you have found out who supports an idea, find out who opposes it. Then look for their backup. Don't be fooled into believing that all ideas are given a fair chance of being heard.

Anytime your representative says "it's a matter of record," check the record. If you don't know how to do that, go to your local legislative-affairs office and ask them how to do it.

How to Read a Legislative Bill

Don't read legislative bills alone. That's not your job. It's too easy to be fooled. But it is the job of your legislator and his or her staff. They work for you. Make them earn their money. Call them and ask for a copy of the bill, a review of the bill done by the legislative legal staff, and copies of any legislative reporting service on the "status of the bill." Also tell them you want the same information on any similar bills in the system. If they claim they don't know what you are talking about, don't believe them. Ask again. Finally, don't feel bad about asking your legislative staff to service your problem. *you* are paying them.

Once you have all the reference material, look at the bill from three angles:

1. Where is the bill? If it's a House bill, close to the end of the second session, in its first committee of referral, and there's no similar senate bill, forget it. It's not going to pass.

2. If it looks like the bill is moving, what changes have been made in committee? Is the bill properly funded? Can it be enforced? Who is going to do the enforcing? Has the legislature given that organization the money to do the enforcing?

    Don't be fooled into believing that a problem is solved because a law is passed. If there's no money attached, you are being snookered. For instance, making it illegal to drive over fifty-five miles per hour is not going to stop people from speeding. If no money is given to hire more traffic officers, the law is just hot air.

3. Even if properly enforced, does the law have teeth? If is turns out that the penalty for people who double-park is ten dollars, who is going to care? Don't waste your time supporting a bill that no one takes seriously.

4. Read the fine print. Legislators are famous for "slipping one over" in the bottom sections where it looks like just numbers are listed. If you don't have a copy of the legislative review of the bill or a legal opinion — which is a risky way to read a bill — look for numbers that are out of place.

5. Ask questions.

How to Propose a Legislative Bill

1. Give your legislator your opinion on bills. If you have an idea, speak up.

2. Give your legislator backup material. Make it readable and easy to follow. After all, you're the expert on your bill.

3. Don't lie. The legislator's staff will be looking into the idea. If a lie is discovered, the feeling will be that you are being less than honest and that more lies are hidden in the material.

4. Listen to your sponsoring legislator. If he or she tells you to start a letter-writing campaign. Do it. If not, stay clear of it. Just because you think it's a good idea doesn't mean that it will work.

Ten Free Ways to Stay Informed at Home

It always pays to be informed of what's happening in the world and in your community. The best way to keep on top of things is to put yourself on every mailing list you can find. Here's a list of places to start:

1. The Public Relations Society of America in your community.

2. Your local legislative information office. Specify what you're interested in and what you want sent. If you don't know what's available, that's the first question to ask.

3. Your United States congressmen and senators.

4. The consumer protection organizations in your area. Often they're associated with a college or university.

5. The U.S. Consumer Information Center, P.O. Box 100, Pueblo, Colorado 81002. Also ask for their list of free pamphlets.

6. Check your phone book for listings of toll-free numbers. Go through and choose those associations in which you have an interest and ask to be put on their mailing list.

7. Your community-service or community-council office. It can usually be found under the school district listings in the phone book.

8. Many communities have activities or arts hotlines. Get these numbers from your local chamber of commerce.

9. National nonprofit agencies. You can find their addresses and phone numbers in classified ads in many large magazines. Many of them have toll-free numbers.

10. Finally, don't forget to get your name on the mailing list of your own political party.

Information Sources

There is an old adage, more apt today than ever before, that "knowledge is power." Below is an annotated list of indexes and and directories to help you find the information, and power, you need. The following list is a potpourri of different sources. It is not meant to be all-encompassing, but it should give an example of the wide range of information sources available in your public library.

Encyclopedia of Associations. (Gale Research, Book Tower, Detroit 48226.) This is a complete listing of all associations and organizations in the United States. This encyclopedia is particularly helpful if you are looking for an individual. For instance, if you're trying to find a pyschologist, you can call the American Psychological Association for their membership list.

International Organizations. (Gale Research)This is a complete listing of major international organizations. Its listings are similar to the Encyclopedia of Associations.

Federal Assistance Programs Retrieval System (F.A.P.R.S.) This is a federal access program which pairs your needs with federal funding sources. Contact your United States Senator's office for details.

Franchise Opportunity Handbook. (U. S. Department of Commerce, Minority Business Opportunity, Washington, D. C.)

Franchise News Annual. (728 Center Street, P.O. Box 550, Lewiston, New York 10492 tel. 716-754-4669)

Congressional Directory. (U. S. Congress, Washington, D. C.)

Statesman Yearbook. (St. Martin's Press). This is a complete listing of who's who in the world of international politics. For instance, it can identify the French Secretary of Commerce or the mayor of Torino, Italy.

Foundation Grants Index. (Foundation Center, 79 Fifth Avenue, New York, New York 10003) This is complete listing of all foundations and all information necessary for grant applications.

Computers and Computing Information Directory. (R. R. Bowker)

Who's Who. There are a great number of *Who's Who* books including *Who's Who in Art*, *Who's Who in the West*, *Who's Who in Canada*, *International Who's Who*, *Who Was Who*, etc.

Information America. (Neal-Schuman, New York) This a directory of nonprofit organizations and their publications.

International Business Organizations, Agencies and Public Directories. (Gale Research)

Directory of Conventions. (tel. 1-800-624-6283)

National Trade and Professional Associations. (Columbia Books, Washington, D.C.)

National Directory of State Agencies. (Information Resources Press)

Land Drilling and Oil Well Service Contractors. (Penwell Publications)

Consultants & Consulting Organizations Directory. (Gale Research)

Marketing Information. (Georgia State University Press)

Directory of Directories. (Gale Research)

Handbook of Construction Management and Organizations. (Van Nostrand Reinhold Co.)

International Marketing Handbook. (Gale Research)

Biographical and Geneological Master Index. (Gale Research)

CORPORATE COMMUNICATION

Communicating within the Organization

In the development of an organizational structure, communication channels are an important consideration. The manager in a hierarchical system becomes a link in the communication chain. It is the hierarchical system that gives direction to and imposes restrictions upon the flow of communications. Management decision and directions flow from higher to lower levels in the organization. Managers also spend time communicating with their peers. Therefore, we see from the outset that communications must function effectively in a lateral direction, as well as downward and upward.

Committees influence the communication process within an organization. A well-run committee can serve as a supplementary link in the communication chain and provide a means for disseminating information. However, committees often fail to ensure that Managers A and B tell each other what they wish or need to know.

Although they cannot give directions or issue procedures, staff members influence the communication process within an organization. The advice or recommendations of staff members are accepted by subordinate managers because of the anticipated support by the staff member's superior. When a staff member is given functional decision prerogatives, he essentially assumes the same status as his superior with respect to such matters.

J. C. Warner, President Emeritus of Carnegie-Mellon University, believes that "one's accomplishment is . . . in a very real sense dependent upon the quality of the communication with others." And John T. Connor, Chairman of the Board of Allied Chemical Company, says that "there is no more valuable asset in business life than the ability to express one's thoughts with clarity and precision."

The Communication Process — To set the stage for information and message flow through an organization, let's review the basic elements of the communication process. These elements include: someone to send the message (the encoder), some means for channeling it, someone to receive it (the decoder) and a feedback mechanism. A multiplicity of encoders, channels, decoders and feedback mechanisms can be used. However, for the information in a message to be processed clearly, quickly and with a minimum amount of degradation, management must establish clear, formal communication channels.

Let's assume the message to be transmitted originates with the manager, or that he is serving as the agent for passing along a message from another source. Regardless of the source, the message passes through his (the sender's) filter before it reaches the intended recipient. The sender injects his attitudes and perceptions into the message; determines who should receive it; and the channels through which it should flow, i.e., upward, downward, laterally or a combination of these. The attitudes and perceptions of the recipient, of course, influence the message translation, as well as the feedback he provides.

Peter F. Drucker, noted exponent of good management practices, says in his book *People and Performance* (Harper and Row, 1977):

> The manager has a specific tool: information. He doesn't "handle" people, but instead he motivates, guides, organizes people to do their own work. His tool—the only tool—to do all this is the spoken or written word or the language of numbers. It does not matter whether the manager's job is engineering, accounting or spelling. To be effective, a manager must have the ability to listen and to read, and the ability to speak and to write. Managers need skill in getting their thinking across to other people.

This describes quite adequately the manager's role in the communication process.

The Communication Channels — The communication channel selected for transmitting a message plays a significant role in maintaining the quality of the original message in its passage from the sender to receiver. The sender, given the opportunity to weigh the merits of using an oral or written communication, or a combination of the two, selects the most effective for the situation.

Regardless of the communication channel selected, the sender will encounter obstacles. Considering the possible barriers, the sender must choose the channel which he feels will best guarantee transfer of the essence and meaning of his message without misunderstanding or distortion.

To counteract possible interference in the communication channel, the message should attract attention, contain redundancy, continue repetition, or use a combination of these approaches.

To attract attention, the message must be different from others competing for the recipient's time. A short handwritten message instead of the usual typed message is one method that can attract attention.

To provide redundancy, the message must be rephrased several times (the technique used in newspaper articles), and/or summarized in the final paragraph. The sender should avoid too much redundancy because this tends to clutter the communication channel.

To provide repetition, the message must be transmitted through more than one channel, as in spoken and written form, or transmitted more than once through the same channel, as in TV advertising.

Now, let's turn our attention to the basic communication channels within an organization. There are three channels:

1. Formal. The communication within the formal organizational structure that transmits goals, policies, procedures, and directions.

2. Informal. The communication outside the formal organizational structure that fills the organizational gaps, maintains the linkages, and handles the one-time situations.

3. Unofficial. The interpersonal communication within (or among) the social structure of the organization that serves as the vehicle for casual interpersonal exchanges, and transmittal of unofficial communications.

A more detailed examination of each of these communication channels will provide a better understanding of these functions.

Formal Communication — Whether written or oral, formal communication follows the chain of command of the formal organization; the communication flows from the manager to his immediate subordinates. Each recipient then retransmits the message in the selected form to the next lower level of management or to staff members, as appropriate. The message progresses down the chain of command, fanning out along the way, until all who have a need to know are informed. Formal communication also flows upward through the organization on the same basis.

Formal communication normally encompasses the transmittal of goals, policies, instructions, memoranda and reports; scheduled meetings; and supervisory-subordinate interviews.

Informal Communication — No organization operates in a completely formal or structured environment. Communication between operations depicted in an organizational chart does not function as smoothly or as trouble-free as the chart may imply. In most organizations operating effectively, channels of communication have developed outside the hierarchical structure.

The informal communication process supplements the formal process by filling the gaps and/or omissions. Successful managers encourage informal organizational linkages and, at the same time, recognize that circumvention of established lines of authority and communication is not a good regular practice. When lines of authority have been bypassed, the manager must assume responsibility for informing those normally in the chain of command of the action taken.

There is a fine line between using informal communications to expedite the work of the organization and the needless bypassing of the chain of command. The expediting process gets the job done, but bypassing the chain of command causes irritation and can lead to hard feelings. To be effective, the manager must find a way to balance formal and informal communication processes.

Unofficial Communication — Astute program and functional managers recognize that a great deal of communication taking place within their organizations is interpersonal. News of reviewed policies and procedures, memoranda and minutes of meetings are subjects of conversation throughout the organization. These subjects often share the floor with discussions of TV shows, sports news, politics and gossip.

The "grapevine" is a part of the unofficial communication process in any organization. A grapevine arises because of lack of information employees consider important: organizational changes, jobs or associates. This rumor mill transmits information of highly varying accuracy at a remarkable speed. Rumors tend to fall into three categories: those reflecting anxiety, those involving things hoped for and those causing divisiveness in the organization. Some rumors fade with the passing of time; others die when certain events occur.

Employees take part in the grapevine process to the extent that they form groups. Any employee not considered a part of some group is apt to be left out of this unofficial communication process.

The grapevine is not necessary good or bad. It serves a useful function when it acts as a barometer of employees' feelings and attitudes. Unfortunately, the information traveling along the grapevine tends to become magnified or exaggerated. Employees then become alarmed unnecessarily by what they hear. It is imperative that a manager be continually alert to the circulation of false information. When discovered, positive steps should be taken to provide the correct information immediately.

Coordination — One of the major functions of the communication process in an organization is effective coordination. Information available within the various functional groups is normally routed to key decision centers. It must be complete, accurate and timely. When decisions are made, they must be transmitted to all concerned groups within the organization. The messages containing the decisions must be clear and precise. The success of the response to each message is dependent upon the preciseness of the original message, the communication channel used for transmitting it, the interpretation and understanding of the receiver and the channel selected for transmitting the feedback.

Lawrence A. Appley, former Chairman of the Board of American Management Associations, states:

> There is little risk of oversimplification in saying that good managers are good communicators; poor managers are usually the opposite. If an individual has a sincere desire to clarify his thinking, there is no better way to do it than to put it in writing.

Communication Problems — Management must be continually aware of the barriers to effective communication and take steps necessary to keep the channels open. These are some of the most effective approaches to solving communication problems:

1. Try to maintain a good relationship. A poor superior-subordinate relationship hampers the communication process.

2. Don't overlook the importance of upward communication from a subordinate, or lateral communication with a peer. This can hamper the communication process.

3. Don't clog the channel of communication. Its value may be reduced by a delay in receipt of the communication.

4. It is better for you as a manager, to pass too much information down the chain of command than to pass too little. The receipt of more information gives your subordinate a feeling of confidence and security; lack of information promotes insecurity and a feeling of not being trusted. The problem in many organizations is that too little information is passed down the chain of command, and too much information is required to be passed up the chain. This problem is discussed in more detail later.

5. Pay attention to the selection of the form in which the message will be conveyed. A message not conveyed in an acceptable form may fail to pass the barriers in the communicating channel, regardless of whether it is moving down the chain of command, up the chain, or laterally.

Overloading — Much attention has been focused on the direction of the communicating flow, but very little attention on the quality of information in the communication chain. In your organization, is the daily message flow high and low? In most cases the organization would operate more effectively if the message flow increased; however, there is a limitation on the number of messages an organization can handle.

The free flow of information within an organization is an ideal to be achieved. When the information received far exceeds that required, the recipients cannot give proper attention to what is really needed. Much valuable time is devoted to the sorting and selection process. One of the problems of using redundancy and repetition to minimize breakdown in the communicating process is possible overload. Therefore, these techniques must be used with caution. If you are spending an increasing amount of time on the communication process, it is imperative to your future success that you develop an efficient information-processing skill.

How can an organization cope with an information overload situation? There is no one best way. The techniques that have been developed are often used in conjunction with one another. One technique involves filtering the messages so that the important ones, those requiring immediate action, get to the decision-maker first. Another technique involves delegating and decentralizing the decision-making process so messages do not go to a single executive. Still another technique involves carefully selecting information sources and eliminating those proven inaccurate or unreliable.

The Need and the Benefits — Sometimes top executives come to grips with basic practical viewpoints which, when carefully articulated, can help all of us. In a presentation to undergraduates at Oklahoma Christian College in 1978, chairman and CEO of the Continental Oil Company Howard W. Blauvelt said, "Business needs skilled communicators." This is a more kindly stance than that taken by many leading educators who are appalled at the inability of undergraduates to spell, write simple effective English or express themselves orally. "The ability to listen, digest, distill and further communicate information is fundamental," Blauvelt said. His message is clear.

Robert W. Sarnoff, chairman of the RCA Corporation, has said:

> Today's leaders are frequently men and women who have mastered the art of communication. They know how to get their ideas across. And successful people—those who are continually sought for key positions—effectively combine their ability to communicate with a solid foundation of knowledge. For knowledge is the predominant quality in the transmission of ideas.

Do you have the basic knowledge to function effectively in your position? Assuming you have, have you developed the necessary communication skills to impart this knowledge to others?

In *Leadership is not a Bowler Hat* (David & Charles Ltd., 1977), Peter J. Prior says,

> A major factor which must be considered, if the benefits of leadership are to be given full rein in an organization, is the existence of a good communications system, from top to bottom and across. . . . This is an area where a pinch of good practice is worth a pound of good theory.

Are you employing that "pinch of good practice," or are you bogged down with "a pound of theory?"

Harry O. Bercher, President of International Harvester Corporation, said, "The accurate transmission of ideas and facts from one mind to another is a complex process with many pitfalls." Success in program or functional management may depend on your skill in applying the communication process effectively in your day-to-day activities.

Conducting Successful Meetings

Was your last meeting successful? Were you an effective chairman or an active participant? Were those who had a contribution to make invited? Did the meeting accomplish the stated purpose?

These questions and many more need to be asked and answered

affirmatively if organizational meetings are to be successful. The chairman—the one who plans, hosts, and leads a meeting—must establish a proper environment. The environment, and the feeling conveyed to the participants by the chairman, will have a great impact on the outcome of the meeting. The chairman must stimulate, guide, clarify, control, summarize, and evaluate the discussion, keeping in mind his responsibility to accomplish the meeting objectives. If he fails to perform his role effectively, the meeting may turn into meaningless discussions of irrelevant subjects, a series of pointless power plays, and even boring monologues.

Meetings are essential and can serve as an effective method of communication within an organization. They have been rightfully categorized by some managers as timeconsuming, high-priced, and unproductive, but this need not be the case. Sometimes we expect too much from a meeting. When it fails to meet our expectations, we may be too quick to criticize. William E. Utterback, author of *Group Thinking and Conference Leadership*, said, "It must not be supposed that the conference table possesses the magic property of generating wisdom when rubbed simultaneously by a dozen pairs of elbows."

Meetings are helpful means of achieving coordination. When there is a gathering of people with a mutual interest, the results may be as follows:

1. Encourage participation in the subject of concern;
2. Integrate interests;
3. Broaden perspectives and change attitudes;
4. Improve decision-making; and
5. Motivate and commit participants to courses of action.

The fundamental decision concerning meetings is not whether to hold them, but how to make them effective. Recent studies show that members of middle management spend 30 percent of their time in meetings. Unproductive meetings can result in substantial loss to an organization. On the other hand, a productive meeting becomes a tool for effective management communication, and serves as a vehicle for development of specific plans or the organization of specific tasks. In any case, successful meetings don't just happen; they occur as a result of careful planning, good leadership, and close attention to details before, during and after the session.

The Planning Process — The key steps to be taken by the chairman in planning a meeting are as follows:

1. Establish the meeting objectives;
2. Prepare the meeting agenda;
3. Determine timing and physical arrangements;
4. Identify and invite participants; and
5. Consider matters of protocol.

Meeting Objectives — Why is the meeting being held? What will it accomplish? Meetings are usually held for one or more of the following reasons:

1. To disseminate new information or provide feedback;
2. To receive a report;
3. To coordinate efforts of a specific nature and obtain group support;
4. To win acceptance for a new idea, plan or system;
5. To reconcile a conflict;
6. To negotiate an agreement;
7. To motivate members of a group;
8. To initiate creative thinking within a group; and
9. To solve a current problem within a group.

The meeting plan should not be too broad or the meeting may be doomed from the beginning. Therefore, a wise chairman identifies realistic objectives for the meeting and is prepared to meet them.

Meeting Agenda — Is an agenda necessary? How long will it require to carry out the agenda? Would the meeting run smoothly and be just as successful without it?

The agenda should crystallize the intended meeting objective(s) and establish the time available to accomplish them. Whether the agenda is in writing or stated verbally by the chairman, it provides the framework to keep the meeting on target. Furthermore, it permits the chairman to devote his attention to managing the interplay of the participants.

The meeting should focus on the objective(s) and also on reaching the objective(s) in a preestablished, finite time schedule. Meetings that exceed established time limits usually are not constructive because opinions begin to replace facts. Such meetings are apt to go astray and may even disintegrate into personal contests or power plays between participants.

There are several other points to consider during preparation of the agenda. Notable among them are:

1. Focus the agenda on items relating to the same general topic, if possible. Begin with a discussion of topics of major concern to participants; then, if necessary, discuss related topics of lesser importance. A meeting of this type requires fewer attendees and generates better participation in the discussion.

2. Schedule fewer agenda items when the topics cannot be related. It is difficult for most participants to come to a meeting completely prepared on a wide variety of topics. The more concise the agenda, the better.

3. Attach background data for each topic to be discussed, when the agenda is distributed. This will ensure that each participant has some familiarity with the items before arriving at the meeting.

4. Establish a time limit and priority for each agenda item. Consider whether the topic to be discussed is familiar, new, controversial, or complex.

5. Don't have the meeting run too long. One hour is usually the norm for busy middle- to upper-level managers. When the meeting is scheduled on a quarterly, semi-annual, or annual basis, it may run longer to accomplish the objectives. Schedule a "break" when the meeting is expected to take over two hours.

6. Submit the agenda to the participants, with the background data, as early as possible. This will give each participant more time to prepare for the meeting.

The chairman should be sure the meeting is needed. If the need disappears, he should cancel the meeting.

Time/Physical Arrangements — When should the meeting be held? Where should it be held? There are several necessary considerations regarding time and physical arrangements for the meeting. Among the more important are:

1. The convenience of the place.
2. The size of the room. It should not be too large or too small. If

the right-size room is not available, it is better to select a small room, rather than too large a room. A small room presents a friendlier atmosphere than a large, sparsely filled one.

3. The seating arrangement and the availability of extra seats if needed.

4. The lighting, heating and ventilation.

5. Any visual aids required and their proper use.

6. Availability of extra paper and pencils.

7. The need for name plates or name tags.

8. The handling of messages.

It is the chairman's responsibility to begin and end the meeting on time. It is the responsibility of attendees to arrive on time. Two techniques proved effective in cuing cases of chronic tardiness are (1) to ignore latecomers; and (2) to make no attempt to bring late-comers up to date.

Meeting Size — How many persons should be invited to the meeting? What is the purpose of inviting each person? The attendees should be viewed as management resources—each able to contribute to the meeting through knowledge or experience or both. It is wise to include some of the persons in the organization to whom action items may be given after the meeting. This tends to encourage better support for the topics to be discussed. Attendance by disinterested persons tends to increase non-relevant discussion and impede the meeting. Thus, the chairman should invite as many people as necessary, but no more.

The size of the meeting tends to affect the way it functions. For example, if attendance exceeds seven, there is a tendency for communication to become more centralized, and participants have less opportunity to communicate directly with one another. As the number of people invited increases, the ability of the chairman to predict the interaction that will take place becomes more difficult.

It is important to have all relevant points of view on a particular subject under consideration represented at the meeting, even if this makes it a large meeting. A large meeting requires increased formality and extra time for each topic to ensure adequate communication between participants.

Proponents of the "small group" theory consider seven to be the maximum number of participants for a productive meeting. However, if a problem-solving type of meeting is to be held, some authorities claim that up to 12 participants can be accommodated effectively. If the number of participants exceeds 18, the chairman may find it almost impossible to accomplish the meeting objectives.

On the other hand, in a meeting involving only three participants there may be a tendency for two of them to form a combination against the third participant. This could be disastrous so managers should guard against organizing too small a meeting.

Matters of Protocol — Why should the chairman be concerned about protocol? How can this affect the success of a meeting? One of the initial steps to ensure a successful meeting is to give adequate consideration to protocol. Protocol might be defined as the application of common sense courtesy.

Some steps the chairman might take to avoid protocol problems are:

1. Notify participants well in advance of the meeting date, and provide them with an agenda and background data.

2. Notify department heads when subordinates with expertise are needed.

3. Make sure that arrangements with resource persons outside the organization are completed before the meeting.

4. Introduce resource persons and newcomers at the start of the meeting. Also, make their affiliations and expertise known to the other attendees.

5. List participants in alphabetical order in the meeting announcement and minutes, unless someone present far outranks the others. In that case, list this person first.

6. Express gratitude to those from outside the group as well as to those within the group, for significant contributions to the success of the meeting.

7. Advise those invited to attend the meeting of postponement or cancellation as far in advance as possible.

Running the Meeting — The chairman should make the meeting as relaxed and informal as possible. He should resort to Robert's Rules of Order only when attendance is large or debate becomes heated. The chairman should "manage" the meeting, speak when appropriate, encourage discussion, seek a consensus and summarize. Under no circumstances should the chairman be unprepared, "hog" the discussion, play the comic, chastise a participant or let the meeting run by itself.

The meeting will not get off the ground unless the participants know where they are going. Therefore, it is important that the chairman make a concerted effort to ensure that:

1. Every participant has a clear understanding of the meeting objectives at the start of the meeting.

2. Each agenda item has a time allocation. The time limit for the meeting should be announced when the agenda is published, or at the beginning of the meeting.

3. The objective(s) remain valid throughout the meeting. If not, they should be revised.

Meeting objective(s) can be communicated more readily if the chairman does not try to force them on the participants. A consensus about the objectives at the beginning will vastly improve chances for success of the meeting. Do you play your role well at a meeting? For a meeting to succeed, the chairman must display strong leadership and he and the participants must be willing and determined to:

1. Become acquainted with each of the participants and carry on a light conversation with them during the "warm up" session at the beginning of the meeting.

2. Give the other participants an opportunity to present their ideas, opinions and recommendations without interrupting or degrading their comments.

3. Listen wisely and well to the other participants.

4. Accept new or fresh thoughts and ideas expressed by other participants, provided those thoughts and ideas support the objective(s) of the meeting.

5. Assist in the process of arriving at a consensus by combining ideas with those of others, reconciling them through compromise or coordinating them with other ideas.

6. Do away with non-relevant issues, perceptions or personal conjectures as soon as they arise and before they can become disruptive.

7. Always be patient and flexible (but with caution).

Major Problems in Running a Meeting — One of the major problems a group often faces at the beginning of a meeting is reaching agreement on both top level and sub-level objectives. The objectives must be agreed upon before the meeting proceeds, if it is to be successful.

A second major problem concerns the personalities of participants. For example, the chairman may be dominant/submissive, have a desire to be liked, or want to impress his superiors. On the other hand, the invited participants may be self-centered, talkative/shy, aggressive/

defensive, argumentative/unresponsive. The participants may have trouble communicating because of differences in age, rank, expertise, and prestige. The ideas of some participants may be ignored and others ridiculed. The mood of the group may be one of elation, depression, or regression. There is no way to avoid these personality problems; therefore, the challenge facing the chairman is how to deal with them effectively. The answer is based upon creating an environment for effective communication. The problems can usually be resolved if the participants can communicate with one another. The problems will not be resolved if they remain hidden. A firmly established, finite time limit for the meeting is the single most effective means of eliminating non-contributory discussion. It gives the group a common purpose and helps the chairman police inappropriate comments.

Another major problem that groups sometimes face is having participants become lost in the problems they are attempting to solve. When this happens the chairman must take positive action to bring the meeting back on target. He can do this by taking one of the following two courses of action:

1. Halting the discussion and redirecting the meeting.
2. Halting the discussion and trying to find out where it is heading. If it is heading in a direction the participants feel is proper, he can allow the discussion to continue where it left off. If the meeting is heading in the wrong direction, he can change the direction.

The latter is preferable. Failure to do anything almost guarantees failure of the meeting. Halting the discussion and redirecting the meeting without providing an opportunity for participants to comment tends to create a debilitating emotional reaction. This might lead to withdrawal of some participants from further discussion, or precipitate aggression. When the participants pause to consider where the discussion is heading, there will be few adverse effects and the progress of the meeting may be enhanced.

A fourth major problem a group might face is how to make a decision at the proper time. If the chairman feels a consensus has been reached, he should cut off further discussion. A decision reached by consensus is the one most likely to be carried into action effectively. Decisions imposed on a minority by the majority of participants, or on the participants by the chairman, are not likely to be lasting or effective.

Groups often fall short in trying to reach decisions. Outside pressures or deadlines tend to foster majority-type or chairman-type decisions. Therefore, it is imperative that the chairman attempt to create an environment to make a consensus easier to obtain. Such an environment develops when each participant is given an opportunity to be heard or to voice an objection. In any case, before the meeting time limit expires the chairman should try to get the participants to agree that a decision is necessary, even if it falls short of unanimity.

Coping with Weaknesses — In order to make meetings more effective, one must be acquainted with the major weaknesses and ways to cope with them. The most common weaknesses of meetings are that they are slow, expensive, tend to produce a leveling effect or lead to dilution or division of responsibility. Let's take a closer look at each of these weaknesses.

Meetings tend to be a slow way to get things done. They do not lend themselves to quick, decisive actions. One observer of committee meetings stated, "They keep minutes and waste hours." Delays are not always bad. Delays provide time for objective reviews or ideas, and development and/or consideration of alternatives. Thus, delays can lead to better decisions.

For a meeting to be effective, those with expertise and/or the need for action, should attend. Inviting experts and providing sufficient time to consider alternative solutions to problems increases the cost of a meeting. However, the cost to an organization if the meeting is not held may be far greater.

There is a tendency at meetings to bring the individual thinking of the participants in line with the average quality of the group's thinking. This leveling effect takes place when a participant begins to think less as an individual and adapts the ideas of other participants. The normal tendency is to accept ideas of the most dominant individual at the meeting, although his ideas may not be the best. Leveling is not always undesirable; it tempers unreasonable ideas and curbs autocrats. The chairman should try to curb the leveling tendency. One way to keep a dominating participant in check is to seat him directly to the chairman's right.

The tendency for a decision made at a meeting to dilute or divide responsibility is a serious one. When this happens, weak managers are prone to blame their failures on that decision. Such comments as "I didn't support this approach at the meeting" are used to explain their failure to perform effectively. The chairman must be attuned to decisions that tend to dilute or divide responsibility and find a way to avoid them. All of the participants should be given an opportunity to express their viewpoints before the decision is made.

Wrap-up and Follow-up — The most important part of the meeting is its ending. After all information has been presented, all decisions made, all problem solutions found, or all conclusions reached, the chairman must summarize and solidify the results. He must review decisions and then perceive any conflicts that might result. He must give those who made a major contribution to the meeting the credit they deserve. If no major decisions were reached, he must emphasize progress made and nail down assignments that will lead to a future decision-type meeting. The chairman must always follow through on his promises to the group; otherwise the participants will have no enthusiasm for participating in a future meeting if called upon to do so.

If a meeting is a prologue to action, the epilogue must produce results. When no action follows a meeting, the meeting can be considered a failure. The chairman must never allow himself to think "activity" is the same as "accomplishment."

To translate decisions reached in a meeting into actions, the chairman must conduct the necessary follow-up action. A strategy used by successful chairmen is to:

1. Plan the follow-up procedure before the meeting;
2. Adjust the procedure during the meeting; and
3. Consolidate the procedure after the meeting.

When the chairman follows up on meeting decisions, he demonstrates that meetings can accomplish something. This encourages future participation.

Summary — Meetings are an essential management tool. Meetings can improve communications, promote coordination, develop people, and help to get a job done. Poor meetings waste time and resources and discourage people.

In preparing for a meeting, the chairman should ensure that the agenda focuses on accomplishment of specific objectives. From time to time throughout the meeting, the chairman should take a census to determine whether the objectives are still valid. If not, they should be revised.

For a meeting to be successful, it must be supported within the organization and provide a needed decision or produce worthwhile actions. This will not occur unless several weaknesses related to meetings are overcome: their slowness, expense, tendency to create leveling, and tendency to dilute or divide responsibility.

Also, for a meeting to be successful, consideration must be given to the timing, meeting place, seating arrangements, size of room, and visual aids.The leader of a meeting must have the right attitude; a well-conceived plan; and the ability to direct (focus), control, motivate, interpret, and moderate the meeting. He must recognize that reaching initial or revised objectives of the meeting, and follow-up after the meeting, are essential to its success.

The value of an effective meeting may be summed up as follows: It serves as the cornerstone for successful team building and progress with an organization.

Effective Presentation of Plans or Ideas

Part of every program or functional manager's time is devoted to the presentation of plans or ideas. In this section we will delve in some detail into how this can be done effectively.

Presentation Objective — The first step in preparing a presentation is to establish a purpose or an objective. What is to be accomplished by the presentation? After this has been determined, necessary steps can be taken to support it, and guidelines established to organize it. If the presentation is logically organized by subject matter at the start, it will do much to assure success of the presentation.

A presentation is made to provide information, give instruction, sell a plan or idea, or accomplish a combination of these things. Through words and visual aids, a presentation performs a service to the listener. A carefully worded presentation can translate facts, trends or statistics into basic relationships that will influence policy or actions. Rudyard Kipling has said that "Words are the most powerful drug used by mankind."

After the objective of the presentation has been established, the general form of the presentation must be considered. The message should be communicated in as few words and using as few visual aids as necessary to present a plan or idea effectively. A concise, convincing presentation of l0-minutes' duration may accomplish readily the desired objective—and be more economical—than one lasting an hour. in other words, the effectiveness of the presentation depends more upon the soundness of the message than its length, the presenter's skill in delivery, or the quality of the visual aids. However, too long a presentation, lack of skill in its delivery, and/or poor visual aids could spell disaster.

Presentation Strategy — Once the objective has been established the next step is planning the presentation strategy. The answers to some basic questions will help in this process:

1. What are you selling?

2. To whom are you selling it?

3. Against what are you competing?

4. In what environment do you expect the message to be received?

What are you selling? Why are you making the presentation? Take another look at the objective. Are you selling a plan of action, a need for action, a product, a service, or support for an idea? Pinpoint the reason for making the presentation. Express it in as few words as possible. To quote an old saying, "Never rise to speak until you have something to say, and when you have said it, cease."

To whom are you selling it? If you know your audience, you have some idea of its position on the subject. A presentation that is highly successful before one audience can be a failure before another one. The presentation strategy should be attuned to the audience. Can the people in the audience make a final decision, or must they take your recommendations to a higher authority? Before the presentation, know as much as possible about the people in your audience—their thought patterns, interests, authority and even their emotional needs. Do they prefer a certain type of visual aid, a break during the presentation or coffee service? Is their time limited? Remember, people in the audience will have different likes and dislikes. C. W. Spalding, a writer for the *Bardstown Kentucky Standard* put it this way: "People differ. Some object to the fan dancer and the others to the fan."

Against what are you competing? When you know the emotional needs of your audience, the message can be geared to the listener's viewpoint. The benefits to the listener can be targeted. In making presentations, the most common barriers encountered will be:

1. Fear on the part of the listener that the plan or idea may curtail his/her prestige, authority or prospects for advancement;

2. Unwillingness of the listener to leave the "beaten" path and/or a hesitancy to stick out his or her neck; and

3. The vanity of the listener.

In what environment do you expect the message to be received? There are a number of questions that might be raised to determine the environment in which the presentation will be given. Some of the basic questions are:

1. Will the audience be friendly or hostile, sympathetic or unsympathetic?

2. Will the audience be open- or close-minded?

3. Will you have supporters, or opposition?

4. If there is opposition, will it hold a unified or divided opinion?

There are some other factors that tend to affect the success of the presentation, namely:

1. When will the presentation be given: early in the morning, after lunch, just before the close of the work day or after dinner?

2. Will the people in the audience be in a hurry?

3. Are you "on the spot" for any reason?

4. Do you have to save someone's face?

In the final analysis, the strategy you formulate as a presenter should be based upon a knowledge of what you are selling, to whom you are selling it, the barriers you will be encountering and the atmosphere in which the presentation will be given.

Presentation Organization — A successful presentation contains more than good material and the most convincing arguments. It displays good organization of subject matter. The most forceful and persuasive presenter may fail to have a plan, idea or information accepted by the audience if the message is not organized well.

The introduction and conclusion cannot be neglected. At the outset, the presentation should gain the interest of the audience and convey to the listeners what is to be covered. In the conclusion, the presenter should review the key points of the presentation and pinpoint the action to be taken, if any.

The body of the presentation, located between the introduction and the conclusion, contains the bulk of the message. It should be presented to the listener in a meaningful form. An outpouring of plans, ideas or information without form or relationship will not hold the attention of any audience very long.

Organization of the presentation involves fitting the parts into a coherent whole. The method depends upon the subject matter to be presented and the strategy to be used. The most familiar form of presentation is probably the time sequenced—chronological—approach. The problem-solution pattern is a logical choice for many "in-house" presentations. When there is a need to compare alternative solutions to a problem, the comparison-contrast approach is a good choice. In an informative presentation, a cause/effect technique might be used. When the purpose of the presentation is to clarify or explain the meaning or nature of something, the definition technique is appropriate. Another form commonly used involves discussing the "parts" comprising the whole, such as sub-division of an organization, or sub-system for components of a missile. Related to this technique is the presentation built around systems, functions and qualities—sub-systems of an aircraft, functions of units within an organization, or qualities of an "All American." If the material to be used does not fit into one of the commonly used organizing patterns, the presenter should establish a pattern of his/her own.

When one has an outstanding point to make in a presentation, it should be made normally at the beginning. This has an advantage over "building up" to the main point. If it "sells" the plan or idea, the balance of the presentation then involves "nailing down" the plan or idea. Another reason for leading off with the main point, or points, is that important listeners could be called away before the presenter is finished. If they are, they will not miss the main point.

After a plan or an idea has been sold by citing its major advantage, or advantages, the balance of the presentation should generally be treated as reinforcement of that plan or idea. The points to be made should be presented in descending order of importance. Remember, when the main point fails to deliver the message, the lesser points will not do it! Speaking of ensuring the message comes through clearly, I am reminded of the 10-year-old explaining the plot of "My Fair Lady" to her younger sister. She said, "It's about a dirty girl who gets remedial reading."

A presentation should be long enough to accomplish the objective. Generally, a presentation of less than one hour is best. Most audiences don't absorb too many thoughts at a single sitting. Three or four important points can usually be established firmly. On some occasions, a half dozen points can be made if they are very closely related. Supplementary information should be screened from the subject matter before the presentation is made. Such material can be provided as a hand-out, if it is deemed important enough to convey to the audience.

At the end of the presentation, the audience should be left with a memorable impression of what the presenter said; accordingly, the presenter should recap the main point or points. If the presenter is expecting some action after the presentation, he/she should tell the people in the audience what is expected.

A good speaker rehearses his speeches; he practices what he preaches. After the presentation material has been assembled and organized, an evaluation should be made. This evaluation should include consideration of the factual contents as well as the personal delivery. There is always a possibility that someone in the audience will assume a "so what?" attitude. It is advisable to have a personally selected evaluator state what is clear, what is effective and what should be reworked or eliminated. Undergoing such an evaluation by a friendly "so whatter" can be likened to seeing a dentist—it is not a pleasant thing to do because it may reveal some trouble, but it could be dangerous not to do so.

Someone has said that want of study, and want of knowing what one is driving at, must bear the blame of many a long and weary presentation. Hence, a short talk is usually of a better quality than a long one, and if it is not, it is all the better that it is short.

Presentation Delivery — At the outset, the presenter must establish a rapport with the audience. There must be a flow of understanding and mutual respect between presenter and audience. At the start, the presenter should win the kind of attention needed for the rest of the presentation. His/her walk, posture, facial expressions, hand movements and clothing will be observed by the audience. Early in the presentation, the presenter will be judged, favorably or unfavorably, by the audience. After the audience decides whether it likes the presenter, it will determine whether it can give credence to what the presenter has to say. One story goes that after giving what he considered a stirring, fact-filled campaign speech, a candidate looked at his audience and confidently asked, "Now, any questions?" "Yes," came a voice from the rear, "Who else is running?"

To be successful—assuming the message is good—the presenter must be animated, alert and free from obvious tensions. A simple, indirect, natural, and relaxed style will gain audience acceptance, as will use of variety in voice, body movements and subject content. The presenter must be intimately acquainted with the principal points and the sequence in which they are to be given, so rehearsals are a must. If the presenter wants to "look alive" to the audience, he/she must know the subject, have an intense belief in the subject, confidence in his/her ability to communicate, and an eagerness to communicate effectively.

The power of words was expressed well in a *Look* magazine editorial several years ago. Speaking of words, the editorial said,

> They sing. They hurt. They teach. They sanctify. They were man's first immeasurable feat of magic. They liberated us from ignorance and our barbarous past. For without marvelous scribbles which build letters into words, words into sentences, sentences into systems and sciences and creeds, man would be forever confined to the self-isolated prison of the cuttlefish or the chimpanzee.

When words alone fail to present the message clearly, visual aids become an important part of the delivery. Visual aids can help to isolate ideas and clarify problems or relationships. They can also be very helpful when figures are involved or trends have to be conveyed. In many cases, the audience can grasp a plan, idea or situation more quickly than when the message is conveyed verbally without benefit or aids.

When words will suffice, visual aids should not be used. writer Dallas Williams questions whether one picture is worth a thousand words as has been sometimes stated. Williams says:

> . . . Give me 1000 words and I can have the Lord's Prayer, the 23rd Psalm, the Hippocratic Oath, a sonnet by Shakespeare, the Preamble to the Constitution, Lincoln's Gettysburg Address, and enough left over for just about all of the Boy Scout Oath—and I wouldn't trade them to you for any picture on earth.

Unfortunately, a presenter can't put all of these immortal words together to convey a single coherent message. Therefore, carefully planned visual aids are often helpful and effective in conveying messages to a variety of audiences.

Some Final Thoughts — The cost of a presentation should be justified, unless the presentation has been directed by higher authority and no alternative is possible. If it has not been specifically directed, the cost of preparing and delivering a presentation must be weighed against the value of the objective to be accomplished. The cost of the time required of the listeners also should be considered.

In weighing alternatives, one might ask, "Can the story be told more economically—and, possibly, as effectively—by an interoffice/ interagency memo, letter, meeting in the office or a telephone call?

Finally, let's run down the list of things that you, as a presenter, should remember when you face the audience.

1. Speak up. Make yourself heard.
2. Keep your back to the wall.
3. Avoid any mention of time during the opening comments.
4. Watch the faces of those in your audience. Maintain "eye-to-eye" contact.
5.   Stand erect and control your nervous habits. Don't fuss with your clothes or use annoying gestures.
6. Avoid competing with outside disturbances.
7. Relax and smile. Avoid smoking, if possible.
8. Use stories to make your points.

9. Reaffirm your points at the end of the presentation.

Now, you should be ready to prepare and make an effective presentation. Best wishes for success in the next one.

The above material is reprinted in part from Skill in Communication *by Jack D. Acker, published by Defense Systems Management College.*

GOVERNMENT FREEBIES (AND NEAR-FREEBIES)

Consumer Information Catalog, P.O. Box 100, Pueblo, Colorado 81002. This is a listing of government pamphlets, many of which are free, on a variety of subjects including careers, raising children, small-business subjects, food, education, federal government benefits, health, housing, money management, travel and hobbies. Some of the free pamphlets include: *Consumer's Resource Handbook; How to Buy a Telephone; Antitrust Enforcement and the Consumer; A Consumer's Guide to Life Insurance; Directory of Business Development Publications.*

U. S. Government Books, Superintendent of Documents, U. S. Government Printing Office, Washington, D. C. 20402. This is a catalog of books printed by the United States government. The offerings vary from scholarly history to how-to books on establishing an export business to tips on being a better babysitter. Some of the business books include: *Financial Management: How to Make A Go of Your Business; Franchise Opportunities Handbook; Basic Guide to Exporting; Stress Management in Work Settings; Occupational Outlook Quarterly;* and *Lifeline: A Small Business Guide to Computer Security.* U. S. Small Business Administration, Office of Business Development, Washington, D. C. 20416 (tel. 1-800-368-5855).

Government Periodicals and Subscription Services. Superintendent of Documents, U. S. Government Printing Office, Washington, D.C. 20402. Probably the most under-used federal pamphlet, this is a listing of all federal magazines, news release services, quarterly reports and other data. The subjects of these reports vary from daily treasury reports to the monthly *Social Security Bulletin* to the quarterly *Shirts, Pillowcases and Towels* industrial update.

For consultants and others offering expert services, perhaps the most important publication is the *Commerce Business Daily* which lists all of the federal contracts open for bid, their closing dates, contact administrators and dollar figures.

Directory of Business Development Publications. U.S. Small Business Administration, Office of Business Development, Washington, D.C. 20416 (tel. 1-800-368-5855).

U. S. GOVERNMENT PRINTING OFFICE BOOKSTORES

ATLANTA:

Federal Building
Room l00
275 Peachtree Street NE
P.O. Box 56445
Atlanta, Georgia 30343
(tel. 404-331-6947)

BIRMINGHAM:
O'Neill Building
2021 Third Avenue North
Birmingham, Alabama 35203
(tel. 205-731-1056)

BOSTON:
Federal Building
Room G25
Sudbury Street
Boston, Massachusetts 02203
(tel. 617-565-2488)

CHICAGO:
Federal Building
Room 1365
219 South Dearborn Street
Chicago, Illinois 60604
(tel. 312-353-5133)

CLEVELAND:
Federal Building
First Floor
1240 East Ninth Street
Cleveland, Ohio 44199
(tel. 216-522-4922)

COLUMBUS:
Federal Building
Room 207
200 North High Street
Columbus, Ohio 43215
(tel. 614-469-6956)

DALLAS:
Federal Building
Room 1C50
1100 Commerce Street
Dallas, Texas 75242
(tel. 214-767-0076)

DENVER:
Federal Building
Room 117
1961 Stout Street
Denver, Colorado 80294
(tel. 303-844-3964)

DETROIT:
Federal Building
Suite 160
477 Michigan Avenue
Detroit, Michigan 48226
(tel. 313-226-7816)

HOUSTON:
9319 Gulf Freeway
Houston, Texas 77017
(tel. 713-229-3515)

JACKSONVILLE:
Federal Building
Room 158
400 West Bay Street
Jacksonville, Florida 32202
(tel. 904-791-3801)

KANSAS CITY:
120 Bannister Mall
5600 East Bannister Road
Kansas City, Missouri 64137
(tel. 816-765-2256)

LOS ANGELES:
ARCO Plaza C-Level
505 S. Flower Street
Los Angeles, California 90071
(tel. 213-894-5841)

MILWAUKEE:
Federal Building
Room 190
517 East Wisconsin Avenue
Milwaukee, Wisconsin 53202
(tel. 414-291-1304)

NEW YORK:
Federal Building
Room 110
26 Federal Plaza
New York, New York 10278
(tel. 212-264-3825)

PHILADELPHIA:
Robert Morris Building
100 North 17th Street
Philadelphia, Pennsylvania 19103
(tel. 215-597-0677)

PITTSBURGH:
Federal Building
Room 118
1000 Liberty Avenue
Pittsburgh, Pennsylvania 15222
(tel. 412-644-2721)

PUEBLO:
World Savings Building
720 North Main Street
Pueblo, Colorado 81003
(tel. 719-544-3142)

SAN FRANCISCO:
Federal Building
Room 1023
450 Golden Gate Avenue
San Francisco, California 94102
(tel. 415-556-0643)

SEATTLE:
Federal Building
Room 194
915 Second Avenue
Seattle, Washington 98174
(tel. 206-442-4270)

WASHINGTON, D. C.:
Government Printing Office
710 North Capital Street NW
Washington, D. C. 20401
(tel. 202-275-2091)

or

1510 H Street NW
Washington, D. C. 20005
(tel. 202-635-5075)

or

8660 Cherry Lane
Laurel, Maryland 20707
(tel. 301-953-7974)

THE PROFIT PLAN

If you're interested in starting your own business and you've read Chapter 6, you know all about writing a business plan. But once you've written a successful business plan, presented it to potential investors, and gotten the money you need to open your own business, your job isn't over. It's just beginning. Now you have to make sure that your business stays open. The best way to do that is to prepare a careful annual profit plan. The profit plan helps you do the following:

- Develop a forecast for sales and gross profit.
- Prepare budgets for operating expenses.
- Prepare an estimate of net profit.
- Consider internal and external factors that could affect sales and costs in the coming period.
- Review performance on a continuing basis.

Introduction

Profit planning is simply the development of your operating plan for the coming period. Your plan is summarized in the form of an income statement that serves as your sales and profit objective and your budget for cost.

How is it Used?

The profit plan is used in the following ways:

- Evaluating operations. Each time you prepare an income statement, actual sales and costs are compared with those you projected in your original profit plan. This permits detection of areas of unsatisfactory performance so that corrective action can be taken.

- Determining the need for additional resources such as facilities or personnel. For example, the profit plan may show that a sharp increase in expected sales will overload the company's billing personnel. A decision can then be made to add additional invoicing personnel, to retain an EDP service or to pursue some other alternative.

- Planning purchasing requirements. The volume of expected sales may be more than the business' usual suppliers can handle or expected sales may be sufficient to permit taking advantage of quantity discounts. In either case, advance knowledge of purchasing requirements will permit taking advantage of cost savings and ensure that purchased goods are readily available when needed.

- Anticipating any additional financing needs. With planning, the search for needed funds can begin as early as possible. In this way, financial crises are avoided and financing can be arranged on more favorable terms.

Advantages of Profit Planning

Profit planning offers many advantages to your business. The modest investment in time required to develop and implement the plan will pay liberal dividends later. Among the benefits that your business can enjoy from profit planning are the following:

- Performance evaluation. The profit plan provides a continuing standard against which sales performance and cost control can quickly be evaluated.

- Awareness of responsibilities. With the profit plan, personnel are readily aware of their responsibilities for meeting sales objectives, controlling costs and the like.

- Cost consciousness. Since cost excesses can quickly be identified and planned expenditures can be compared with budgets even before they are incurred, cost consciousness is increased, reducing unnecessary costs and overspending.

- Disciplined approach to problem-solving. The profit plan permits early detection of potential problems so that their nature and extent are known. With this information, alternate corrective actions can be more easily and accurately evaluated.

- Thinking about the future. Too often, small businesses neglect to plan ahead: thinking about where they are today, where they will be next year, or the year after. As a result, opportunities are overlooked and crises occur that could have been avoided. Development of the profit plan requires thinking about the future so that many problems can be avoided before they arise.

- Financial planning. The profit plan serves as a basis for financial planning. With the information developed from the profit plan, you can anticipate the need for increased investment in receivables, inventory, or facilities as well as any need for additional capital.

- Confidence of lenders and investors. A realistic profit plan, supported by a description of specific steps proposed to achieve sales and profit objectives, will inspire the confidence of potential lenders and investors. This confidence will not only influence their judgment of you as a business manager, but also the prospects of your business' success and its worthiness for a loan or an investment.

Limitations of Profit Planning

Profit plans are based upon estimates. Inevitably, many conditions you expected when the plan was prepared will change. Crystal balls are often cloudy. The further down the road one attempts to forecast, the cloudier they become. In a year, any number of factors can change, many of them beyond the control of the company. Customers' economic fortunes may decline, suppliers' prices may increase or suppliers' inability to deliver may disrupt your plan.

The profit plan requires the support of all responsible parties. Sales quotas must be agreed upon with those responsible for meeting them.

Expense budgets must be agreed upon with the people who must live with them. Without mutual agreement on objectives and budgets, they will quickly be ignored and serve no useful purpose.

Finally, profit plans must be changed from time to time to meet changing conditions. There is no point in trying to operate a business according to a plan that is no longer realistic because conditions have changed.

Advantages vs. Disadvantages

Despite the limitations of profit planning, the advantages far outweigh the disadvantages. A realistic plan, established yearly and reevaluated as changing conditions require, will provide performance guidelines that will help you control every aspect of your business with a minimum of analysis and digging for financial facts.

Objectives

In preparing a profit plan, you will learn how to do the following:

- Develop a forecast for sales and gross profit, considering all of the various internal and external factors that are relevant to the forecast.

- Develop budgets for operating expenses to quickly detect excessive expenses so that corrective action can be taken and purchasing commitments held within budgetary limits.

- Estimate net profit so that you can determine whether or not the projected return on your investment is satisfactory. You will also be able to determine how much cash will be generated from operations either for reinvestment in the business or to compensate owners for their investment.

Beginning of Profit Plan

Development of your profit plan should usually begin with a forecast of your expected sales and gross profit for the coming year. The sales and gross profit must be considered together since they are so closely inter-related. Gross profit percentages are determined by pricing policy, which also affects expected sales volume. A decision to increase the expected gross profit percentage will usually tend to decrease expected sales, while reducing the expected gross profit percentage should increase sales.

A second major reason for beginning the profit plan with a sales forecast is that the volume of expected sales often determines a number of other factors such as the following:

- Expected changes in variable expenses, those expenses that tend to change in direct proportion to changes in sales. These could include expenses such as sales commissions or delivery costs.

- The impact of the added sales volume on the various fixed costs of operating your business. These costs, by definition, do not tend to vary in direct proportion to changes in sales volume. However, substantial increases in sales over an extended period can force an increase in many fixed expenses. For example, a sales increase realized through the addition of many new accounts could affect bookkeeping and credit costs.

- The ability of present resources such as storage space, display area, delivery capability or supervisory personnel to accommodate the added volume.

- The need for funds to invest in increased inventory or accounts receivable to accommodate sales increases.

- Cash generated from operations to meet current operating needs as well as expansion requirements, debt repayments and owners' compensation.

Realism

A realistic sales forecast must rely on careful analysis of market potential and the ability of your business to capture its share of this potential. The forecast should not be based upon "what you would *like* to do" or "what you *hope* to do." It must be "what you *can* do" and "what you *will* do."

Any forecast of a sales increase must be supported by realistic expectations for stronger market demand and specific marketing steps that will be taken to capture a share of this market.

The key to successful forecasting is realism. You only fool yourself if you reject reality in forecasting. Such forecasts serve neither as a realistic planning basis nor as a reliable means of performance evaluation.

Your forecast can be the basis for important decisions such as decisions to add personnel, lease additional facilities or increase promotional costs. If these decisions are based upon unrealistic sales expectations, any money expended on them will be wasted.

Forecasts are often presented to lenders or potential investors to guide them in their decisions. If they lack confidence in your forecast, they will certainly be reluctant to commit their funds to your business.

Every forecast should be supported by carefully considered, specific action plans. It is inadequate to forecast a sales increase of 20 or 30 percent without plans for specific actions to achieve the increase. These actions could include the introduction of new products, opening of new branches, market expansion, commitments from new customers, increased requirements from existing customers, additional salesmen or an intensified promotional effort to attract new customers.

Analyzing Current Sales and Gross Profit

Your sales and gross profit forecast begins with analysis of current performance. Sales are usually divided into various categories. Each category is examined individually to determine expected sales for the coming year.

Selecting Sales Categories

The selection of categories will depend upon the nature of your business. For example, a food broker selling to a large number of relatively small accounts might be interested primarily in analyzing sales by product. The owner of a single retail store might choose to analyze sales by selling department, while the owner of a retail chain would probably be interested in analyzing sales by outlet. An insurance broker with several agents might categorize sales by agent. An individual wholesaler might consider sales by sales territory.

Factors Affecting Sales

After categories have been selected and current sales divided among them, the various factors which can affect sales in each category must be considered. These factors could be either *internal* or *external*. Internal factors are those that you can influence. External factors are those that affect the market served by your business, but are generally beyond your control.

Internal Factors — The following are typical internal factors that could influence your sales forecast:

- Promotional plans
- Expansion plans
- Capacity restrictions
- New product introductions
- Product cancellations
- Sales force changes
- Pricing policy
- Profit expectations
- Market expansion to new customers or territories

External Factors — Among the external factors that must be considered are the following:

- Business trends
- Government policies
- Inflation
- Changes in population characteristics
- Economic fortunes of customers
- Changes in buying habits
- Competitive pressures

Analyzing Gross Profit Percentages

It is often useful to begin a sales forecast with an examination of your current gross profit percentage (markup percentage or gross profit percentage). The gross profit percentage is usually the best indicator of pricing policy which can have significant impact on sales volume. To some extent, the gross profit percentage will also reflect the buying economies of your business. However, the range over which costs of purchased goods will vary is not ordinarily as wide as the possible range of prices you may seek for your products.

Three Bases of Comparison

Examination of current gross profit percentages can indicate the need for pricing policy revisions to meet competition or closer attention to purchasing costs in order to provide extra gross profit without increasing prices.

The evaluation of gross profit percentages requires comparison of current performance with three bases:

- Objectives originally set for the current year, if available
- Other businesses in the same industry
- Results of prior years

Comparison with objectives permits you to determine how well you have done compared with your original expectations. Assuming that these objectives were realistic, this is often the best single performance indicator. Deviations from objectives can quickly be identified and explored in detail to determine the cause of the deviation.

Comparison with industry averages permits identification of areas where the experience of similar businesses indicates room for improvement in your own.

Unfortunately, businesses are often too quick to dismiss the applicability of industry averages to their own operation, claiming that "Our circumstances are different." Such an attitude is self-defeating. It prevents you from taking advantage of the experience of others to improve your own sales and profit. A far more productive attitude is to say, "If everybody else can realize a gross profit of x percent, then we should be able to." Until specific circumstances are identified that make it impossible for your business to be consistent with industry averages, every attempt should be made to bring performance in line with the experience of others.

Comparison of current operations with performance in prior periods permits detection of trends so that progress, or the lack of it, can be identified. It also permits evaluation in light of those specific considerations that may be unique to your business. For example, if your gross profit as a percentage of sales is low compared with the industry, analysis of your historic performance may reveal the cause of this apparent deficiency such as reliance upon a major customer where severe competition restricts the available gross profit percentage.

Evaluating Gross Profit Percentages

Refer to Table 1, which is an analysis of gross profit percentages realized by a hypothetical company, Western Appliances, in 1989. Percentages are shown for cost of sales, gross profit, total expenses and profit before taxes as follows:

- 1989 actual (12)
- 1988 actual (13)
- Industry average (14
- 1989 objective 15

Each basis of comparison provides a different viewpoint of the company's operations.

Table 1
Western Appliances, Inc.
Profit Percentage Analysis

	1989 Actual	1988 Actual	Industry Average	1989 Objective
Sales	100.0%	100.0%	100.0%	100.0%
Cost of Sales	80.0%	80.5%	81.8%	80.7%
Gross Profit	20.0%	19.5%	18.2%	19.3%
Total Expenses	17.9%	18.6%	14.7%	17.2%
Profit Before Taxes	2.1%	0.9%	3.5%	2.1%

In 1989, Western Appliances' gross profit was 20.0% of sales. This represented an improvement over their 1988 performance of 19.5%, the industry average of 18.2%, and their 1989 objective of 19.3%. By any of these measures, this should be considered favorable. Apparently, they were able to control their purchasing costs and realize adequate prices in order to improve upon their own previous gross profit performance as well as the industry average.

Conflicts

Sometimes financial analysis can lead to conflicting conclusions derived from identical facts. Comparing Western Appliances' 20.0% gross profit with the 18.2% industry average could raise questions. If Western Appliances were more competitive in its pricing, could it capture a larger market share? A reasonable answer to this question would depend upon thorough knowledge of their operations and the experience of their sales personnel in dealing with specific customers. Perhaps their pricing is fully competitive in their area or local retailers are willing to pay slightly more because of the superior services they offer. If this is the case, price cutting might only trim profit margins with no realistic hope of additional sales volume to offset the effects of the price reduction.

On the other hand, if their gross profit percentage is below that of the industry, a number of other questions would be raised, such as the following:

- Are they purchasing at prices that are too high to provide an adequate gross profit?
- Is their pricing structure so low that adequate gross profit margins cannot be attained?

- Are salesmen too quick to cut prices?
- Is their marketing effort too heavily concentrated in those product lines that offer a relatively low gross profit percentage?
- Is their marketing effort directed toward those high-volume accounts that are so highly competitive that gross profit must be trimmed to an unrealistically low level?

Analysis of Sales Performance

Table 2, shown below, analyzes the 1989 sales of Western Appliances by account. Actual sales, gross profit, and the gross profit percentage are shown individually for major accounts and as a group for smaller accounts. These are reported on the bottom line and represent 50 small retailers served by Western Appliances.

Table 2
Western Appliances, Inc.
Sales Forecast, 1990

Account	1989 ACTUAL			1990 FORECAST		
	Sales	Gross Profit	%	Sales	Gross Profit	%
Giant Discount	$300,000	$45,000	15.0%	$323,500	$45,300	14.0%
Appliance Mart	150,000	27,000	18.0	174,000	31,300	18.0
TV Center	120,000	21,600	18.0	159,000	23,900	15.0
Whitney Bros	80,000	15,200	19.0	100,000	20,000	20.0
Packer Elect.	70,000	14,000	20.0	40,400	8,100	20.0
Consumers Outlet	40,000	7,200	18.0	50,000	9,000	18.0
Other (50 stores)	440,000	110,000	25.0	553,100	142,400	25.7
Total	$1,200,000	240,000	20.0%	1,400,000	280,000	20.0%

Let's consider Appliance Mart, one of the major accounts shown. In 1989, Western Appliances' sales to Appliance Mart were $150,000. These sales generated gross profit of $27,000, or 18.0% of sales.

In 1990, Western Appliances expects a general price increase of 5% with no change in the discount structure available to them from their suppliers.

Appliance Mart's business in 1990 is expected to be affected only by general economic conditions such as the 5% price increase and an expected 10% industry growth in consumer demand for electrical appliances.

Appliance Mart operates a chain of discount stores in an economically stable suburban area. For 1990, they have no plans to add or eliminate any stores. There are no changes expected in Western Applianoes' relationship with them that would materially affect sales.

Therefore, the only factors affecting the sales forecast for Appliance Mart would be the planned 5% price increase and the general 10% increase in demand. Sales to Appliance Mart in 1990 could then be forecast as follows:

1989 Sales	$150,000
+ 5% Price Increase	7,500
= Subtotal	$157,500
+ 10% Demand Increase	15,750
= Total	$173,250

This amount, $173,250, has been rounded to $174,000 and entered in the 1990 sales forecast column.

Since there is no planned change in Western Appliances' discount structure from its suppliers, nor is there any indication that competition for Appliance Mart's business will be any more or less severe, Western Appliances probably should assume that gross profit as a percentage of these sales will remain at 18.0%, the 1989 level. The gross profit expected on these sales could then be calculated as follows:

$$\$174,000 \times .180 = \$31,320$$

This amount has been rounded to $31,300 and entered in the gross profit forecast column.

Subdividing Sales Categories

It is often useful to subdivide sales into more detailed classifications in order to develop a more precise forecast such as potential sales to a single customer. As an example, refer to Table 3, Western Appliances' sales summary by product line to Giant Discount, its major customer in 1989. Sales, gross profit and the gross profit percentage are shown by product line so that each line may be considered separately to determine a realistic forecast for 1990.

Development of the 1990 forecast will assume that Giant Discount's various stores are located in areas that are representative of the general economy and therefore will reflect the industry's expected sales growth of 10%; the price increase of 5% will have no significant effect on Giant Discount's sales; and competition among appliance wholesalers for Giant Discount's business will prevent Western Appliances from increasing its gross profit percentage in any product line.

Table 3
Western Appliances, Inc.
Customer Sales Analysis – Giant Discount

PRODUCT LINE	1989 ACTUAL			1990 FORECAST		
	SALES	GROSS PROFIT	%	SALES	GROSS PROFIT	%
Television	$160,000	$16,000	10.0%	$184,800	$18,500	10.0%
Automotive Radios	20,000	6,000	30.0	—	—	—
Table Radios	30,000	6,000	20.0	34,700	6,900	20.0
Stereo	40,000	7,000	18.0	46,200	8,300	18.0
Small Appliances	50,000	10,000	20.0	57,800	11,600	20.0
Total	$300,000	45,000	15.0%	323,500	45,300	14.0%

The first product line on Table 3, television sales, could then be forecast as follows:

1987 Sales	$160,000
+ 5% Price Increase	8,000
= Subtotal	$168,000
+ 10% Demand Increase	16,800
= Total	$184,800

Assuming that the gross profit percentage of 10.0% on television sales is maintained in 1990, the forecast for gross profit can then be calculated as follows:

$$\$184,800 \times .100 = \$18,480, \text{ rounded to } \$18,500$$

Giant Discount plans to discontinue its sales of automotive radios in 1990. Therefore, sales, gross profit, and the gross profit percentage for all are shown as zero on Table 3.

Sales, gross profit, and gross profit percentages have all been determined for the remaining product lines and shown on the 1990 forecast on Table 3. You will note that the gross profit as a percentage of total sales in the 1990 forecast, 14.0%, is well below the 1989 experience of 15.0% even though the gross profit on each product line remains the same. This is due to the elimination of the highly profitable automotive radio line which produced a 30% gross profit but is being discontinued from Giant Discount's stores. In fact, the net effect of this discontinuation is that Western Appliances will realize additional gross profit of less than $1,000 on sales to Giant Discount despite a sales increase of almost

$24,000. This important fact probably would not have been revealed if sales to Giant Discount had not been subdivided into individual product lines for analysis.

This negligible increase in gross profit will probably be more than offset by normal cost increases in various expense accounts required to handle Giant Discount's business in 1990. At this point, the owners of Western Appliances would be well advised to take a hard look at their pricing strategy to see if more favorable prices can be realized in any product line without any significant sales loss so that the gross profit earned from this, its largest account, can be improved.

Forecasting Expenses

After a realistic forecast has been developed for sales and gross profit, expenses for the coming year must be estimated in order to establish expense budgets and to determine expected operating profit.

Comparisons

As with the forecast of sales and gross profit, expense estimating begins with a review of the current year's performance based upon comparison with the following indicators:

- Performance in prior periods
- Industry averages
- Objectives established for the current year

Expenses as a Percentage of Sales — For purposes of comparison, it is often useful to express each expense as a percentage of total sales. This has been done in Table 4 (see next page) for Western Appliances' 1989 expenses. For example, the owner's salary, $24,000, represents 2.0% ($24,000 / $1,200,000) of 1989 sales.

Comparing Variable Expenses — The use of percentages as a basis of comparison and forecasting is particularly applicable when analyzing variable expenses. Variable expenses are those that tend to change as a result of changes in sales volume. For example, if salesmen's commissions are based upon a percentage of sales, the total dollar amount of commissions earned would increase as sales increase. If sales in a month were 20% higher than expected, commissions paid would also increase 20% as a direct result of the higher sales volume.

Table 4
Western Appliances, Inc.
Sales and Expense Forecast
January 1 to December 31, 1990

	1989 ACTUAL	1989 (% SALES)	1988 ACTUAL	1988 (% SALES)	INDUSTRY (% SALES)	REVISED 1990 FORECAST
Sales	$1,200,000	100.0%	$1,080,000	100.0%	100.0%	$1,400,000
Cost of Sales	960,000	80.0	880,000	81.5	81.8	1,120,000
Gross Profit	$ 240,000	20.0%	$ 200,000	18.5	18.2	280,000
Operating Expenses						
Salary — Owner	$ 24,000	2.0%	$ 20,000	1.9%	1.7%	$ 26,000
Salary — Office Manager	17,000	1.4	16,000	1.5	(Office Sal: 4.9%)	18,000
Salaries — Salesmen	12,000	1.0	11,000	1.0	(Selling & Deliv.	12,000
Commissions — Salesmen	24,000	2.0	22,000	2.0	Expense: 7.6%)	28,000
Salaries — Warehouse	22,000	1.8	18,000	1.7		23,000
Salaries — Clerical	12,000	1.0	10,000	0.9		14,000
Payroll Taxes	9,000	0.8	8,000	0.7		10,000
Employee Benefits	8,000	0.7	6,000	0.6		9,000
Rent	9,000	0.8	9,000	0.8		10,000
Utilities	4,000	0.3	3,000	0.3	0.7	4,000
Telephone	4,000	0.3	2,000	0.2		3,000
Supplies	2,000	0.2	1,000	0.1		2,000
Advertising and Promotion	13,000	1.1	12,000	1.1		15,000
Travel and Entertainment	13,000	1.1	10,000	0.9		13,000
Freight	16,000	1.3	16,000	1.5		18,000
Professional Fees	5,000	0.4	4,000	0.4		5,000
Depreciation	6,000	0.5	5,000	0.5	0.5	8,000
Total Operating Expenses	$ 200,000	16.7%	$ 173,000	16.0%		$ 218,000
Profit Before Interest and Taxes	$ 40,000	3.3%	$ 27,000	2.6%		$ 62,000
Interest	15,000	1.3	12,000	1.1		17,000
Profit Before Income Taxes	$ 25,000	2.1%	$ 15,000	1.4	2.5	$ 45,000
Income Taxes	6,000	0.5	4,000	0.4		15,000
Net Profit	$ 19,000	1.6%	$ 11,000	1.1%		$ 30,000

Comparing fixed expenses — On the other hand, fixed expenses are not directly affected by short-term variations in sales volume. Therefore, a 20% increase in the dollar amount of any fixed expense such as salaries or rent would normally be considered unacceptable even if sales for the period increased by 20%. When comparing fixed expense levels with objectives or from one period to another, it is more realistic to make comparisons in absolute dollars rather than in percentages.

A business has sales and rent expense in January, February and March as follows:

| | | RENT EXPENSE | |
MONTH	SALES	$	% SALES
January	$100,000	$1,000	1.00%
February	80,000	1,000	1.25
March	125,000	1,000	0.80

As a percentage of sales, rent expense was high in February and low in March. However, this does not indicate that control of this expense was more or less effective in either month. It simply reflects the changes in sales volume. In all three cases, the actual rent expense was $1,000.

Long-range considerations — Despite the shortcomings of using percentages to evaluate fixed expense control within the business from month to month, they can be useful when making long-term comparisons or comparisons with industry averages. These averages normally express expenses as percentages of sales, regardless of whether they are fixed or variable.

For example, assume that a business found that its rent expense as a percentage of sales was 2% compared with an industry average of 1%. This differential would have to be offset by better than average performance in gross profit or other expense classifications if the business expects to realize net profit equal to its industry average. Perhaps the reason for the high percentage is due to an exorbitant rental expense, or it may be caused by inadequate sales. In either case, certain questions must be answered. These could include the following:

- Are we renting more space than we need?
- Is our space too expensive for our requirements?
- Could a less elaborate facility be located that would be adequate for our needs?
- Would a less costly location be sufficient?

- Is our space utilization inefficient?

- Will expected sales increases be handled without renting additional space? Will this bring our rent expense percentage in line with the industry?

- Can the terms of our lease be renegotiated?

Similarly, when comparing long-term performance with prior periods, the use of fixed expense percentages can be helpful. For example, if you found that warehouse salaries jumped from 2% of sales to 4%, a number of important questions would be raised. These could include the following:

- Are we now using too many warehouse personnel?

- Are warehouse personnel less efficient?

- Has ineffectiveness crept into the warehouse layout or operating procedure?

- Are warehouse workers overpaid?

- Is warehouse supervision inadequate?

Identifying excessive expenses — At Western Appliances, no objectives were available for 1989 performance. Therefore, excessive expenses can be identified only by comparison with 1988 results, as shown in Table 4, and, in some cases, with industry averages. These averages also appear on Table 4.

Industry Average Comparisons — Comparisons with industry averages are not available in all of Western Appliances' expense accounts. However, this can be determined by examining those accounts on the company's income statement that can be combined for comparison with industry averages. For example, the industry averages in Table 4 show that office salaries for the industry were 4.9% of sales. Examining the operating expense accounts at Western Appliances, the accounts that would appear to fall into this classification are the following:

Salary—Office Manager	1.4%
Salaries—Clerical	1.0%
Salaries—Warehouse	1.8%

The total of these expenses, 4.2% of sales, compares favorably with the industry average of 4.9%.

Comparison with previous periods — The information given in Table 4 permits comparison of all expenses in 1989 with 1988 results. The only variable expense at Western Appliances in 1989 is salesmen's commissions. These represented 2.0% of sales in both 1988 and 1989. Therefore, they would not appear to be excessive.

In the fixed expense accounts, sharp increases could be noted in the following accounts and would warrant review and possible corrective action.

ACCOUNT	1989	1988
Salary-Owner	$24,000	$20,000
Salaries-Warehouse	22,000	18,000
Salaries-Clerical	12,000	10,000
Employee Benefits	8,000	6,000
Utilities	4,000	3,000
Telephone	4,000	2,000
Supplies	2,000	1,000
Travel and Entertainment	13,000	10,000

Comparing Western Appliances' 1989 fixed expenses with its experience in 1988, significant increases are noted in almost every account. Some of these increases should be regarded with more concern than others and therefore given prompt attention. Reasons for the increases and possible corrective action must be determined.

Some increases were probably unavoidable, having been dictated by contract, legal requirements or price increases beyond the company's control. Others could probably be reduced with closer control. For example, travel and entertainment expense jumped from $10,000 to $13,000, an increase of $3,000. This sharp increase should indicate that a closer look at all travel and entertainment expenditures is in order to determine whether or not all were necessary. Could some have been avoided by restricting salesmen's expense accounts? Could more economical means of travel have been used? Could the company eliminate unnecessary trips that resulted in costs far beyond any real value to the business?

Supplies expense doubled from $1,000 to $2,000 although the volume of business increased by only about 10%. This sales increase would not seem to indicate a need for such a sharp increase in supplies usage. Such an expense could be controlled by closer attention to purchasing procedures and supplies issued to employees, use of less expensive supplies where possible, and so on.

Determining Expense Budgets

Budgets for each expense must be established, considering both external and internal factors, as in sales forecasting. From the standpoint of expense budgeting, the following would be considered internal factors:

- Corrective actions planned to bring excessive expenses in line.
- Policy changes such as new commission plans.
- Commitments such as equipment purchases, leases on new facilities, or professional service contracts
- Planned salary increases.
- Planned changes in benefit programs.
- Additional personnel.
- Promotional plans.

External factors could include the following:

- Inflation and its effect on price increases from suppliers.
- Tax rate increases including payroll taxes, local propertytaxes, inventory taxes and so on.
- Utility rate increases.

Additionally, the interrelated effects of expense increases must be considered. For example, payroll increases will increase payroll taxes and, possibly, employee benefits. Rent on larger facilities can also involve additional utilities expense.

Initial Forecast

Table 4 shows Western Appliances' initial forecast for 1990 operating expenses.

- The owner's salary will be increased from $24,000 to $26,000.
- The office manager's salary will be increased from $17,000 to $18,000.
- Salesmen's salaries will remain unchanged.
- The expected sales increase will cause salesmen's commissions, 2% of sales, to increase from $24,000 to $28,000.
- Warehouse salaries will be increased about 5% from $22,000 to $23,000.

- Clerical salaries will be increased about 17% from $12,000 to $14,000.

- Payroll taxes, approximately 8% of total compensation, will increase to $10,000 as a result of the compensation increases.

- Employee benefits expense is expected to increase from the present $8,000 to $9,000. This increase is dictated by increased premium costs for employees' health insurance.

- Rent expense will increase from $9,000 to $10,000 due to a tax escalator clause in the lease agreement and a proposed municipal tax increase.

- Utilities expense is expected to remain unchanged at $4,000.

- Telephone expense is expected to be reduced from $4,000 to $3,000 because of tighter controls introduced by management in response to the sharp increase in 1989.

- New controls on supplies should hold this expense at $2,000 despite price increases.

- To increase sales, the advertising and promotion budget will be increased from $13,000 to $15,000, a 20% increase.

- Through tighter control, the owner expects to restrict travel and entertainment expense to the 1989 level of $13,000 despite the general increase in travel-related costs.

- Freight expense will increase from $16,000 to $18,000 reflecting the increased sales volume and higher freight tariffs.

- Professional fees are expected to remain at $5,000.

- Depreciation expense will increase from $6,000 to $8,000 due to the addition of new receiving equipment being purchased at a cost of $10,000 and depreciated over 5 years.

- Total operating expenses will increase from $200,000 to $218,000. Profit before interest and taxes will be $62,000, an increase from $40,000 in 1989.

Reevaluating the Plan

Once an initial plan has been established, it is often useful to review it in order to identify areas of further improvement. In the example of Western Appliances, the expected profit before income taxes, 3.2% of sales ($46,000 / $1,400,000), is well above the industry average of 2.5% and no extensive reevaluation appears needed.

Summary

Facts vs. Observations — Too often, the owners of small businesses rely upon their eyes and ears to tell them whether or not the performance of their business is up to par. Unfortunately, our eyes and ears often betray us. The sales representative with the glib tongue and quick wit may appear to be your star performer while the facts, actual sales and profit, may show that someone else is doing a far better job. The secretary who constantly appears busy may be far less efficient than another who works in a more organized fashion with fewer errors and less need for duplicate effort.

There are also many aspects of a business that our eyes and ears cannot always sense. Changes in the market, shifts in customers' economic fortunes, and gradual but seemingly irreversible increases in costs can develop into crises unless they are detected at an early stage and effective action is taken promptly.

Performance Evaluation — The establishment of a profit plan permits you to evaluate performance in your business based upon facts, not upon random observations. Certainly, there is no substitute for the "gut feel" of the small business owner in making these important decisions that affect the prosperity of the business. However, the effectiveness of the owner's gut feel, when combined with facts, can dramatically increase the accuracy of management decisions.

Profit Plan — With a well-considered profit plan, out-of-line conditions can be detected at the earliest possible date. Corrective action can be taken promptly, eliminating the erosive effect of continuing losses as well as the need to react in a time of crisis. The profit plan also permits the owner to agree upon specific responsibilities with all employees who are in a position to influence sales or costs. Their performance can be evaluated and any deficiencies brought to their attention so that they can participate in the development of corrective action plans. As a further plus, the disciplined thinking about the future will permit you to foresee many problems before they occur and assist you in anticipating opportunities in your market that will permit you to build your business for greater sales and profit.

The above material is taken from The Profit Plan, *a booklet printed by the Small Business Administration.*

BIBLIOGRAPHY

The following books can be found in bookstores or any major library.

Allen, Robert. *Nothing Down.* New York: Simon & Schuster, 1986.

Andrews, Markita. *How to Sell More Cookies, Condos, Cadillacs, Computers — and Everything Else.* New York: Vintage, 1986.

Augustine, Norman R. *Augustine's Laws.* New York: Viking, 1986.

Baugh, L. Sue. *Handbook for Business Writing.* Lincolnwood, IL: NTC Business Books.

Bear, John. *Bear's Guide to Money for College.* Berkely, CA: Ten Speed Press, 1984.

Bivins, Tom. *Handbook for Public Relations Writing.* Lincolnwood, IL: NTC Business Books.

Blanchard, Kenneth. *Power of Ethical Management.* New York: Fawcett, 1989.

Bloch, Arthur. *Murphy's Law, Book Two, More Reasons Why Things Go Wrong.* Los Angeles: Price Stern Sloan, 1980.

Bloom, Alan. *The Closing of the American Mind.* New York: Simon and Schuster, 1987.

Bolles, Richard Nelson. *What Color is Your Parachute?* Berkley, CA: Ten Speed Press, 1971.

Boyer, Richard and David Savageau. *Places Rated Almanac.* New York: Prentice Hall, 1985.

Cappiello, Frank and Karel McClellan. *From Main Street to Wall Street.* New York: John Wiley & Sons, 1988.

Cobb, Douglas, and the Cobb Group. *Excel in Business.* Redmond, WA: Microsoft Press, 1986.

Colwell, Marian. *Think Like an MBA.* New York: Dell, 1984.

Cone, E. Paul. *What You Need to Know About Computers.* New York: Dell, 1984.

Cook, Wade B. *How to Build a Real Estate Money Machine.* Scottsdale, AZ: Regency Books, 1983.

Currier, Chet, and the Associated Press. *The Investor's Encyclopedia.* New York: Franklin Watts, 1985.

Dickhut, Harold W. *The Executive Resume Handbook.* New York: Prentice Hall, 1987.

Donner, William, and William Proctor. *How to Go from Rags to Riches in Real Estate.* New York: Morrow, 1982.

Downes, John and Jordan E. Goodman. *Barron's Finance and Investment Handbook.* Hauppauge, NY: Barron's Educational Series , Inc. 1986.

Industry Norms and Key Business Ratios. New York: Dun & Bradstreet.

Edelhart, Mike. *Breaking through the Job Barrier: Real Life Success Stories.* New York: Anchor Books, 1981.

_____. *College Knowledge.* New York: Anchor Books, 1979.

Fast, Julius. *Body Language.* New York: Pocket Books, 1979.

Foster, Richard. *Innovation: The Attacker's Advantage.* New York: Simon & Schuster, 1986.

Frank, Milo O. *How to Get Your Point Across in 30 Seconds or Less.* New York: Simon & Schuster, 1987.

Frankel, Sandor and Robert Fink. *How to Defend Yourself Against the IRS.* New York: Simon & Schuster, 1986.

Freudberg, David. *The Corporate Conscience.* New York: Amacom, 1986.

Friedman, Michael and Jeffrey Weiss. *Power Sell.* New York: Tern Enterprises, 1986.

Golde, Roger A. *Can You Be Sure of Your Experts?: A Complete Manual on How to Choose and Use Doctors, Lawyers, Brokers, and All the Other Experts in Your Life.* New York: Macmillan, 1969.

Harris, Thomas Anthony. *I'm Ok; You're Ok.* New York: Harper & Row, 1969.

Heller, Robert. *The Naked Manager: Games Executives Play.* New York: E.P. Dutton, 1985.

_____. *The Great Executive Dream: The First Myth of Management Is That It Exists.* New York: Delacorte, 1972.

Henry, Rene A. Jr. *How to Profitably Buy and Sell Land.* New York: John Wiley & Sons, 1986.

Hickman, Craig and Michael Silva. *Creating Excellence.* New York: New American Library, 1986.

Holland, Gary. *Running a Business Meeting.* New York: Dell, 1984.

Hornstein, Harry A. *Managerial Courage.* New York: John Wiley & Sons, 1986.

Irwin, Robert. *How to Find Hidden Real Estate Bargains.* New York: McGraw-Hill, 1986.

Jobst, Katherine. *Internships 1990.* Cincinnati, OH: Writer's Digest Books, 1981.

Johnson, Spencer, M.D. and Larry Wilson. *The One Minute Sales Person.* New York: Avon, 1986.

Keeslar, Oreon. *Financial Aids for Higher Education.* Dubuque, IA: William C. Brown Group, 1988.

Korda, Michael. *Power: How to Get It, How to Use It.* New York: Ballantine, 1976.

Kyle, Robert C. and Jeffrey S. Perry. *How to Profit from Real Estate.* Chicago: Longman, 1987.

Lesko, Matthew. *The Investor's Information Sourcebook.* New York: Harper & Row, 1988.

Levering, Robert, Milton Moskowitz and Michael Katz. *The One Hundred Best Companies to Work for in America.* New York: New American Library, 1987.

Levitt, Theodore. *The Marketing Imagination.* New York: McMillian, 1986.

Lewis, Adele Beatrice. *Barron's Getting a Job in Today's Competitive Market.* Hauppauge, NY: Barron's Educational Series Inc., 1982.

Loeb, Marshall. *Marshall Loeb's Money Guide.* Boston, MA: Little, Brown & Company, 1986.

Lowry, Albert J. *How You Can Become Financially Independent by Investing in Real Estate.* New York: Simon & Schuster, 1981.

Maccoby, Michael. *Why Work?: Leading the New Generation.* New York: Simon & Schuster, 1988.

McGill, Michael. *American Business and the Quick Fix.* New York: Henry Holt, 1988.

McGrath, Phyllis. *Communicating with Professional Investors.* New York: The Conference Board, 1974.

Marlin, John T., Immanuel Ness, and Stephen T. Collins. *Book of World City Rankings.* New York: Macmillan Publishing Co., 1986.

McCormack, Mark. *Succeeding and Rising to the Top of Any Corporation.* New York: Warner Books, 1986.

_____. *What They Don't Teach You at Harvard Business School.* New York: Warner Books, 1986.

Machiavelli, Niccolo. *The Prince.* New York: New American Library, 1952.

Merrell, V. Dallas. *Huddling: The Informal Way to Management Success.* Books on Demand, 1979.

Messner, Stephen D., Irving Schreiber, and Victor Lyon. *Marketing Investment Real Estate.* Chicago: Realtor's National Marketing Institute, 1985.

Miller, Martin R. *Climbing the Corporate Pyramid.* New York: AMACOM, 1973.

Miller, Peter G. *Successful Real Estate Investing.* New York: Harper & Row, 1989.

Miller, Robert B., and Stephen E. Heiman. *Strategic Selling.* New York: Warner Books, 1986.

Molloy, John T. *Dress for Success.* New York: Warner Books, 1978.

Molloy, John T. *The Woman's Dress for Success Book.* New York: Warner Books, 1978.

Nauheim, Ferd. *The Retirement Money Book: Ways to Have More Income When You Retire.* Washington, D.C.: Acropolis Books Ltd., 1982.

Nierenberg, Gerard I. *Workable Ethics.* New York: Nierenberg & Zeif, 1987.

Oxford Analytic. *America in Perspective.* Boston, MA: Houghton Mifflin, 1986.

Parker, Yana. *The Damn Good Resume Guide.* Berkley, CA: Ten Speed Press, 1986.

Perkins, Gail and Judith Rhoades. *The Women's Financial Survival Handbook.* New York: New American Library, 1980.

Peter, Laurence J. *The Peter Prescription.* New York: William Morrow, 1972.

_____. *The Peter Pyramid.* New York: William Morrow, 1986.

_____. *Peter's Quotations.* New York: Bantam Books, 1979.

Peter, Laurence J. and Raymond Hull. *The Peter Principle.* New York: Bantam Books, 1984.

Peters, Thomas. *Thriving on Chaos.* New York: Alfred A. Knopf, 1988.

Peters, Thomas and Nancy Austin. *A Passion for Excellence.* New York: Random House, 1986.

Pritchard, Robert E., Gregory C. Potter and Larry E. Howe. *Be Your Own Financial Advisor.* New York: Prentice Hall, 1988.

Reimold, Cheryl. *Being a Boss.* New York: Dell Books, 1984.

_____. *How to Write a Million Dollar Memo.* New York: Dell Books, 1988.

Renetzky, Alvin. *Directory of Internships, Work Experience Programs and On-the-Job Training Opportunities.* Santa Monica, CA: Ready Reference Press, 1986.

Rees, Alan M., and Jodith James. *Money Management Information Source Book.* New York: R. R. Bowker, 1983.

Ries, Al and Jack Trout. *Marketing Warfare.* New York: New American Library, 1986.

Rosenberg, Claude. *Investing with the Best: What to Look for, What to Look Out for in Your Search for a Superior Investment Manager.* New York: John Wiley & Son, 1986.

Rosenberg, Jerry Martin. *Investor's Dictionary.* New York: John Wiley & Sons, 1986.

Ruff, Howard. *Making Money.* New York: Simon & Schuster, 1984.

Sevareid, Eric. *The Making of Business in America.* New York: McGraw-Hill, 1983.

Shanahan, William F. *Guide to Apprenticeship Programs.* New York: ARCO, 1983.

Shanahan, William F. *Resumes for Computer Professionals.* New York: ARCO, 1983.

Shook, Robert L. *The Entrepreneurs.* New York: Harper & Row, 1980.

Silk, Leonard. *Ethics and Profits: The Crisis of Confidence in American Business.* New York: Simon & Schuster, 1976.

Skacel, Robert K. *The Marketing Plan: How to Prepare It, What Should Be in It.* Lincolnwood, IL: NTC Business Books, 1987.

SRI International Staff. *Investor Information Needs* and *The Annual Report.* Financial Executives Research Foundation, 1987.

Strunk, William and E. B. White. *The Elements of Style.* New York: Macmillan Publishing Co., 1979.

Study Abroad. White Plains, NY: UNIPUB, 1987.

Townsend, Robert. *Up the Organization.* New York: Alfred A. Knopf, 1970.

Tracy, Diane. *The First Book of Common Sense Management.* New York: William Morrow, 1989.

Troy, Leo. *Almanac of Business and Industrial Financial Ratios.* New York: Prentice Hall, 1988.

Jones, H. Stanley. *Planning Your Financial Future.* New York: John Wiley & Sons, 1988.

Westoff, Leslie Aldridge. *Corporate Romance: How to Avoid It, Live through It, or Make It Work for You.* New York: Times Books, 1985.

Wright, John W. *American Almanac of Jobs & Salaries.* New York: Avon, 1987.

Ziglar, Zig. *See You at the Top.* Gretna, LA: Pelican Pub, 1984.

Zweig, Martin. *Martin Zweig's Winning on Wall Street.* New York: Warner Books, 1986.

BOOKS TO HELP YOU WITH YOUR WRITING

How to Write a Million Dollar Memo, Cheryl Reimold (Dell, 1984)

The Elements of Style, William Strunk and E. B. White (Macmillan, 1979)

The Art of Writing Advertising, Denis Higgins (NTC Business Books, 1988)

Handbook for Business Writing, L. Sue Baugh, Maridell Fryay and David A. Thomas (NTC Business Books)

Handbook for Public Relations Writing, Tom Bivins (Crain Books, 1987)

GLOSSARY

Analog — A gradient system with continually variable degrees, such as a mercury thermometer or standard clock dial. See also digital.

Artifical Intelligence — The ability of computers and software programs to imitate human brain activity.

Baud — A unit of speed for data communications.

Binary Code — A computer language made of combinations of 0 and l arranged to represent computer instructions.

Bit — Smallest piece of computer information.

Book — A storehouse of entertainment, knowledge and advice. It can be found in bookstores or libraries.

Bug — An error in the computer program. In the early days of computers, the machine emitted so much heat that the windows to the room had to remain open. The heat, alas, attracted insects which flew into the computer and shorted out the system when they struck sensitive circuits. These bugs caused computer error. The insects are now gone but the term remains.

Business Plan — A written plan, created before you start a business, which outlines how you intend to run your enterprise. The Business Plan also includes hypothetical spread sheets, income projections, proforma cash flow analysis, as well as an explanation in script of how the business will be run. A Business Plan is also needed when an enterprise seeks investment capital or a loan. In a nutshell, a Business Plan is the enterprise's prescription for success.

Byte — Eight bits.

CC — Abbreviation for correspondence copy appended to a letter or memo.

CD — Abbreviation for certificate of deposit, a federally-insured investment purchased for a fixed period of time, providing a specified rate of return.

Cellular Phone — A telephone not requiring wires or wall sockets. A cellular phone may be used anywhere within the geographic reach of the cellular stations. Someday soon, this reach will be the entire United States.

CEO — Abbreviation for chief executive officer.

Chip — A fingernail-sized flat piece of silicon which, when placed in an integrated circuit, forms the "guts" of a computer.

Collections — The function of collecting money owed for services rendered.

Cordless Phone — See electronic phone.

Corporation — A legal entity formed by an individual or individuals to financially protect themselves personally from the actions of the group.

CYA — Abbreviation for cover your ass, the ongoing activity of making sure, on paper, that you have fullfilled all of your obligations and responsibilities, spoken and unspoken, and have proof of your following-through on every assignment.

DBA — Abbreviation for doing business as.

Digital — A system based on numbers in definite predetermined intervals, ie., in a system such as volume, typing in "7" will set the volume at 7. You cannot fine tune the volume to 7.23 or 7.54. See analog.

DINK — Acronym for double income, no kids.

Downside — Opposite of upside, a negative consequence. In the making of a decision, there is usually a positive reason for choosing an option, the upside, as well as a possible negative conseqence, the downside. For example, if a bookstore chooses to sell Salman Rushdie's *Satanic Verses*, the upside is that the bookstore will make a lot of money. The downside is that Muslims in the community may not do their book shopping there anymore.

Electronic Phone — A cordless phone which can operate within a few hundred feet of its power station, but which does not utilize cellular technology.

Electronic Mail — Communication between computers on a telephone hookup.

Error of Idiots — Changing jobs just to escape someone with whom you work.

Error of Similarity — Changing jobs to escape an unpleasant task that is part of your profession, i.e. a high school teacher who becomes a college instructor to escape the tedium of grading papers.

Error of Timing — Changing jobs at the wrong moment. Change jobs when it fits your schedule, not your supervisor's.

FAX — Common name for a facsimile machine, a device that takes a signal from a phone line and creates a paper duplicate of the document being transmitted by another FAX machine.

Final Placement — The position at which a worker has reached his or her "level of incompetence" and is sitting out the years until retirement. See Peter Principle.

Fixed-Pie Assumption — The assumption in negotiating that the only issues to be discussed are already on the table. This leads to the assumption that someone has to lose if someone else is to win.

GIGO — Pronounced "gee-go." A computer term for "garbage in, garbage out." If you put bad information into your computer, you will get bad information out of your computer.

GO Bonds — Abbreviation for general-obligation bonds, a financial instrument offered by a government agency that is guaranteed by the full faith and credit of the issuing entity. GO bond revenue is tax-free.

GONGO — Pronounced "gone-joe." The term describes the lowest, most menial job on a project. For example, on a construction project, gongos will do all the manual labor that machines can not.

Headhunters — Executive recruitment officers.

Horizon Thinking — To think three or four years into the future. Horizon thinkers make decisions today that will still be valid in three years.

Instrument — A financial term meaning any investment that is designed to earn money, such as a stock, bond, CD, TB or IRA.

IRA — Abbreviation for individual retirement account. A personal retirement account that is tax-free if the person doing the investing is not covered by another retirement program. An IRA is different from a KEOGH plan in the amount of money that may be invested. Both the IRA and KEOGH plans are only tax-free in the sense that the tax will be collected when the money is withdrawn at retirement.

KEOGH — A retirement plan for a taxpayer covered under no other program. A KEOGH is different from an IRA in the amount of money that may be invested. Both the IRA and KEOGH are only tax-free in the sense that the tax will be collected when the money is withdrawn at retirement.

KISS Principle — Acronym for Keep It Simple, Stupid. You should not make simple things complex. In a speech, for instance, don't stretch a thirty-second idea into a twenty-minute speech.

Lateral Promotion — Promotion sideways in which someone is given a raise in dollars and a new title but no responsibility. A lateral promotion means one of three things: 1) you are no longer in the career track, 2) you are in Final Placement, or 3) someone is trying to force you into Final Placement.

Memo — An informal letter routed within the office.

Mouse — An electronic pointer on analog computers.

Networking — Developing personal contacts who can assist your career just as you assist theirs. A printer and writer would network. The printer will pass along any writing assignment possibilities to the writer, who will in turn pass along any possible print jobs to the printer. In this way both writer and printer have access to more people.

NIMBY — Acronym for "Not in My Backyard." This describes the attitude of many Americans when the United States Congress or state legislators discuss where to put a prison or nuclear power plant.

Office Terrorism — A VERY dangerous method of harassing a supervisor.

Old Guard — Powerful supervisory personnel of the corporation who have been in place for ten years or longer.

Orphan an Idea — To formulate an idea, develop it, research its feasibility, supply prudent backup information, collect statistics, identify case studies and then allow a superior to "discover" the idea in such a way that he or she thinks that it is his or hers, not yours.

Paper — In the investment community, paper is any document which indicates ownership of an asset. Most frequently it means a CD or TB.

Paper Trail — The collection of documents tracing the origins of any decision.

Partnership — An organization of two or more individuals who operate as a business. There are two types of partnerships: limited, where an investor has no say in the operations of the business, and general, where the investor may participate in decision-making but also has financial liability.

PC — Abbreviation for personal computer.

Peter Principle — Principle of life put forward by L. J. Peter in *The Peter Principle*, which states that an individual will rise to his "level of incompetence."

Punk Rule of Consulting — In every department there is someone who knows what should be done to remedy the situation that the consultant has been called in to fix. Management is not listening to that person, because he or she is viewed as a punk, lightweight or royal pain. All a good consultant has to do is find that person.

Push/Pull Rule — When you are trying to convince someone of the superiority of your idea, you have to PUSH them away from competing ideas and PULL them to your project.

Quick Fix — The decision to solve a problem for the short term with no regard for the long term. The quick fix usually ends up causing as much difficulty as the original problem.

RAM — Acronym for random access memory, a computer memory which allows for storage of information without disturbing other memory bits.

Reader's Guide to Periodical Literature — An index of articles on a wide variety of subjects in most national magazines. It comes in book and microfilm form and allows a researcher to find published references to any subject very quickly.

Reasonable Man Test — A test of the safety of your place of business. In protecting your corporation from the risk of a liability suit, look around your place of business and ask yourself, "Is there any danger here to a person who acts in a reasonable manner?" If the answer is "Yes," there is potential for a liability suit.

Résumé — A short, typed profile of an applicant's education, experience and ability. The best resumes are short, concise and complete.

Revenue Bonds — Bonds which are offered for sale to pay for a specific, revenue-producing project. The bonds will be paid back from the revenue earned from the project. Revenue bonds are not guaranteed.

Reference Librarian — A divine gift to people who need information immediately. These angels of mercy can also be reached by phone, and are paid by the federal, state and local government to answer your questions. You can find them in the government section of your local telephone directory.

SINK — Acronym for single income, no kids.

Solangic — Logical or rational behavior without the benefit of a brain. For example, suppose a problem arises where an executive decision has to be made immediately, but no executive can be found. A worker who makes the correct decision without "going through channels" is said to have made a "solangic" decision.

Sole Proprietorship — A business which is owned and operated by one person.

Stock — A share of a company.

TB — Abbreviation for treasury bill, a federally-insured investment in which one lends money to the federal government for a specified time at a specified rate of return.

Tidal — Usually used to refer to the normal flow. Tidal paperwork, for instance, is that paperwork which is normal.

Time Share — The using of a computer memory by more than one person at the same time. At a library, for instance, hundreds of people may be using the memory bank at any given moment. The computer is programed such that it responds to a request and then moves on to the next request. However, because the computer responds so quickly, it is unlikely any of the users will notice a delay.

Upside — Opposite of downside. See downside.

Vacuum Thinking — Thinking in the negative, trying to see what is NOT there. In reading a contract, for instance, a good reader is just as concerned with what is not included as what is written.

WIIFM — Pronounced "whiff-'em." Acronym for "What's in it for me?"

Writer's Market — An annual listing of national publishers and all major publications. It is an excellent source of magazines that can help your career.

YUFFY — Young urban failure, a comic response to YUPPY.

YUPPY — Young urban professional.

Zap — The destruction of a program or hardware due to an electrical charge such as a spark or surge. You can protect your equipment with a surge protector, which costs about ten dollars at any computer store. You can reduce static charges with a hard plastic sheet on the floor beneath your computer desk.

BUSINESS TERMS — A MATTER OF INTERPRETATION

Appropriate — Originally meant the action involved met an industry standard; now it means that the standard is set by the corporation. Additionally, when used in terms of a written project, it implies length.

Budget — Originally a firm guideline for the allocation of money; now a much more flexible target that is not always expected to be met. Be sure, though, just how flexible before going over budget.

Concise — Originally it meant short; now it means as lengthy as appropriate.

Duties — Originally they were part of your job; now they are extra projects you are expected to do beyond your normal job requirements.

Electronic Phone — Originally a car phone; now it means any phone that can be used free of a cord within a few hundred feet of its power station.

Girl Friday — Originally a person, usually a woman, who would do a wide variety of office jobs but was not necessarily a secretary. It comes from Robinson Crusoe's servant, Friday. Now the term has sexist overtones and should be avoided or at least replaced with "gal/guy Friday."

Golden Rule — Originally meant, "Do unto others as you would have them to do unto you;" now it means, "He who has the gold makes the rules."

Pacific Rim — Originally Japan, Korea, Taiwan and the United States; now it means all thirty-eight nations and commonwealths which border on the Pacific Ocean.

Plan C — Originally meant a backup to Plan A and B; now the implication is that if Plan A and B did not work, Plan C is to give up. If it didn't work after two tries, don't waste your time on it.

Secretary — Original term for the person who handled the nuts-and-bolts, day-to-day office functions; now that person is usually called "staff" or "assistant."

Staff — Originally meant the support personnel for mid-level management; now it means anyone in a support position, including secretaries.

INDEX

ABOUT THE AUTHOR

Steven C. Levi is a free-lance writer living in Alaska. He is the author of fourteen books. His most recent releases were *Deadwood Dick*, a Western; *The Alaskan Traveler*, a travel guide; and the first high-school textbook about the Pacific Rim.